Friendly Fire

FRIENDLY FIRE
● ● ● ● ● ● ● ● ●

American Images of the Vietnam War

Katherine Kinney

OXFORD
UNIVERSITY PRESS
2000

OXFORD
UNIVERSITY PRESS

Oxford   New York
Athens   Auckland   Bangkok   Bogotá   Buenos Aires   Calcutta
Cape Town   Chennai   Dar es Salaam   Delhi   Florence   Hong Kong   Istanbul
Karachi   Kuala Lumpur   Madrid   Melbourne   Mexico City   Mumbai
Nairobi   Paris   São Paulo   Shanghai   Singapore
Taipei   Tokyo   Toronto   Warsaw

and associated companies in
Berlin   Ibadan

Published by Oxford University Press, Inc.
198 Madison Avenue, New York, New York 10016

Oxford is a registered trademark of Oxford University Press

Library of Congress Cataloging-in-Publication Data
Kinney, Katherine, 1959–
Friendly fire : American images of the Vietnam War / Katherine Kinney.
p.   cm.
Includes index.
ISBN 0-19-511603-8; 0-19-514196-2 (pbk)
1. American Literature — 20th century—History and criticism.
2. Vietnamese Conflict, 1961–1975 —Literature and the conflict.
3. National characteristics, American, in literature.
4. War stories, American —History and criticism.
5. War poetry, American —History and criticism.
6. Group identity in literature. I. Title.
PS228.V5 K56 2000
810.9'358— dc21   00-022892

Portions of chapter 2 are reprinted by permission of *American Literary History*.
Other portions of chapter 2 appeared in *Post National American Studies*, edited by
John Carlos Rowe et al. (Berkeley: University of California Press, 2000).
An earlier version of parts of chapter 5 appeared in *Fourteen Landing Zones*,
edited by Philip K. Jason (Iowa City: University of Iowa Press, 1994).

Cover image and "Girls Say Yes to Boys Who Say No" archival poster provided by
the Center for Political Graphics, a non-profit, tax-exempt educational archive
that collects, preserves, documents and exhibits domestic and international posters
relating to historical and contemporary movements for peace and social justice.
8124 West Third Street, Suite 211, Los Angeles, CA 90048-4309.

9 8 7 6 5 4 3 2
Printed in the United States of America
on acid-free paper

For Geoff — *rave on*

ACKNOWLEDGMENTS

I have been unusually fortunate in the number, variety, and verve of the intellectual communities which nurtured my thinking and research about this project. Betsy Erkkila helped me understand the infinite complexity of my conviction that history matters. Houston Baker said, "Yes, of course, Vietnam!" at the critical first moment of my thinking and particularly enabled the writing of chapter 3. Cindy Fuchs got the joke—without her as fellow traveler I would have never gotten started. The Vietnam War section of the Popular Culture Association was the first audience for much of this work and the insight and knowledge I gained there could never be adequately cited—particular thanks to Brad Christie, Renny Christopher, Dan Duffy, David DeRose, Phil Jason, Paul Lyons, J. J. Malo, Steve Potts, Dan Scripture, Kali Tal, David Willson, and, again, Cindy Fuchs.

The English department of UC Riverside has been an unfailingly supportive and challenging intellectual home. Special thanks to my writing group: Jennifer Brody, Joe Childers, George Haggerty, and Traise Yamamoto. Carole-Anne Tyler, Parama Roy, Emory Elliott, and Steve Axelrod gave intellectual and practical support too various to do justice to here. Two resident research fellowships at the University of California Humanities Research Center not only gave me release time for research but challenged my thinking about race, nation, and American studies. My thanks to Valerie Smith, convener of the second year of the Minority Discourse project, and John Carlos Rowe, convener of the Post-National American Studies research group, as well as to the members of both seminars. At UC Riverside a quarter at the Center for Ideas and Society in the company of Traise Yamamoto, Piya Chattejee, Steffi San Buenaventura, Devra Weber, Pat Tuck, viii Acknowledgments

and Paulette Browe-Heines became the ideal place to finish chapter 5. Mary Hunter, Devin Orgeron, Daphne Renfrow, Allison Smith, and Karen Polster did excellent and irreplacable research and editorial work. Special thanks to Scott Andrews for his tireless work on picture research. Kim O'Doherty made me think about audience in ways that will stay with me far beyond this book. John Newman and the staff of the Vietnam War Literature Archive at Colorado State University were tremendously helpful in the initial stages of the project.

My thanks to Elliott Gruener and Gorden O. Taylor for their careful and sensitive readings of the manuscript. Two editors at Oxford University Press were crucial to the completion of this book. My thanks to T. Susan Chang for her patience and sound advice and to Elissa Morris for bringing new enthusiasm to the final stages of publication.

Margaret Kinney always believed I would write a book. Pat O'Doherty made it possible for me to write this book. Warren Cohen kept me reasonably honest in my historical thinking. Betty Loverich, RoseAnn Hill, and Jan Prichard Cohen lent aid and comfort more times than can be counted. Walter Kinney did not live to see this work, but he in many ways began it when he watched "combat theater" with me on Saturday afternoons and made me understand that war movies were not real but they were important. Tess Cohen and Grace Cohen keep me sane. Geoff Cohen makes the impossible happen every day.

CONTENTS

Friendly Fire

INTRODUCTION

At the end of Oliver Stone's 1986 film, *Platoon*, the protagonist, Chris Taylor (Charlie Sheen), offers the quintessential statement of what I call the trope of friendly fire. In a voiceover Taylor tells us, "I think now looking back that we did not fight the enemy, we fought ourselves and the enemy was within us." In *Platoon*, this story of Americans killing Americans in Vietnam is both literal and allegorical. At the heart of the film is the epic struggle between the evil sergeant Barnes, the figure of the war's self-consuming violence, and the regenerative promise of Elias, the Christ-like figure of goodness sacrificed on the battlefields of Vietnam. The plot demands that Barnes kill Elias and that Chris Taylor, in turn, kill Barnes. *Platoon* is quite simply the story of the Manichaean struggle for a young man's soul. Despite this overtly symbolic structure, the film has been often praised for its realistic depiction of the war. Tellingly, not only is *Platoon*'s allegorical structure defined by this trope of friendly fire, but its most realistic gesture is shaped by it as well.

Framing the final deadly struggle between Taylor and Barnes is an apocalyptic battle at the height of the Tet Offensive. When the North Vietnamese Army (NVA) overruns the American encampment, the unit captain calls in an air strike on his own position. "Be advised," he tells the bomber pilot over the radio, "we have zips in the wire." When the pilot responds that they have struck as close as they dare to the American position, the captain makes a terrible decision: "For the record, it's my call. Dump everything you've got left on my pos[ition]. I say again. Expend all remaining within my perimeter. It's a lovely fucking war. Bravo 6 out." The captain then hangs up, puts on his helmet, and waits for the devastating power of American bombs to fall. The captain's intentional use of friendly fire figures the real-

3

istic heart of the "lovely fucking war" in Vietnam, measuring the limits of what men can and must do in a war in which boundaries refuse to remain secure. This gesture of realism is deepened by the casting of Dale Dye, a veteran of the war, who appears briefly in Michael Herr's *Dispatches* and who is listed in the film's credits as "Military Technical Advisor, Captain Dale Dye, United States Marine Corps (retired)."[1] The doubling of Dye's role on and off screen underlines the authority of experience used to authenticate many representations of the Vietnam War and the need for that experience to be presented in the veteran's body, not simply through the transmission of any particular knowledge a veteran might have.

The idea that we fought ourselves, literalized in the repetitious image of Americans killing Americans, is, I would argue, virtually the only story that has been told by Americans about the Vietnam War. In novels, memoirs, oral histories, plays, and films the image of friendly fire, the death of one American at the hands of another, structures the plotting of both realist gestures toward "what really happened" in Vietnam and symbolic expressions of what Vietnam meant. From the orders to "terminate" Col. Kurtz in *Apocalypse Now* to the fragging of an officer in Tim O'Brien's *Going After Cacciato* and the bootcamp stabbings of David Rabe's *Streamers*, Americans are portrayed as the victims of their own ideals, practices, and beliefs, while the ostensible enemy, the regular forces of the NVA and the Viet Cong guerrillas, remain shadowy figures glimpsed only occasionally.

This figuration of the war has historical roots in the tactical frustrations of fighting a war against an elusive enemy and in the frequent accounts of American soldiers burned by napalm, caught by U.S. artillery, and shot reentering their own perimeter, the specific military meaning of "friendly fire." Friendly fire was and is not unique to Vietnam; it is endemic to mass warfare and to the technological firepower of modern war. But whereas the novels of Ernest Hemingway or James Jones, for example, describe incidents of being shelled by one's own artillery, friendly fire does not organize the plots of World War I or World War II in the conspicuous way it does those of the Vietnam War. Furthermore, as *Platoon* makes clear, this plotting of friendly fire very often involves the act of "fragging," the intentional murder of superior officers. Fraggings are the most dramatic example of the breakdown in army discipline which became increasingly conspicuous in the last years of the war. But whereas statistics regarding fraggings are notoriously hard to come by, certainly such incidents were not as common during the war as they are in representations of it.[2] Rather, the ubiquity of the fragging plot reflects the war's deep connection to the contemporary domestic challenges to traditional American authority. The perceived breakdown of American world hegemony in Vietnam occurred concurrently with an attack on the categories that defined and upheld that power: race and gender. In challenging the status quo, movements such as Black Power and Women's Liberation sought to rewrite the past as well as the present.

The violent solipsism of Vietnam War narratives reflects this very material struggle to redefine American identity.

If the trope of "friendly fire," a term I use to include all acts of Americans killing Americans, testifies to the subversion of traditional American orders of meaning, the story it ultimately tells is not necessarily subversive. First, as the example of *Platoon* once again testifies to, the trope often recapitulates the pattern Richard Slotkin has so resonantly named "regeneration through violence." Chris Taylor comes to the realization that "the enemy was within us" while literally rising above the scarred battlefield of Vietnam on a helicopter. Having survived the mythic "scenario of separation [and] temporary regression to a more primitive or 'natural' state,"[3] Chris ends the film with a classic statement of regeneration:

> The war is over for me now, but it will always be there the rest of my days—as I'm sure Elias will be, fighting with Barnes for what Rhah called possession of my soul. There are times since I've felt like the child born of those two fathers. But be that as it may, those of us who did make it have an obligation to build again, to teach to others what we know, and to try with what's left of our lives to find a goodness and meaning to this life.

It is only through violence, the physical and symbolic killing of Barnes, that Chris comes to this higher truth, lifted quite literally into a blinding white glow. As Susan Jeffords has persuasively argued, Chris's rebirth as "the son born of these two fathers" marks a conspicuously gendered regeneration of an exclusively masculine cultural identity.[4]

Even more obviously, imagining the war as something Americans did to each other displaces the Vietnamese as historical agents in the war. They typically serve as little more than the exotic backdrop for the American encounter with "the heart of darkness" within itself. But this familiar, even cliched imprint of the imperial in representations of the war marks the curious doubleness of the trope of friendly fire as an agent of both historical memory and amnesia. When Dale Dye tells the bomber commander in *Platoon*, "Be advised, we have zips in the wire," his dispassionate, professional assessment of his specific situation is underwritten by the racialized nightmare voiced moments earlier by a hysterical soldier who appears out the gloom and climbs into Taylor's foxhole: "They're all over the place, hundreds of them." The camera shots of Vietnamese soldiers preparing for attack, reading maps, tying up their pants legs, hiding weapons in trees, do not justify this level of fear. We see only a few soldiers. And although Stone may want the scene to be read under the sign of realism, an image of how men can panic under the stress of battle, the fear is understood more viscerally as the realization of the cultural threat of the "yellow peril" or "the rising tide of color": the imperial nightmare of being overwhelmed by the

Asian Other. This fear supports, in turn, the audience's understanding of Dye's rational decision to call in the air strike on his own position when the line between "us" and "them" has dissolved: "Exterminate the brutes." Barnes may be the ultimate savage in Platoon, but the moral struggle at the heart of the film trades on a racialized imperial memory without ever critically engaging its terms.[5] Vietnam becomes yet another site of the "inscrutable," that which Americans cannot understand.[6]

Platoon is emblematic of the ways in which the trope of friendly fire imperfectly turns a critical eye on the American involvement in Southeast Asia. The relation between realism and allegory, memory and amnesia is awkwardly animated in its plot. Certain transgressive memories and images, such as the indiscriminate violence of American technology, are frequently foregrounded by friendly fire, while others, particularly the imperial nature of American military and political power, are made visible only intermittently, and often only by reading against a given text's directing of its narrative meaning. The domestic social upheavals of the period are typically invoked but not engaged. Most telling are the frequent references to hippies or antiwar protesters, often figured in relation to a girlfriend in college and thus suggestively linked to women's liberation or changing gender roles. Similarly, the iconography of black nationalism, particularly the elaborate handshake known as the "dap" and the raised-fist salute of Black Power, are common gestures, albeit frequently deployed as signs of interracial solidarity. Although such references to the contemporary social fissures along class, race, gender, generational, and ideological lines seem necessary for purposes of verisimilitude in depictions of the war, the violence plotted by friendly fire is rarely, if ever, openly motivated by ideology. Black soldiers do not typically shoot white soldiers; Americans do not kill each other over their positions on the war. One result has been a certain conspicuous level of political incoherence, measured not only by the heated critical debates about the "conservative" or "liberal" politics of any number of films but even more tellingly by the ability of audiences to simultaneously embrace both *Rambo* (1985) and *Platoon* (1986) not only as box office hits but as cultural events.[7] In Rambo, too, "we fought ourselves"; the enemy, even upon going back to Vietnam, is American—the spies and bureaucrats exemplified by the computer that betrayed the loyal American soldier.

The stories told by friendly fire are so dramatically conflicting because the trope is not so much a historical narrative as the marker of its absence. Unlike the World War II trope of the flag raising on Iwo Jima, which was able to secure cultural order and a stable American identity out of the unprecedented violence of the Pacific theater, friendly fire figures the compulsive need to return again and again to the cultural trauma of the Vietnam War. Iwo Jima haunts Vietnam War literature as the key sign of what Tim O'Brien in *Going After Cacciato* calls "the things they didn't know," such as "raising a flag and calling it victory."[8] In Larry Heinemann's novel *Paco's*

Story, a World War II veteran retells to a Vietnam veteran the story of flag raising.

> Iwo Jima was this bullshit little island, see . . . out in the middle of no fucking place. . . . About all I remember is the fucking smell—of which there was plenty, you understand? Sulphur sand. Gunpowder smoke. Greasy sweat. Diesel fumes. Tons, it must have been *tons* of shit—human and otherwise—there were four Marine divisions and more than 20,000 Japanese, see, everybody eating and shitting. And we were dying like flies. The Japs were dying like flies—there were fucking corpses sticking up out of the dirt and everywhere. . . . The day we put the flag up—it wasn't me but I was near there—why, everybody on that island stopped to watch. . . . Everybody felt that all that fucking work was worth something, though the fighting went on for three more weeks. Couple of years ago I was traveling through Washington, D.C., on my way to my sister's in Virginia Beach, and happened to drive near that Iwo Jima statue that's over by the cemetery, and you could see it from clear across the river. Six guys breaking their balls, muscling that goddamn flag up. . . . Work's work but I tell you from the bottom of my heart that Iwo Jima was a sloppy, bloody butt-fuck.[9]

Heinemann's obscene, embodied language is deeply familiar to readers of Norman Mailer and James Jones. It reinvests Iwo Jima with the bodily horror evacuated from the popular memory forged by the famous photograph, the memorial sculpture, and the John Wayne film. But this realistic turn to the body does not void the power of the memorial gesture. Ernest, the veteran, retains his personal memory of the physical trauma of the battle for Iwo Jima, but the larger-than-life inscription of the flag raising on the national landscape marks narrative closure and gives the veteran somewhere to place the horror. Earlier Ernest says, "Guadacanal about broke my fucking balls . . . but Iwo Jima was my goddamn declaration of independence."[10] Alleviating the bitterness of Ernest's irony, the bronze soldiers take on the memory of this "ballbreaking" effort and free Ernest from the exclusive burden of the past. Paco, the veteran of Vietnam, tells no stories; instead he dreams, his body contorting with the uncontrollable force of memories which are nowhere registered with the coherence of the Iwo Jima memorial.

The image of the flag raising works as cultural shorthand for a popular narrative with a logical beginning, the bombing of Pearl Harbor, and ending, the dropping of the atomic bomb, a narrative which succeeds in making sense out of the most violent conflict in human history. But there is nothing like this level of historical consensus regarding the Vietnam War. Among scholars, statesmen, and citizens there is open disagreement about when the war began, why we fought, who we fought, or when and how and why and if we lost. In the face of this lack, the veteran's authority of experience has come to define the Vietnam War in American culture. The war has become knowable primarily through the arbitrary boundaries of the soldier's 12-month tour of duty. This emphasis on what the soldier knows about war turns again and again to the body. Obscenity and atrocities, whether the kind of gross violation of the "proper" use of force typically represented by My Lai or the technically acceptable horrors of battlefield wounding, forge one standard by which to judge how close representations have come to what the war was really like—literally showing us the things histories do not tell.

The bloodiness so characteristic of representations of the Vietnam War testifies to Elaine Scarry's observation that "war is relentless in taking for its own interior content the interior content of the human body."[11] The purpose of war, Scarry argues, is to confer upon ideology the "incontestable reality of the body," a reality which is made "compelling and vivid" through wounding.[12] But, the reality marked by wounding has a "referential instability"; the body may be claimed by either the side for which it suffered or the side that wounded it.[13] To the victor goes the right to claim the bodies and their reality conferring power. In Vietnam the United States suffered defeat yet refused to admit it. Diplomatic recognition of a unified Vietnam was withheld for more than 20 years. Friendly fire, with its retelling of Vietnam as a domestic American war, supports this official denial. By fighting ourselves, Americans surreptitiously claim the victor's right to the bodies' substantiating reality. The Vietnam Veterans Memorial institutionalizes this counting of the American dead, even as it subverts other ideological imperatives of war's memorialization.[14]

But the subterfuge underwriting this claim to the bodies of war prevents the act of memorializing from fully translating bodily reality into a coherent and stable national self-image in the way that happened after World War II. This failure is typically voiced in terms of a deeply conservative sense of nostalgia for the "good war." Ironically, however, it forms one of friendly fire's most potentially radical historical possibilities: a deconstruction of war's power to make men, culture, and, in Scarry's terms, "the world." The incoherence of the Vietnam War carries with it a deeper if hidden suggestion that what has been forgotten in the act of historical memory is more compelling, more meaningful than what is remembered, encouraging a more contentious and unruly conception of the national body even while openly desiring the narrative orderliness of World War II. If the wounds of Vietnam have failed to heal, as politicians, artists, activists, and pundits have claimed with tiresome frequency, perhaps it is because the wounded national body displays valuable meanings and memories concealed in purified bodies like the bronze giants of the Iwo Jima memorial.

In searching out the meanings opened by the wounds of the Vietnam War, it is, however, crucial to avoid a dangerous nostalgia for the body as a reliable source able to directly counter the notorious dissimulation and dissembling associated with the war. The memories and bodies of veterans are not immune to the transformations of time or representation. When Ron Kovic's autobiography *Born on the Fourth of July* was published in 1976, its emotionally wrenching account of his wounding and paralysis offered a devastating repudiation of the baby-boomer desire to be John Wayne or Audie Murphy. But his 1986 presence at the Academy Awards and nomination for an Oscar for the screen adaptation of his story suggests in terribly ironic ways that he has, in fact, become the Audie Murphy of his generation —rewriting if not actually replaying his combat role on screen. Or, to return to the example with which I began, Dale Dye's embodied veteran's experience has literally been incorporated. Since the success of *Platoon*, Dye has formed a corporation, "Warriors Inc.," which advises Hollywood on accuracy in representations of war, including the much acclaimed *Saving Private Ryan*, in which Dye once again has a cameo role.[15] Kovic and Dye are highly dramatic examples of the intimate relation between fiction and experience located in the veteran's body.

As Elaine Scarry notes, the injured body's "reality-conferring function" is also a "fiction generating" one. Scarry calls this the "as-if" function of injury, which "acts as a source of apparent reality for what would have otherwise been a tenuous outcome, holding it firmly in place until the postwar world rebuilds the world according to the blueprint sketchily specified by the war's locus of victory. . . . what it substantiates is *not untrue*: it is just *not yet* true."[16] I do not distinguish "reality" and "fiction" in the substantive way Scarry does but would argue instead that the fiction-generating power of war and the injured bodies at its core *are* what confer a sense of reality— what Kaja Silverman has called the "dominant fiction."[17] If World War II seems to present an example of a world literally built, building by building, government by government, alliance by alliance, on the "blueprint" of the surrender of Germany and Japan, the retelling of Iwo Jima in *Paco's Story* reminds us that it is the quality of the "fiction," the iconic story rather than the embodied reality, which most powerfully differentiates World War II from Vietnam. Furthermore, I hope to show that as fiction World War II is itself vulnerable to being rewritten by the American involvement in Vietnam, for Vietnam was one of the least successful sites of post-World War II "rebuilding." The definitional struggles over French Indochina and Vietnam, over colonialism, nationalism, and communism, were at their deepest levels simultaneously material and narrative.[18]

It is the reality-conferring power of fiction, in Fredric Jameson's term, "the socially symbolic act of narrative," and war's privileged place in twentieth-century fictions with which I am most concerned in this study. This fictiveness is not the exclusive province of any genre or medium, as the ingeniousness of twentieth-century technologies of propaganda, whether centered in the Kremlin or Madison Avenue, the Pentagon or Hollywood, testify. Even so, my opening discussion of *Platoon* is to a degree misleading. In this study I have focused primarily on postmodern inheritors of modernism; writers whose self-reflexive understanding of the complicity of fiction tremendously complicates their desire to tell some version of the truth about the war. As I demonstrate in my study of John Wayne, the movies are, however, a key trope for the complex relationship of reality to fiction for the generation who fought in Vietnam and the generations who now seek to learn the war's history. Whatever claims of truth are made here are decidedly contextual rather than absolute and reside within the frame of fiction even when appealing to historical sources of evidence. In short, I am not offering an argument about what happened in Vietnam but attempting to understand the reality-conferring fictions that are the legacy of the war.

The five chapters that follow offer readings of a variety of literal and symbolic scenes of friendly fire: accidental shootings and fraggings, the cultural revolt against John Wayne, the domestic scene of battle at Kent State and the assassination of Martin Luther King, fantasy elaborations in Africa and Iran, and literalization of the ideological struggle between black and white men or between men and women. At stake is a demystification of the Vietnam War as a truth known only to veterans. The cultural authority placed on the experience of the Vietnam veteran has done little to ease the material suffering that has so often been the personal legacy of the war. As Bobbie Ann Mason's *In Country* testifies in its very title, the radical difference attributed to Vietnam often covertly doubles an image of home. It is this idea of home with which this study is most fully concerned: the America that was constructed against the otherness of Vietnam, through both the orientalized obsessions of the Cold War and the more enduring figure of Vietnam as a war, place, and time (categories barely distinguishable from one another) which mark the nadir of American self-conception.

Chapter 1

INDIAN COUNTRY REVISITED

The Persistence of John Wayne

Does the picture tell the truth
or will the young people
of today have reason to say they
were misled by propaganda?
Office of War Information question
to film makers during World War II.[1]

"I think I'm going to hate this movie"
— Joker in *The Short-Timers*

In a 1992 analysis of the questions surrounding presidential candidate Bill Clinton's draft status during the Vietnam War, David Lamb of the *Los Angeles Times* posed the following rhetorical question:

If the war was so unpopular, if it was a misadventure, as is now widely believed, why should Clinton be penalized for deciding, as an anguished young man, not to rush off to the jungles of Vietnam? After all—John Wayne—deferred from the World War II draft because of his age (34) and a football shoulder injury—and Army Captain Ronald Reagan—who spent the war years making military movies in Hollywood—are viewed as patriots. Why, then, should we care if a candidate served in Vietnam or legally avoided it?[2]

Rhetorically in this passage the Vietnam War is the question and John Wayne (along with Ronald Reagan) is the answer. The passage is particularly illustrative because this rhetorical structure holds even when Vietnam is characterized as something less than Ronald Reagan's noble cause and the ironic distance between John Wayne as man and as image is foregrounded. The often bitterly ironic invocation of John Wayne has been one of the most prominent, persistent, and analyzed images in representations of the Vietnam War.[3] Yet his image has survived this continual discrediting —so much so that at the end of the Gulf War, the site of a conspicuous re-circulation of his patriotic image, the *Los Angeles Times* could report that President Bush was being "spoken of as something like John Wayne with an Ivy League education."[4] The irony this time is meant to be more admiring than critical.

In representations of the Vietnam War, the irony associated with the image of John Wayne promises to assert a more devastating critique. Novelist Larry Heinemann perhaps best captures John Wayne's emblematic role in establishing the American identity that went to war in Vietnam and the ironic approach veterans' texts take in retrospect. In the first chapter of *Close Quarters* (1977), Philip Dossier, a soldier new to Vietnam, wonders:

> What in the world am I doing here? My parents raised me on "Thou-shalt-nots" and willow switches and John Wayne (even before he be-came a verb), the Iwo Jima Bronze and First and Second Samuel, and always, always, the word was "You do what I tell you to do." The con-cept around our house was everybody takes his own lickings. But what in the name of God had I done to deserve this one?[5]

John Wayne reigns here among absolute authorities, a god from popular culture, equaled to the patriarchs of home, heaven, and country. In this passage, and many others like it in Vietnam War literature, John Wayne is the model by which young American men learn to accept duty and re-sponsibility. But as this passage also testifies, when faced with Vietnam, the concepts of duty and justice on which that vision rests are thrown into doubt. From this fallen point of view, John Wayne's presence becomes ironic, a flag that should have served as an early warning that the founda-tions of his world were not sound.

In scores, if not hundreds of novels, memoirs, poems, films, plays, and works of criticism about the Vietnam War, John Wayne is parodied, de-bunked, reviled, rejected, and metaphorically and sometimes literally shot dead. But somehow he always returns, like Michael Herr's "character in pop grunt mythology who is dead" but "too stupid to lie down."[6] This ob-session with John Wayne exemplifies the solipsism of American narratives of the Vietnam War, the self-referential quality that displaces the historical struggles within Vietnam with a spectacle of American culture at war with itself. At the most literal level, the ironic association of John Wayne with the Vietnam War testifies to the crude fictionalizing of the historical record that came to be known as the "credibility gap" in the Johnson administra-tion. Peter McInerney has argued that "the tension in the record between fact and fiction is its single most reliable feature."[7] John Wayne, as it has been frequently suggested, exemplifies not so much the tension as the di-vorce between fact and fiction during the Vietnam War. In Toby Herzog's analysis, for example, John Wayne is emblematic of the "innocence" of the 1950s which was destroyed by the "experience" of Vietnam.[8]

Herzog's archetypal model, however, can hardly account for the persistence of John Wayne images within representations of the Vietnam "experience" itself and its disquieting effect on critical attempts to draw lessons from the war. Richard Slotkin's discussion of *Full Metal Jacket* is a case in point.

> . . . several members of "the platoon" respond to the presence of the TV camera with the joking invocations of movie myths ("Is that you, John Wayne? Is this me?") and historical mythology ("I'll be General Custer. But who will be the Indians?"). By making no distinctions between the "real" historical figure and the make-believe heroes of the movies, the dialogue suggests that there is no "reality" to which one can appeal for an antidote to the poisonous illusion of "John Wayne."[9]

Slotkin here reifies an opposition between "reality" and "illusion" which is figured more subtly and ambivalently elsewhere in his study of twentieth-century constructions of the frontier. Slotkin's larger reading of John Wayne's association with the Vietnam War stresses the relation of Wayne's anticommunist patriotism and its self-conscious staging in such films as *The Alamo* and *The Green Berets* as the "reality" that demystifies Wayne's connection to Vietnam.[10] But the scene from *Full Metal Jacket*, which foregrounds the presence of the camera and the soldier's self-conscious talking back to the camera, poses another "reality," the practical impossibility of getting behind the camera as Slotkin seems to do with Wayne. John Wayne was always already an "illusion," an effect of the very camera that offers to present the "reality" of the war. This is not to say that there is no historical frame of critical appeal. The question "who will be the Indians" in the command performance demanded by the camera carries considerable critical possibility, appealing not simply to the historicity of the Sioux at Little Big Horn but to the generations of framings and reframings of the event which Slotkin himself has so powerfully analyzed. With Eric Lott, I would argue that popular culture can "best thought of as a realm of counterfeits— contradictory popular constructions that were not so much true or false as more or less pleasurable or politically efficacious in the culture that embraced them."[11] Rather than rejecting John Wayne as a figure of false consciousness we need to examine what John Wayne "did" once he "became a verb."

As a suitably ironic starting point, I begin with the death of John Wayne at the precise historical moment in which the Kennedy administration was committing to the disastrous course of action in Vietnam.[12] In 1962 John Ford released his study of the death of the West, the Western, and its hero, *The Man Who Shot Liberty Valance*. The challenge posed in the film by the text of John Wayne's dead body is to interrogate the relationship of myth to history, to discover whether or not it is possible to make myth responsible to history. John Wayne dies old, forgotten, and poor in *Liberty Valance*, his body laid out in a crude pine box, without guns or boots, headed for potter's field. In the narrative frame, Jimmy Stewart's Senator Stoddard stands before an old wreck of a stagecoach, one of many nods to the first major Ford/Wayne collaboration, suggesting that genre as well as conveyance is now an anachronism. Ford's signature use of the epic spaciousness of the Western landscape retreats into the cramped interiors and backlot streets of *Liberty Valance*'s Shinbone.

These revisionary images have received a great deal of commentary, but perhaps the most interesting historicizing gesture is the pointedly aged faces of John Wayne and Jimmy Stewart. In the flashback sequences, they are much too old for the parts they play as young men creating a new society in the West. At the age of 55, Wayne is no longer the raw-boned Ringo Kid of *Stagecoach* who can make a new start with a marriage and a homestead. Stoddard's tale, although offered as the truth which will overturn the myth, is built on the impossible nostalgia their aging faces suggest. The fresh faces in this Western belong to Lee Marvin and Lee Van Cleef, a new generation of actors who herald a new type of Western, one defined by levels of violence which the Western's traditional narrative structures cannot contain.[13] The sadistic viciousness of Liberty Valance is defeated not by Stoddard's rule of law or Wayne's self-reliance but by a shot without warning from a dark alley. In *Red River*, Montgomery Clift assures one of the men that Wayne would not pick a man off in the dark, but in *Liberty Valance* he does, and that act of violence marks the West's entrance into the modern world.

In retrospect, these revisionary figurations seem full of portents of the Vietnam War. But to the amazement and confusion of most critics, John Ford continued to the end of his life to affirm his allegiance to the sentiment of the film's end—"when the legend becomes fact, print the legend." As he told Peter Bogdanovich, "I think it's good for the country." One of Ford's most perceptive and sympathetic critics, Tag Gallagher, seems to feel that Ford's comment was made in bad faith: "Really? How come, then. . . . Ford 'prints' the facts, while exploding (and explaining) the legends?"[14] But this seems to assume that to explain is to explode, an assumption shared by most of the attacks on John Wayne in Vietnam War literature; that to point out the ironic distance between image and event will collapse myth's power to persuade.

As an alternative to this ironic focus, which is aimed at destroying myth, Roland Barthes advocates a "dynamic" approach which "consumes the myth according to the very ends built into its structure: the reader lives the myth as a story at once true and unreal." In this way, one can "connect a mythical schema to a general history . . . explain how it corresponds to the interests of a definite society, in short . . . pass from semiology to ideology."[15] Barthes begins this process by asking a simple question: "How does [the reader] receive this particular myth *today?*" (129). By locating the meaning and function of myth in the reading of a specific reader (or group of readers) at a specific point in time, Barthes provides a model for analyzing the relationship between an icon of popular culture like John Wayne, an historical event like the Vietnam War, and the body of self-conscious literature which the war has produced. Toward this end, I pose three questions: What did John Wayne signify before Vietnam? What does he signify in postwar texts of Vietnam veterans, such as Ron Kovic's *Born on the Fourth of July* and Gustav Hasford's *The Short-Timers?* And what does John Wayne come to mean after reading those texts? Through a comparative reading of these successive "John Waynes" I would offer a model of "rereading" which seeks not to banish John Wayne from American culture but to more fully describe the ideological assumptions he both embodies and erases.

During the Vietnam War, John Wayne presents an almost too perfect place from which to trace the movement from image to ideology. *The Green Berets* can be seen as the final act in Wayne's personal audition to play the mythic embodiment of the American ideologies that went to Vietnam: anticommunism, racism, and imperialism masked by the rhetoric of manifest destiny and mission. In a 1972 *Life* magazine interview, Wayne offered a paradigmatic example of his views:

> "Your generation's frontier should have been Tanganyika," he [Wayne] contends, recalling the African country—independent Tanzania now—where he made *Hatari.* "It's a land with eight million blacks and it could hold 60 million people. We could feed India with the food we produced in Tanganyika! It could have been a new frontier for any American or English or French kid with a little gumption! Another Israel! But the *do-gooders* had to give it back to the Indians!
>
> "Meanwhile, your son and my son are given numbers back here and live in apartment buildings on top of each other."[16]

Note the casual opposition of "blacks" and "people," the us-and-them thinking which breaks along color lines, the patriarchal concern for the son's inheritance, the conviction that the power to transform a desert into a garden is a question of Western character in both its American and European frames of reference. Wayne's two directorial efforts, *The Alamo* (1960) and *The Green Berets* (1968), affirm the connection between Wayne's personal ideology and his on-screen mythic persona as the hero of the West and of the U.S. Armed Forces. David Thompson makes perhaps the most clever and biting indictment of Wayne's self-aggrandizing patriotism when he points out that Wayne's famous line from *The Alamo*, "Republic, I like the sound of the word . . . ," becomes more than a little ironic when you remember that Republic was the studio that launched Wayne's career.[17]

If John Wayne made himself the easy target of the left in the 1970s, much as Jane Fonda did for the right, Eric Bentley makes a more serious case for respecting Wayne's virulent expressions of anti-communism. In "The Political Theatre of John Wayne," Bentley writes,

> The most important American of our time is John Wayne. Granted that all good things come from California, Richard Nixon and Ronald Reagan are only camp followers of Wayne, supporting players in the biggest Western of them all, wagons hitched to Wayne's star. In an age when the image is the principle thing, Wayne is the principle image, and if the soul of this image is *machismo*, its body is the body politic, and its name is Anti-Communism.[18]

Bentley emphasizes Wayne's role as president of the Motion Picture Alliance for the Preservation of American Ideals, founded in 1944 to combat "the growing impression that this industry is made up of, and dominated by, Communists, radicals and crack-pots," and its link to the naming of names before the House Un-American Activities Committee.[19] HUAAC's Hollywood investigations, Bentley argues, coerced the members of the entertainment industry not only to defend themselves as not communist but to become "anticommunist," thus moving the center to the right and paving the road to Vietnam. "Wayne was the icon," Nixon the "iconographer," Bentley asserts, and compelling though his formulation may be (especially after eight years of President Ronald Reagan), Bentley assumes a singular and readily ascertainable definition of Wayne's image. His essay offers no readings of Wayne's films, no allusions to the roles he has played, evidently deeming it unnecessary to show how Wayne animated his opinions in popular imagination. But this precludes the possibility that there might be iconographers of the Wayne myth other than Richard Nixon (not even John F. Kennedy or John Ford, let alone Ron Kovic or Gustav Hasford) who might be relevant to considerations of the American involvement in Vietnam.

The Green Berets is the film most often used to illustrate the link between Wayne's political views and his image. Toby Herzog notes that "movie critics" found the film "filled with cliche, propaganda, unintentional humor, and the plot and values of many previous John Wayne westerns and World War II movies." Comparing *The Green Berets* specifically to *Sands of Iwo Jima*, Herzog continues, "The setting is different from Wayne's W.W.II movies, and the Viet Cong have replaced the Japanese. But the message, characters, and portrait of conflict remain the same."[20] The articulation of the message in *The Green Berets* is, however, conspicuously different than in *Sands of Iwo Jima*. As Kathryn Kane notes, typically in World War II combat films, "there is a sense that the war is too complex for ordinary men . . . to understand."[21] The answer to "why we fight" is generically framed in terms of personal loyalty and duty to the socially symbolic platoon rather than in a direct appeal to history or ideology. *The Green Berets*, in contrast, opens with an explicit presentation of public relations in which an audience of common citizens and a skeptical reporter (David Jansen) is apprised of the political situation in Vietnam and given a demonstration of the counter-insurgency tactics of the Green Berets. Jansen is, in fact, the key character in the film, who must be converted from his knee-jerk suspicion of the government to an appreciation of the necessity of the battle against communism. The World War II John Wayne film which *The Green Berets* most closely resembles is *Back to Bataan*, which also attempts to historicize war, as John Wayne seeks to valorize the spirit of Philippine resistance to American imperialism in an effort to turn it against the Japanese. When Anthony Quinn, cast as the son of an Aguinaldo-like Philippine nationalist, turns to American adviser John Wayne and says, "I know you're a better Filipino than I am . . .," the narrative's logic collapses in the same sort of absurdity that has made *The Green Berets* infamous.

For as Richard Slotkin has noted, "myth does not argue its ideology, it exemplifies it."[22] John Wayne left his mark on the literature of the Vietnam War and on American culture, not as an idealogue but as an actor, a player of parts, literally a body who came to carry the resonances of myth. And between his opinions and his best performances there is often as much tension as correspondence. The most obvious example here is *The Searchers* where the determination, self-reliance, and racism Wayne personally espoused and celebrated in interviews is opened to scrutiny and criticism not only by the film's narrative structure, which collapses the self he would protect and the Other he would destroy, but in Wayne's own performance. In John Wayne's persona, all the "isms" of ideology become the god-given strength of a self-reliant man. And here, Barthes tells us, we find the "very principle of myth: it transforms history into nature" (129). In *The Searchers*, the Comanche call Wayne "Big Shoulders," naming his body as the site of signification, the natural symbol of the material power of his culture.

Few actors have been so identified by their physical presence as John Wayne. With its tremendous stature and lurching, determined walk, the body of John Wayne offered a near-perfect symbol of American power in the post–World War II era. Although possessing an often copied voice, John Wayne is most often remembered as the man of action not words. This active capacity, however, is dramatic rather than historical. In essence John Wayne is revered in American culture for having pretended to do things. Wayne's nearest rival in Vietnam lore, Audie Murphy, underlines this point. Murphy's fame originates less in his historical place as the most decorated soldier of World War II than in his Hollywood recreation of those acts. It is *To Hell and Back* that is remembered. This privileging of the copy over the original is central to the workings of popular culture but also dramatizes Barthes' critique of myth as "depoliticized" speech "which is trained to *celebrate* things, and no longer to act them" (144). John Wayne was carried to Vietnam as a celebration of American power. John Wayne made to act—in Larry Heinemann's resonant phrase, once he "became a verb"—became a figure of folly. "To John Wayne" in grunt lore is to act on the battlefield as if before a camera, and to die. Tellingly, Audie Murphy also died in Vietnam, in Joseph Mankiewicz's 1958 adaptation of *The Quiet American.*[23]

The persona "John Wayne" was born of two roles, the Western individualist and the World War II marine, both of which represent a nostalgic yearning for the innocence of the past at critical moments of modernization in American history: the closing of the frontier and the ascension to superpower status in World War II. In Vietnam War literature, the nearly exclusive identification of John Wayne with war movies such as *Sands of Iwo Jima*, even in narratives set in the "Indian Country" of Southeast Asia, testifies to the establishment of an unambiguous and essentialist definition of American power. In the westerns, John Wayne's backward glance is a desire to return to the moment when the West, and thus America, was pure possibility, but this utopian moment is acknowledged to be permanently lost in a breech of American myth-history typically signified by the Civil War. In these films, the effort to ignore becomes the act of acknowledging what Richard Slotkin has called "the Frontier Myth's dark side of racism, false pride and the profligate wastage of lives, cultures and resources," which became fully apparent in Vietnam.[24] In World War II films by contrast, the nostalgic and equally innocent desire for the isolationism of a peaceful domestic life serves to reinforce the vision of American power as a natural fact: We didn't want it, we just had it. In the act of accepting this responsibility, all self-interest is erased: American power and goodness are reified as absolute and identical terms.

THE CRUCIAL IMAGE THAT IDENTIFIES JOHN WAYNE WITH the American victory in the "good war" is the raising of the flag on Iwo Jima. As not only Larry Heinemann but the memoirs of Philip Caputo and Ron Kovic testify, the image of John Wayne that young men carried to Vietnam was the persona of the World War II combat films, specifically the role of Sgt. Stryker in *Sands of Iwo Jima*. In *A Rumor of War*, Philip Caputo recalls meeting the Marine recruiter at his college:

> Already I saw myself charging up some distant beachhead, like John Wayne in *Sands of Iwo Jima*, and then coming home a suntanned warrior with medals on my chest. The recruiters started giving me the usual sales pitch, but I hardly needed to be persuaded. I decided to enlist. (6)

It would be hard to overestimate the influence of this film. More than any other single film, *Sands of Iwo Jima* defined the image not only of John Wayne but of war and the Marine Corps for the generation that fought in Vietnam. The film marked the turning point in Wayne's career. He was second choice for the part, but his performance as the sergeant who is initially hated by his men as inhumanly harsh but comes to be respected and revered from

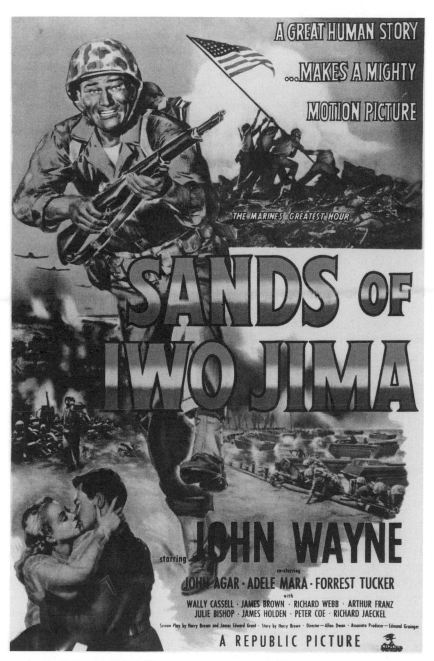

In Sands of Iwo Jima *John Wayne became the embodiment of the World War II soldier for the Vietnam generation. From author's collection.*

the mature perspective of combat garnered Wayne his first Oscar nomination (his only other came 26 years later for *True Grit*) and made him the number-one box office attraction for the first time. Wayne remained among the top 10 for the next 24 years. According to Lawrence Suid, as late as 1975, after the final withdrawal of American soldiers from Vietnam, Marine recruiters were claiming that "volunteers still increase whenever the movie appears on television."[25]

The film was conceived by producer Edmund Grainger, who began with the title, a phrase he had remembered from a newspaper article, and the image of Joe Rosenthal's photograph of the flag raising on Mount Suribachi for the film's climax[26]—the same image replicated by sculptor Felix W. De Weldon in the Iwo Jima Bronze invoked by Heinemann which stands at Arlington National Cemetery and the Marine Training facility at Parris Island. De Weldon, in fact, served as technical adviser in shooting the climactic scene of *Sands of Iwo Jima*. Although often hailed as one of the most technically and historically accurate of Hollywood combat films, *Sands of Iwo Jima*, as De Weldon's participation suggests, is ultimately a reenactment not of a military event but of a self-conscious act of representation.

Charges that Joe Rosenthal's photograph of the flag raising had been staged further remove the possibility of locating a reliable point of historical origin. There were two flag raisings on Mt Suribachi on February 23, 1945. The first signified the Marine's success in taking control of the island. The second was the result of orders to find a "bigger flag" which would better represent the American accomplishment.[27] It was this second flag raising that was immortalized by Joe Rosenthal and reinscribed in bronze and on celluloid. When Ron Kovic "cried in his seat" as a boy watching the flag being raised as the Marine Corps hymn played in his local theater, he was watching actors, advised by a sculptor, recreate a photograph of an event which had been ordered to improve the symbolic character of an historical moment.

The ultimate triumph of this image, its ability to freeze history in a single moment of American purpose and accomplishment as the group of Marines strains to raise the pipe bearing the flag over the war-torn terrain, can perhaps be best measured by the way in which Caputo and Kovic misrepresent Wayne's role in the film. When Caputo imagines himself returning from war the suntanned hero who stormed a beachhead like John Wayne in *Sands of Iwo Jima*, he seems to have forgotten that John Wayne dies at the end of the film and in any case had no home awaiting his return. In the film, Sgt. Stryker is a brave and coolheaded soldier in battle, but on leave he drinks himself into oblivion. His dedication to the Marine Corps has cost him his wife and son, who needed "something more" than he could offer between tours of duty.

Ron Kovic knows that Wayne dies but remembers a more overtly glorious and patriotic death than the film offers:

The Marine Corps hymn was playing in the background as we sat glued to our seats, humming the hymn together and watching Sergeant Stryker, played by John Wayne, charge up the hill and get killed just before he reached the top. And then they showed the men raising the flag on Iwo Jima with the Marines' hymn still playing, and Castiglia and I cried in our seats.[28]

In the film John Wayne does charge up a hill and wipe out a Japanese gun placement, but it is not Mt. Suribachi; it is, in fact, not even on Iwo Jima but on Tarawa. After Iwo Jima is declared secure, Stryker, having a cup of coffee with his men, is killed by a sniper's bullet. The flag raising is the backdrop against which Stryker's death occurs, a tragedy without any purpose or meaningful result. As Thomas Doherty has observed, Stryker's death is "as radically disruptive as anything in the Vietnam film genre."[29]

Sands of Iwo Jima takes pains to render the inglorious cost of such history making. In her historical and formal study of the genre, *The World War II Combat Film*, Jeanine Basinger gives a sensitive reading of the film's overt message. Noting that *Sands of Iwo Jima* belongs to the cycle of postwar films about World War II, Basinger emphasizes the significance of Wayne's death occurring after the battle is over. "In this sense we must have a film in which we kill John Wayne. . . . By killing him, we rid ourselves of the war and of wartime attitudes."[30] Basinger emphasizes the role of the John Agar character, the recruit who resents and resists Marine Corps definitions of masculinity. Agar is reconciled to Wayne right before his death and vows to finish the letter Wayne had tried to write to his son. As Basinger points out, "the more tender and sympathetic John Agar" is held up as "the father we will need for the post war age, one who could give his son Shakespeare instead of the Marine manual."[31]

Stryker's encounter with a prostitute is one of the important "subplots involving women and family structures" that Basinger argues carry the film's anti-Stryker "undercurrent."[32] At one level the scene does radically challenge the righteousness of Stryker's commitment. Accepting an offer of company during one of his drunken binges, Stryker goes home with a woman in a long black dress named Mary. "The long arm of coincidence" Stryker calls it; Mary is his wife's name. Mary is in essence all the women whom soldiers have left behind. At her apartment, money changes hands as Mary goes out for liquor, a surprisingly frank acknowledgment of her status as prostitute. Alone in the apartment, Stryker discovers a baby playing in the next room, completing the radical collapse of wife, mother, and prostitute. "There are a lot tougher ways to make a living than going to war," she tells him upon her return, reprimanding Stryker along with the father of her child for abandoning them for the war. Mary presents a biting indictment of the personal cost of war and the willingness to "bear any burden" that threatens not only the soldier's life but the very home he is charged with protecting.

But this scene also demonstrates the ultimate failure of the film's realism to counter the mythic characterization of John Wayne. As Stryker begins to mix pablum, Mary softens. "You know about babies," she says in surprise. Entering the baby's room for the first time, he drops a wad of cash into the crib and walks back out the door, cured forever of his alcoholic regret. Throughout the film, Stryker's drunken binges signify his nostalgic longing for what he has left behind, the peace of domestic life. They are testimony to his essential sensitivity and humanity, proof that he is not a monster who "loves war." "You're a very good man" Mary tells Stryker, and we are meant to have been privy to his true self. But by affirming the fact that Stryker could be something other than a soldier, Mary fulfills his nostalgic desire and ultimately deflects the blame she originally directed toward him. His motives are restored to innocence, much as her image is transformed from opportunistic whore to loving mother. Stryker may not want the terrible responsibility the war has thrust upon him, but it is his by virtue of those "big shoulders" and he can bear it. Stryker's power and goodness, heretofore seen as oppositional characteristics, are revealed to be one and the same thing.

Basinger's less suspicious reading is rooted in her own experience of World War II. In her acknowledgments, she presents herself as the ideal reader of the film's 1949 message.

> I felt it was my personal responsibility to be organized for attack, and I worried alone at night in my bed, hideously aware that the rest of the family did not seem alert to the impending arrival of the Japanese and Germans in our back yard. I expected them because I went to the movies every Saturday and Sunday night—and God knows there they were. . . . These powerful and dark films about war stayed with me for many years. . . . They very definitely taught me that war is a terrible thing, a lesson I've never forgotten.[33]

Having lived through the war, Basinger is attuned to the changing needs and reactions of the audiences who struggled through the early years of defeat in the Pacific to ultimate triumph and peace. Basinger's experience of war taught her that peace is its object and that demobilization requires a major cultural rethinking. Her readings reflect that assumption.

But for the baby-boomers like Philip Caputo and Ron Kovic, peace was both the status quo to be taken for granted and a falsehood, the placid exterior of a deadly cold war. John F. Kennedy's "ask not what your country can do for you," which serves as the epigraph to *Born on the Fourth of July* and echoes throughout Vietnam literature, pointed the finger of mythic self-sacrifice at the Vietnam generation, intensifying their desire "to find in a common place world a chance to live heroically" (Caputo 5). *Sands of Iwo Jima* creates such an opportunity by submerging its careful delineation of personal loss and effective use of realistic documentary footage in the final image of the flag raising, an image unmoored from historical circumstance. In Barthes's words, "history is changed into a gesture," a gesture which in this film is made virtually irresistible by its familiarity. It is the expected image of triumph which signifies rather than the unexpected image of John Wayne's death. Or, rather, the familiarity of the image of the flag raising demands that the viewer forge a connection between the two events which the overt narrative seeks to diminish. Barthes calls this the "button-holing" characteristic of myth: "It comes and seeks me out in order to oblige me to acknowledge the body of intentions which have motivated it" (125). To a youthful audience John Wayne becomes the unambiguous embodiment of mythic, epic possibilities in spite of the specific attempts to burden his character with a more pedestrian identity.

WHERE MYTH MAKING IN *SANDS OF IWO JIMA* TAKES PLACE at a subtextual or extratextual level, in John Wayne's classic Western films, the tension between history and myth is itself a key part of the story.[34] Often in these films the Civil War is presented as the site of rupture which reveals the unnaturalness of myth. In Howard Hawks's *Red River*, the adopted son (Montgomery Clift) returns from the war to a confused and angry father (John Wayne) and an inheritance literally devalued by the turmoil of Reconstruction. In John Ford's *The Searchers*, John Wayne's delayed return from the war presents him as man alienated from family, society, and self. "Unreconstructed," Wayne's Ethan Edwards continues to declare his allegiance to a world, only symbolized by the Confederacy, which no longer exists. The film's narrative brings this alienation to a crisis, sending Ethan to look for a niece captured by the Comanche whom he comes to realize has likewise ceased to exist; time has transformed her into the enemy.

In both of these films the unity of society and history is ultimately reasserted through family reunion and marriage. But this turn to familial regeneration to explain, resolve, and dispel the tensions of history attests to the naturalizing quality of myth. In *The Searchers* and *Red River*, the naturalness of family unity is itself questioned by heirs who are adopted, sons who are made not born. The restitution of the family and the resolution of the plot in these films necessitates a forgetting of such differences, of the past itself. The films are about this very act of forgetting and thus become acknowledgments of the historical amnesia which gives birth to myth.

John Ford's *Fort Apache* directly addresses this disjunction between history and myth. As an indirect retelling of the Custer story, *Fort Apache* offers an image, like that of *Sands of Iwo Jima*, which is insistently familiar. What an artist later depicts as "Thursday's Charge" is presented by Ford in traditional Custer iconography: Col. Thursday (Henry Fonda) stands among the small knot of men taking careful aim, an image frozen as the thundering hooves of the Apache charge drowned out the voices of the men. But where *Sands of Iwo Jima* presents its mythic image as a naturally occurring

event (albeit one underscored by a military drum roll), the Last Stand in
Fort Apache is an event with a series of audiences, each further receding
from the actual event. Released in 1948, the film marks, as Tag Gallagher
argues, an important turn in the career of John Ford toward a self-conscious
interrogation of myth and myth making.[35] The film looks forward to the
battle between facts and legend which concerns *Liberty Valance* and is particularly interesting in its use of Wayne as the witness to history who in-
herits the legend.

In a film insistently about family, Wayne's Capt. Kirby York stands outside intimate relations. He is neither one of the fathers to young Lt. Michael
O'Roarke (John Agar)—that role is filled to bursting by Ward Bond as Sgt.
Major O'Roarke and the other noncom "Uncles," Irishmen or ex-rebels all
—nor a rival suitor to Philadelphia Thursday (Shirley Temple). He is pe-
ripheral to all relationships and action in the film with one exception: He is
the link to Cochise. And in this one connection the most salient characteristic of Wayne's Western persona is forged. As Richard Slotkin has argued,
"the most potent recurring hero-figures in our mythologies are men in
whom contradictory identities find expression: the white man with knowledge of the Indians, the outlaw who makes himself an agent of justice or
even law" ("Myth" 86).[36] *Fort Apache* places Wayne as a liminal character
throughout, containing although not resolving the conflicts between honor
and duty, white and Apache, past and present, history and myth.

These precariously balanced oppositions are thrown into crisis at the
moment of enacting the Last Stand. Knowing that his arrogant commanding officer, Col. Thursday, is about to lead his men into an ambush that
will mean certain slaughter, York rides out of rank to confront Thursday,
throwing down his gauntlet in challenge. York's attack is on the man, however, not the institution, and so cannot alter events; he will not mutiny.
Ordered to the dishonorable position of a safe vantage point, York watches
the debacle through binoculars, suggesting just how close and how far he
is from the inevitable massacre. Significantly, it is Cochise who returns
York's authority, planting the captured colors of the company standard at
York's feet. York is restored to his position of powerful ambivalence.

In the coda with which Ford ends the film, York has taken command of
Fort Apache and in an office now dominated by a portrait of the martyred
Thursday, he answers reporters' questions. Newspaper readers "back East"
are clamoring for more stories of "the great hero." York does not seek to
deflate their illusions, answering instead in carefully circumscribed truths,
"No man died more gallantly. Nor won more honor for his regiment." The
irony in the scene is terrible but not overpowering, because the popular
myth of Thursday's heroism does not fully displace the historical memory
of his deadly arrogance. York does carry the burden of Thursday's mythic
presence. The standard Cochise returned to York is now part of the shrine to
Thursday. As York gives his "official but convincing" respects to Thursday,[37]
he turns away from the portrait, but the image stares down over Wayne's

shoulder, a key light further privileging its position. It is York who will lead the inevitable reprisals against the Apache.

But the memory of what actually happened at Thursday's charge is not fully obscured. As York leaves the office, standing in the foyer are his new adjutant, Lt. Michael O'Roarke, and O'Roarke's family—mother, wife, and son. The next in command is another witness to Thursday's debacle, one for whom the price, the death of his father, was terrible and personal. But as Philadelphia Thursday's husband, O'Roarke, no less than York, is Thursday's literal heir. The two Mrs. O'Roarkes embody this double and contradictory heritage, as does the small son with the impressive name, "Michael Thursday York O'Roarke." The family testifies to history as "sensuous human activity" in their immediate connection to the possibilities and actions swept aside by the reporters.[38] Framed between the door to the commander's office, which enshrines myth, and the family tableau, which embodies history, is an open door beyond which are visible the open spaces whose grandeur Thursday refused to see in the film's opening sequence. It is out in that space, which in this film and in American iconography belongs to John Wayne, that the double and contradictory burden of myth and history can be born. The excessive spaciousness of Monument Valley becomes the "elsewhere" which Barthes notes myth always has at its disposal: "The meaning is always there to *present* the form; the form is always there to *outdistance* the meaning. And there is never any contradiction, conflict, or split between the meaning and the form: they are never at the same place" (123).

Like *Sands of Iwo Jima*, *Fort Apache* has its Vietnam-era reader. In *Dispatches*, Michael Herr writes:

> Mythopathic moment; *Fort Apache*, where Henry Fonda as the new colonel says to John Wayne, the old hand, "We saw some Apache as we neared the Fort," and John Wayne says, "If you saw them, sir, they weren't Apache." But this colonel is obsessed, brave like a maniac, not very bright, a West Point aristo wounded in his career and his pride, posted out to some Arizona shithole with only marginal consolation: he's a professional and this is the only war we've got. So he gives the John Wayne information a pass and he and half his command get wiped out. More a war movie than a Western, no jive cartoon either where the characters get smacked around . . . broken like a dish, then up again and whole and back in the game, "Nobody dies," as someone said in another war movie. (48)

The competition between careerist officers, the racist devaluation of an elusive enemy, and the refusal to revise tactical assumptions in the light of experience have, as Herr points out, obvious resonance in Vietnam. His formulation of the "mytho*pathic*" moment reflects as well the film's overt concern with the deluding quality of myth which deforms historical experience and gets people killed.

But Herr, like Kovic and Caputo invoking *Sands of Iwo Jima*, misremembers the film's final scenes. Near the end of *Fort Apache*, John Wayne's final speech does in fact attest to the fact that "nobody dies" in war. Looking out a window on which the reflection of marching cavalry overlays Wayne's own image, and beyond which stretches Monument Valley, York celebrates the nameless soldiers who make history and live on in regimental identity. But in Vietnam, the "elsewhere" of American myth ceased to exist—form and meaning were violently brought together. For Michael Herr it was no longer possible to posit an innocent belief that accepting myth in the face of history's contradictions could be "good for the country." The contradictions Ford could explore without exploding as late as 1962 moved beyond closure in the Vietnam War. After Vietnam, *Fort Apache* acquires (or requires) a different ending.

RICHARD SLOTKIN HAS NOTED THAT THE "THE ONE LANGUAGE the grunts demonstrably shared with their military and bureaucratic superiors was [the] language of Cowboys and Indians" (71). But in spite of the pervasiveness of Western metaphors and images, in the context of the Vietnam War, John Wayne remains the World War II Marine and not the ambivalent figure of the Western. Even for Michael Herr, who can quote John Wayne as the ironic critic of American self-aggrandizement, the cultural icon "John Wayne" functions primarily as a figure of delusion—"the lowest John Wayne wetdream" of winning wars singlehandedly (Herr 20). We have seen how the text of *Sands of Iwo Jima* leaves room for such misapprehension, but the privileging of the Stryker role also lays bare the ideology that reconstructed John Wayne in these terms. Ron Kovic's *Born on the Fourth of July* offers a reading of the John Wayne myth which fully articulates the "contingencies of social and personal life" which produced its relevance to Vietnam (Slotkin 80).

In the third chapter, Kovic goes back to "the beginning," his birth on July 4, 1946, a date which extends Kovic's own story beyond the personal to national history. The ultimate "baby-boomer," Kovic's birthdate marks him as the child of victory and the heir apparent of American history. The nation is in effect reborn in him; "every birthday after that was something the whole country celebrated" (46). The chapter is in many ways a disarming series of recollections which recreate a 1950s childhood: baseball, television, movies, the Cold War. But coming as it does after chapters describing Kovic's wounding in Vietnam, his confinement to a wheelchair, and humiliating rounds of treatment in hospitals, these childhood memories take on the sinister weight of formative experience, stepping-stones on his road to Vietnam. The chapter ends with Kovic's enlistment in the Marine Corps.

Kovic's memories of John Wayne lead associatively into Sputnik and the defining cultural terms of the Cold War. Kovic vividly recreates the powerful emotions he felt watching Audie Murphy in *To Hell and Back* and John

Wayne in *Sands of Iwo Jima* and traces, with no apparent irony, the way he and his friends would reenact these cinematic battles using Mattel machine guns in their backyards. Playing war is a game like baseball, Kovic suggests, noting how he and his friends would pore over the Marine Corps handbook and dream of becoming a Marine "just as we dreamed of playing for the Yankees someday" (56). The two all-American uniforms seem interchangeable. From dreams of the Marines there is a logical transition to memories of the cub scouts where they marched in memorial day parades and "built fallout shelters out of milk cartons," which leads us to Sputnik and communists and finally Kovic's determination "to build a strong and heathy body" (56, 61).

The transitions in this section, as in most of the book, seem "natural" and thus "artless," functions of what Kovic remembers, of what his life was "really like." The mode appears to be directly mimetic. But broken down into its component parts—John Wayne, Mattel machine guns ("made by Mattel" was the favorite grunt joke about the M-16's tendency to jam), Marines, cub scouts, bomb shelters, Sputnik, the body—Kovic's boyhood appears less a catalogue of personal events than an assemblage of ideological signifiers associated with Vietnam. Kovic presents his valorization of John Wayne in *Sands of Iwo Jima* simultaneously as a boy's "natural" desire to be a hero, to be more than a checker at the "A&P" like his dad, and as the inevitable product of the Cold War. For Ron Kovic, growing up at a time when the "Communists were all over the place," the sacrifices of Sgt. Stryker did not appear as things of the past (60). Sputnik meant that "America wasn't first anymore," and Kovic's birthright, his identification of self and country, demanded that he reestablish American preeminence (59). The ubiquitous presence of militarism and anticommunism—on television, in movie theaters, in school, in his backyard—ensures that Kovic will not miss his calling.

Kovic's overt references to the Cold War are comic, almost innocent, in their absurdity and ignorance. At one point, Kovic is convinced that a teacher made speechless by the idea that there would soon be "one billion Chinese" was a communist. Ironically, it is Kovic's dedication to sports which best defines his ideological orientation. Becoming a Marine *is* like playing baseball in a world in which global politics is organized as a contest between two sides. There is no room here for the ambiguities of Wayne's Western persona. Only when the rules of the game are broken, when John F. Kennedy is assassinated, do Western images suggest themselves; "It all seemed wild and crazy, like some Texas shoot-out" (72). Actual violence momentarily transforms the simplified, progressive image of JFK's New Frontier.

When Kovic's high school coaches tell him, "Wanting to win and wanting to be first, that's what's important. . . . Play fair, but play to win" (62), they do not sound that different from Sgt. Stryker, the harsh preacher of discipline. To win, Kovic is told, "You're going to have to drive your bodies far beyond what you think you can. You have to pay the price for victory" (62). Just as John F. Kennedy inaugurated his New Frontier with the Presidential Fitness Program in American schools, so Ron Kovic responds to the communist "invasion" by strengthening his personal defenses.[39] His new awareness of his body, his determination to be strong, becomes the internalization of this ideology of power, another imitation of John Wayne. Here Eric Bentley's formulation of the body of John Wayne as "the body politic" gains force and substance.

The structure of Kovic's memoir, as N. Bradley Christie has pointed out, demands "re-reading."[40] The body we see being built in John Wayne's image in chapter 3, has already been broken. In chapter 2, Kovic comes to understand the true nature of his wound "watching his legs become smaller and smaller, until after a month the muscle tone had all but disappeared" (31). The overt comparison between the John Wayne Kovic wanted to be, the physical embodiment of strength and manhood, and the "sexless man" left by the war, leaves Kovic howling with betrayal. "I gave my dead dick for John Wayne. . . . Nobody told me I was going to come back from this war without a penis" (112). At this level of terrible emotional pain, Kovic indicts the culture which compelled him to volunteer for duty in Vietnam. "In one big bang they have taken it all from me" (38), Kovic thinks in the hospital, externalizing completely the responsibility for what has happened to him and apparently destroying the identification Kovic felt with his country.

But Kovic's body does in fact continue to figure the American body politic. The poem with which Kovic begins his memoir both introduces and redefines the very terms of his upbringing and reasserts his exemplary Americanness.

> I am the living death
> the memorial day on wheels
> I am your yankee doodle dandy
> your John Wayne come home
> your fourth of july firecracker
> exploding in the grave (i)

Ron Kovic's broken body reflects a body politic shattered by the war in Vietnam. "John Wayne come home" carries the stigma of the war's self-consuming violence. In the images of the "war at home," the violent confrontations of police and antiwar demonstrators, Kovic himself beaten, handcuffed, and arrested, we see the cultural manipulations of the Cold War give way to overt government coercion. Significantly, it is the killings at Kent State which first motivate Kovic to participate in demonstrations against the war.

The image of Americans killing Americans over the war in Vietnam recapitulates what Peter McInerney calls the "secret history" of Kovic's text:

Kovic's killing of an American corporal in battle. Suppressed in the early chapters, the corporal from Georgia lies at the heart of the emotional breakdown that parallels Kovic's physical debilitation. McInerney sees a discrepancy in Kovic's "attack on American culture" and his account of killing the corporal, specifically in Kovic's dual citing of these events as explanations of how he came to be wounded in Vietnam. But Kovic's exploration of his own complicity deepens rather than, as McInerney argues, contradicts "the text's thesis of cultural manipulation" (199). Accidentally killing another American in battle throws into crisis Kovic's ideological assumptions, much as the killings at Kent State would later.

> He had panicked with the rest of them that night and murdered his
> first man, but it wasn't the enemy, it wasn't the one they had all been
> taught and trained to kill, it wasn't the silhouette at the rifle range he
> had pumped holes in from five hundred yards, or the German soldiers
> with plastic machine guns in Sally's Woods. He'd never figured it
> would ever happen this way. It never did in the movies. There were al-
> ways the good guys and the bad guys, the cowboys and the Indians.
> . . . The good guys weren't supposed to kill the good guys. (194–195)

The trope's significance lies not in assigning guilt, as McInerney assumes, but in its radical reorientation of the self. Kovic returns to the terrain and assumptions of his childhood, replaying the narrative that no longer fits his experience. The opposition of self and other on which the Cold War narrative depends breaks down in violence. The experience of friendly fire signals the death of John Wayne in Kovic's imagination.

At the very end of *Born on the Fourth of July*, Kovic returns in his imagination to the backyard of his childhood, where he was young and strong and free. In this memory John Wayne no longer contends with Mickey Mantle as Kovic's hero. It is the Cub Scout, not the Marine Corps, manual they study. *Sands of Iwo Jima* is banished along with all those traces of militarism and Cold War ideology which stigmatized chapter 3. If there is a point of profound disjunction in Kovic's text, it is here. Kovic is attempting to present the best of what was lost in Vietnam; but in his very understandable desire to preserve that space where his body was whole, he risks recreating the body politic in the nostalgic terms of depoliticized myth.

"It was all kind of easy. It was all come and gone," Kovic tells us, but if we are to believe the rest of his memoir it also never existed. The childhood which throughout the memoir is leading inexorably to Vietnam is suddenly torn from this context. Even on the page, italicized, the memory is distinguished from the text that proceeds it. Kovic isolates one perfect moment:

> *There was this song called "Runaway" by a guy named Dell Shannon play-*
> *ing one Saturday at the baseball field. I remember it was a beautiful spring*

*day and we were young back then and really alive and the air smelled fresh.
The song was playing and I really got into it and was hitting baseballs and
feeling I could live forever.* (224)

Kovic removes baseball from the competitive "us and them" ideology of a
Cold War childhood, but this is not to demythologize it, only to dehistoricize
the process of myth making. As a creation of the rapid industrialization of
nineteenth-century America, baseball preserves the green pastoral space of
the American past in the middle of an urban, industrial society and thus
embodies an essential quality of American myth. As Richard Slotkin has
noted, "Through myth we imaginatively hoard away the cake we have eaten
and voice our affection for a precapitalist Eden even while we affirm our
affiliation with the values and priorities of the bourgeois society."[41] Kovic's
final nostalgic image creates the imaginative space ("the backyard, that was
the place to be") where he can live on as an innocent true believer in himself, but also in the myth of America which that self represents throughout
the text. Ironically, by banishing John Wayne Kovic simply recuperates the
nostalgic backward glance so central to the Wayne mythos.

BY THE TIME JOHN WAYNE MAKES HIS ENTRANCE ON THE
second page of Gustav Hasford's novel *The Short-Timers*, he is already dead,
but, as noted earlier, like Michael Herr's "character in pop grunt mythology," he's "too stupid to lie down" (74). John Wayne is in fact one of the
"undead," not unlike the werewolves and vampires who haunt Hasford's
surreal novel. Deepening the connection in Kovic's text between the trope
of friendly fire and the death of John Wayne, Hasford moves beyond ironic
repudiation to the increasing violence that marks the consumption of this
particular myth to "the ends built into its structure." Unlike Kovic, Hasford
posits no "before" Vietnam, no backyard to invest with innocent, nostalgic
desire. The first chapter of *The Short-Timers* begins with an epigram from
Michael Herr's *Dispatches*: "I think that Vietnam was what we had instead
of happy childhoods."[42] Hasford's narrative, although drawn from his personal experience as a Marine combat correspondent in Vietnam, expresses
a postmodern acknowledgment of its status as "already written" rather
than the emotional purity of Kovic's *cri du coeur*.

   Instead of a classic move from innocence to experience, or even from
"naivete to cynicism,"[43] there is in *The Short-Timers* an escalating scale of
violence committed by Americans against themselves and fought over the
dead body of John Wayne. Each of the novel's three parts is structured
around an act of murder which attacks the John Wayne myth at increasingly deeper levels. Leonard's killing of Sergeant Gerheim in basic training
makes good the overt ironic comparison of Parris Island and John Wayne
movies. The fragging of Shortround and Joker's killing of the female sniper
undermine the humanistic code of honor Wayne represented and unmask
the racial and sexual hegemony on which that code rests. Finally, Joker

must kill Cowboy, his best friend, to prevent his squad from "committing suicide for a tradition" which however corrupt still compels allegiance. This cycle of violence turning ever further inward unmasks the internalization of ideology which John Wayne represents.

Hasford's characters arrive in bootcamp making John Wayne jokes. The first reference to Wayne in *The Short-Timers* is a statement of irony and an act of mimicry, elicited by the insults of an "obscene little ogre in immaculate khaki," Gunnery Sergeant Gerheim, the senior drill instructor.

> A wiry little Texan in horn-rimmed glasses the guys are already calling "Cowboy" says, "Is that you John Wayne? Is this me?" Cowboy takes off his pearl gray Stetson and fans his sweaty face.
>
> I laugh. Years of high school drama classes have made me a mimic. I sound exactly like John Wayne as I say: "I think I'm going to hate this movie." (4)

In Hasford's profoundly fallen world, John Wayne is an echo, a mask, a joke—no longer a body but a voice. This is not a world in which boys become men but in which actors play parts. The irony here is not simple, however; it embodies rather than displaces John Wayne's persistent presence in the novel. It is the John Wayne joke which names the novel's two main characters and forms the basis for their friendship. The narrator is dubbed "Private Joker" when Sgt. Gerheim hears his act of mimicry, naming irony itself as but another part to play. Cowboy remains "Cowboy" in quotes; he's too short and he wears glasses, but he's from Texas and plays the part to the hilt, beating his Stetson on his thigh, complaining that there are "no horses in Vietnam." In spite of the obvious irony of the allusions, we never know him by any other name than "Cowboy."

John Wayne becomes an unplayable role only when confronted with violence. Hasford/Joker's most direct repudiation of the John Wayne image of Marine Corps concerns the beatings the drill instructors administer during training.

> Beatings, we learn, are a routine element of life on Parris Island. And not that I'm-only-rough-on-'um-because-I-love-'um crap civilians have seen in Jack Webb's Hollywood movie *The D.I.* and in Mr. John Wayne's *The Sands of Iwo Jima*. Gunnery Sergeant Gerheim and his three junior drill instructors administer brutal beatings to faces, chests, stomachs, and backs. With fists. Or boots—they kick us in the ass, the kidneys, the ribs, any part of our bodies on which a black and purple bruise won't show. (7)

Violence, not sentimentality, is the true core of Gerheim's being and the essence of the esprit de corps he drills into the men. He literally writes this lesson on the bodies of the recruits.

There is no trace of the double identity of the John Wayne sergeant in Gerheim, a fact illustrated by Hasford's account of bayonet training. In *Sands of Iwo Jima*, Sgt. Stryker singles out a recruit who cannot master his bayonet and nearly breaks the kid's jaw with his rifle butt. The on-set technical adviser from the Marine Corps objected to the scene during the shooting, but it was ultimately approved because of the humorous companion scene that marks the completion of the recruit's training. Making good Stryker's original promise that "if I can't teach you one way, I'll teach you another," the sergeant finally teaches the recruit to master the bayonet by dancing the Mexican hat dance with him. "You lead," John Wayne orders the kid, and they proceed to dance a sprightly jig. The scene ends with a privileged shot of Wayne smiling as the kid yells "Hey Sarge, I got it!" The role of violence in Stryker's training is clearly defined; it is what you are trained to guard against. It is a threat from outside the self against which the American soldier must employ all his abilities.

In *The Short-Timers*, Hasford names the opening section on basic training "The Spirit of the Bayonet"; that spirit is violence, the form and substance of Marine training. Gerheim's instruction of the troops in the proper use of the bayonet directly parodies the portrayal in *Sands of Iwo Jima*. "During bayonet training," Joker begins, Sgt. Gerheim "dances an aggressive ballet" (14). Where Wayne's dance was the path to physical skill and refinement, a testament to cooperation and diligence, Gerheim's is a ritualistic celebration of violence; "The purpose of bayonet training, Sergeant Gerheim explains, is to awaken our killer instincts" (14). "Sgt. Gerheim demonstrates effective attack techniques to a recruit named Barnard, a soft-spoken farm boy from Maine. The beefy drill instructor knocks out two of Private Barnard's teeth with a rifle butt" (14). Unlike John Wayne's recruit, Barnard is picked out for injury at random. He demonstrates no special deficiency that requires the harsh lesson. Permanently marked by Gerheim's lesson, Barnard is not shown to heal physically or emotionally as does the soldier in *Sands of Iwo Jima*. But he does learn Gerheim's lesson well. As Gerheim preaches his gospel of strength and self-reliance, "Every Marine must be the instrument of his own salvation," Barnard, "his mouth a bloody hole, demonstrates that he has been paying attention. . . . [He] bayonets Sergeant Gerheim through the right thigh" (15). Gerheim's response is to knock Barnard unconscious and then to praise him. Promoting the "unconscious Barnard" to squad leader, Gerheim announces, "Goddamn it, there's one little maggot who knows that the spirit of the bayonet is to *kill*! He'll make a damn fine field Marine" (15).

When John Wayne is injured training his men, it is the result of an act of salvation, not aggression. He shields a recruit with his own body when a grenade is misthrown during practice. The contrast between these two injuries defines Hasford's essential revision of the Wayne myth. In talking with the Marine advisers to the film, Wayne was told "that the Marines didn't train men to die for their country. They were trained 'to live for their country and to live to fight again. It was survival training.'"[44] Before landing at Tarawa, Wayne tells his men, "Let the other guy die for his county," an overt reference to the anti-Japanese propaganda that depicted enemy soldiers as suicidal fanatics.[45] Gerheim tells his men that he won the Navy Cross on Iwo Jima for "teaching young Marines how to bleed" (20). Gerheim's revision is historically resonant; nearly 7,000 Americans died in the 36 days of fighting on Iwo Jima and more than 19,000 were wounded, a casualty rate of 1:3.[46]

If Gerheim represents a revision of the John Wayne image of Marine mythology, he does not signify a demystified Corps. Much of what Gerheim tells the men is in fact familiar to Hollywood audiences: Marines are faster, tougher, cleaner. The Marine Corps motto is *Semper Fidelis*, "Always Faithful," and "Gung Ho" is Chinese for "working together." Most of all, "It is a Marine Corps tradition that Marines never abandon their dead" (18). But Hasford's focus on the violence and sexual intimidation used in Marine training shifts the significance of this valorization of the dead away from honor, glory, and duty to the bloody exchange between body, corpse, and Corps. "Marines die—that's what we're here for—but the Marine Corps will live forever," Gerheim tells the men (9), transforming even as it echoes John Wayne's final speech in *Fort Apache*.

John Wayne's "living" body, the celluloid image of his actual performance, although it articulates many of the Corps' cherished principles, can no longer fully embody this myth because it does not bleed. Wayne's death in *Sands of Iwo Jima* is completely bloodless. Late in his career John Wayne complained about the realistic violence that came to characterize the movies. "I never used things like animal livers to show someone getting shot. That's just bad taste."[47] Hasford's vicious irony, which, as Thomas Myers has noted, aggressively employs bad taste, purposefully sullies the image of John Wayne, not to destroy it but to show how its debased remains still signify.[48]

Gerheim's mythology is built on a marriage of those elements carefully censored in John Wayne's image, sex and violence, in the union of a Marine and his rifle, "the deadliest weapon in the world" (13). The recruits who arrive on Parris Island are named by Gerheim "pukes, you are scumbags, you are the lowest form of life on Earth. You are not even human. You people are nothing but a lot of little pieces of amphibian shit" (4). Such prehuman matter is most frequently referred to as "ladies." Gerheim's "comprehensive" imagination, which returns again and again to sexual humiliation, serves the same purpose as the beatings; it ties the recruits to their bodies, a state of debased imminence named female. Masculinity is created, asserted through training. "Sound off *like* you've got a pair," Gerheim tells the men when they arrive, a direct acknowledgment of manhood's metaphorical and thus mythical nature (5, emphasis added). The rifle is the instrument that transforms ladies into men. As Gerheim orders his recruits to march around the barracks with their rifles in one hand and their penises in the other, singing, "*This is my rifle, this is my gun; One is for fighting, and one is for fun,*" the metaphorical exchange between history and nature that characterizes myth can be seen taking place (12).

The body as the site of sexuality and violence that is hidden in John Wayne's films is exposed by Gerheim so that he can displace it in the mythology of the rifle. For the rifle is not only the phallus named and recognized but the soldier's object of desire as well. Gerheim orders each man to give his rifle a girl's name. "This is the only pussy you people are going to get," he tells them. "You're married to *this* piece, this weapon of iron and wood" (13). In spite of his apparent ironic detachment, Joker assimilates this schizophrenic mythos easily enough. The pun on "piece" is exactly the sort of cultural collapse in which Joker's humor feels most at home. But two moments of an uncharacteristic lack of self-awareness on Joker's part reveal the degree to which Joker has also come to live the metaphor that the struggling recruit Leonard tragically enacts. By the sixth week of training, Joker wakes up in his bunk to find his rifle in bed with him. "I don't know how it got there," is Joker's only comment. Confronted with Leonard's erotic handling of his rifle, Joker thinks of his girlfriend, Vanessa. "I'm fucking her eyes out. But my favorite fantasy has gone stale. Thinking about Vanessa's thighs, her dark nipples, her full lips doesn't give me a hard-on anymore. I guess it must be the saltpeter in our food, like they say" (27). Joker, who never takes anyone's word for anything without putting an ironic spin on it, settles for it here, refusing to make the obvious connection that he too has entered the absurd marriage of body and weapon, human and machine.

Hasford fully exposes Gerheim's own displacement of the body in the final confrontation with Leonard, in an elaborate interplay of body and voice, metaphor and allusion. When the all but hopeless Leonard is finally beaten into shape by his fellow recruits, he seems to lose his voice even as his body fulfills the tasks demanded of it. It is not until late in training that Leonard begins to speak again, reciting the "Rifleman's Creed" at the top of his lungs. Following graduation, Leonard's voice disturbs the peace of the final night on Parris Island. He is talking to his rifle, having a lover's quarrel with "Charlene." "He begins to field-strip his weapon. 'This is the first time I've seen her naked,'" he tells Joker. Leonard proceeds to literalize his training. "Gently, he inserts the metal magazine into his weapon, into Charlene," consummating their marriage (27).

The "live" ammunition that Leonard is now packing unmasks Gerheim's mythic persona. Awakened by Leonard's dialogue with Charlene, Gerheim announces his presence with the capitalized insults that mark his character. But once informing Gerheim that Pyle has "a full magazine locked and loaded," Joker sees the sergeant in a new light.

Gunnery Sergeant Gerheim looks more than a little ridiculous in his pure white skivvies and red rubber flip-flop shower shoes and hairy

legs and tattooed forearms and a beer gut and a face the color of raw
beef, and, on, his bald head, the green and brown Smokey the Bear
campaign cover.

Our senior drill instructor focuses all of his considerable powers of
intimidation into his best John-Wayne-on-Suribachi voice . . . (29)

In the face of actual violence, the metaphoric violence of Gerheim's mythology is emptied of authority. His threat of castration ("I'M GOING TO TEAR
YOUR BALLS OFF") is undercut by the "virility" of Leonard's loaded weapon.
His voice, which had apparently shouted down the anachronistic fiction of
John Wayne, is revealed to be but another echo. His body is not a figure of
power but an absurd assemblage of Marine cliches. Sgt. Stryker gone to
pot; Gerheim is killed by his own creation.

Leonard has fulfilled the promise of training, but having revealed the
contradictions of its mythology, that the weapon is more powerful than the
body that wields it, Leonard must complete his "consumption" of the myth
to the "ends built into its structure." "Leonard takes the black barrel into his
mouth" and pulls the trigger, rendering his body an "awful lump of blood
and facial bones and sinus fluids and uprooted teeth and jagged, torn flesh"
(31). In this purposefully graphic image of "sensuous human activity," myth
collapses into history for the reader, although not for Joker and the other
recruits. "The skin looks plastic and unreal," Joker says of Leonard, remaining inside the mythic discourse of the Marine Corps: "Private Pratt, while a
highly motivated individual, was a ten percenter who did not pack the gear
to be a Marine in our beloved Corps" (31). Joker's dreams that night are not
of the terrible vulnerability of human flesh but of the "holy relic," his rifle,
"Vanessa."

Parodied, debunked, and shot dead in part one, John Wayne returns on
the second page of part two in a suitably debased vehicle, *The Green Berets*.
Joker compares the dirty, unshaven, rowdy grunts in the theater to the
"beautiful soldier . . . sharply attired in tailored tiger-stripe jungle utilities"
up on the screen (38). Seizing on the film's most famous unconscious irony,
Joker describes its ending:

> . . . John Wayne walks off into the sunset with a spunky little orphan.
> The grunts laugh and whistle and threaten to pee all over themselves.
> The sun is setting in the South China Sea—in the East—which makes
> the end of the movie as accurate as the rest of it. (38)

Joker's reading of *The Green Berets* reiterates the terms of the ironic rejection of John Wayne's image in part one. Vietnam is clearly not an orderly
and sentimental place. But *The Green Berets* becomes increasing less laugh-
able as the novel continues.

In its concern with propaganda and power, part two of *The Short-Timers*,
"Body Count," exposes the conspiratorial ideology which keeps an obvi-

ously expired John Wayne at the center of the war's iconography. John Wayne's version of Vietnam is no more ridiculous than the assignments Joker is given as a reporter for the Marine Corps newspaper, *Leatherneck*. Returning from the movie, Joker writes a "masterpiece"—"it takes talent to convince people that war is a beautiful experience" (45). This talent is the Marine Corps' secret weapon and John Wayne is the spearhead. Captain January, who spends the war playing Monopoly, observes, "the lesser services like to joke about how every Marine platoon goes into battle accompanied by a platoon of Marine Corps photographers. That's affirmative. Marines fight harder because Marines have bigger legends to live up to" (62). John Wayne embodied the photograph which embodied the Marine legend—the flag raising at Iwo Jima. The official "cooperation" between Hollywood and the Pentagon which created the World War II combat film is, in Captain January's terms, "good business," suggesting deals based on profit and loss and not, to use Slotkin's term, the seemingly "occult" influence of national character or culture.

The continuing but ironic presence of John Wayne in Vietnam reflects the class split between grunts who are "prisoners of the war" and the "lifers" or "poges" who run it.[49] From the top, John Wayne is "good business," but business as represented by the Monopoly game which Captain January orders his subordinate, Mr. Payback, to play. Rather than a free market there is a fascistic centralizing of power for which the Marine Corps is only a symbol. The "good old boy" General Motors, "who likes to keep in touch with his Marines," is the closest thing to a John Wayne-style officer in *The Short-Timers*, with his starched uniform and "tough but sensitive face" (50). But as his name suggests, his Hollywood perfect image is cynical public relations. Recalling the observation that "what's good for General Motors is good for the country," and the business-like approach Robert McNamara took from Ford Motors to the Defense Department and on to Vietnam, Hasford's General Motors embodies the public relations effort to keep a human, John Wayne face on a technocrat's war.

From the bottom of this bifurcated hierarchy of power, the John Wayne image is quite simply ridiculous. But in its symbolic function of keeping a human face on the war, the grunts instinctively cling to it. It is at the theater showing *The Green Berets* that Joker and Cowboy renew their boot-camp friendship. In their hatred of the "poges," the bureaucrats and officers who keep the war going from air-conditioned offices in the rear, the grunts reject the cynical view of John Wayne as a commodity to be bought and sold. In a world of carefully controlled and circumscribed imagery, John Wayne remains the only part they have to play, so they transform it, "consume it to the ends built into its structure," make it their own (Barthes 128). All of the most "sympathetic" characters (an admittedly relative term in Hasford's hard-boiled world) are called John Wayne at one point or another: Mr. Payback, Lt. Shortround and Cowboy. Shortround, and Cowboy give the role's command performances and pay the price, shot by their own men in the end.

Mr. Payback preaches the gospel of violent return which begins the redefinition of John Wayne in the grotesquely bloody terms of Vietnam. "Payback is a motherfucker, New Guy," he tells the combat neophyte, Rafter Man. "When Luke the gook zaps you in the back and Phantoms bury him in napalm canisters, that's payback. When you shit on people it comes back to you, sooner or later, only worse" (64). Joker softpedals Mr. Payback's message, "Don't listen to any of Mr. Payback's bullshit, Rafter Man. Sometimes he thinks he's John Wayne" (65). But he is John Wayne forbidden to fulfill his assigned role. The drafted Monopoly partner, Mr. Payback is the ultimate "prisoner of the war." As Top Sergeant, he is an initiator of the new guys, but one who teaches them that their powerlessness within the war can only be transcended by embracing the violence that threatens them. Rafter Man learns this lesson well. When later that night, Rafter Man has his first taste of enemy fire, he holds on to a souvenir.

> He's looking at Mr. Payback. The object in Rafter Man's hand is a piece of flesh, Winslow's flesh, ugly yellow, as big as a John Wayne cookie, wet with blood. We all look at it for a long time.
>
> Rafter Man puts the piece of flesh into his mouth, onto his tongue, and we think he's going to vomit. Instead, he grits his teeth. Then, closing his eyes, he swallows. (74)

Like Leonard, Rafter Man seeks to "consume" John Wayne's body in a travesty of communion which nonetheless seals his membership in the brotherhood of bad taste, those who bleed in graphic and prolific ways, the grunts.

Lt. Shortround is a more traditional John Wayne, one whose precarious balancing act between the discipline and violence needed to fight a war collapses in mutiny. Animal Mother is the squad's soul of anarchic violence, the soldier whom the leader must curb in order to maintain his authority. Shortround seeks to do it in the classic tradition of honor—"our John Wayne Lieutenant" Cowboy calls him (87). When Shortround draws the line with Animal Mother, he doesn't pull rank but invokes the moral force of a man-to-man confrontation. Told that Animal Mother had been chasing a 13-year-old girl around "with his dick hanging out," Shortround replies, "You harass one more little girl and I'm going to put my little silver bar in my pocket and then you and I are going to throw some hands" (92), just as John Wayne does with a soldier he suspects of cowardice in *Sands of Iwo Jima*. But as Animal Mother points out, the enemy has been young and female before, and then he was entitled to rape and murder.

The break between Shortround and Animal Mother comes, however, not in a moral confrontation but in a divided reading of the John Wayne mythos. When members of the squad are pinned down by a sniper and dismembered bit by bit, Animal Mother wants to go in after them, to "pull a John Wayne," enacting the Vietnam vintage definition of the role. Shortround insists on the discipline of Sgt. Stryker, refusing to allow his emotions to be manipulated by a ruthless enemy. He "lets hands fly" at Animal Mother, but the argument is postponed although not decided when the sniper kills the Americans.

Animal Mother does get his payback. He frags Shortround during a firefight and then invents a suitably John Wayne-style death to cover his act of mutiny. "'The platoon radioman was down. . . . The Skipper went out to get him. A frag got him. A frag got them both. At least . . .' Cowboy turns to look at Animal Mother. 'At least, that's how Mother tells it'" (106). None of the others believe Animal Mother, but to shed the admittedly contrived structure of the John Wayne narrative is to face without protection the violence Mother embodies. So they tell the story, looking over their shoulders the whole time, trying to outdistance the reality that surrounds them.

This distance collapses in the killing of the sniper, "no more than fifteen years old, a slender Eurasian angel with dark, beautiful eyes, which, at the same time, are the hard eyes of a grunt" (116). The clear delineation of self and other on which the orderly world of John Wayne depends collapses utterly in this enemy who is simultaneously child and adult, male and female, white and Asian, seductive and deadly. Rafter Man shoots her in his final act of initiation. He "loses his cherry," making good the bootcamp psychology that preaches a violent loathing of the female. But the girl refuses to die. Her assumption of power has already turned the mythic manhood of the squad against itself and will not conform easily to its narrative. To kill her, Joker must step out of his role as mimic, removing himself from even the ironic model of John Wayne, and kill her in cold blood. But the female no longer exists in a position of "natural" weakness which confirms male power. The small, weak, dark-skinned enemy outshoots the Americans. The ideological underpinning of John Wayne's world collapses in violence one more time.

Significantly, Cowboy has been unconscious during the final encounter with the sniper and wakes up to assume the leadership of the squad. In Cowboy, John Wayne walks once again, and in the final section of the novel, the squad moves into "Indian County." Like Kovic retrieving baseball from the ideological complicity of his childhood, Cowboy clings to Western images of personal freedom and individualism as an alternative dream world to the nightmare of violence and corporate cooptation in Vietnam. Remembering his life before the war, Cowboy tells the others, "After school, I shucked pennies out of parking meters. I had a red wagon to pour the pennies in, and I had a blue cap with a silver badge on it. I thought I was hot shit. Now all I want is a ranch with some horses. . . . " (160). In Cowboy, John Wayne is reinvested with the Western nostalgia for a simpler, freer world—one without uniforms to define a man's relationship to his society. Cowboy's ranch echoes the Texas spreads to which the Civil War veterans return in the movies of John Ford and Howard Hawks. But "there's not one horse in all of Viet Nam," as Cowboy himself is the first to point out (41). The means of this redemption are beyond the reach of the grunts trapped inside the war.

The novel's end replays the confrontation with the sniper in part two, marking finally the limits of mimicry and the John Wayne joke. On patrol in the jungle, Alice, the point man, is shot by a sniper as he enters a clearing. Cowboy calls for air support but is refused and then the sniper shoots the radio. Alice loses a foot, then a hand to bullets, and begs Cowboy for help. It is like a horror movie being replayed. Cowboy holds his men back, but he is arguing against their best and deepest instincts. The medic, the soldier designated to heal and feel compassion, goes in and is dropped by the sniper as well.

In Hasford's perfect replaying of the Vietnam-as-quagmire metaphor, Cowboy is faced with the impossible decision of sacrificing his friends in order to avoid losing more men to a hopeless situation. He tries to make the call, but the Marine Corps ethos runs too deep. The New Guy "charges," firing blind. "He thinks he's John Wayne" (172). The sniper shoots him in the throat, silencing his imitation. Cowboy orders the men pull out but faces the same force Shortround did. Animal Mother reminds him, "Marines *never* abandon their dead or wounded, Mr. Squad Leader, *sir*" (173). The embodiment of viciousness becomes the voice of the most honorable of Marine traditions and forces Cowboy to play out his tragic role. Like Sgt. Stryker on Tarawa, Cowboy refuses to risk more men, choosing to go himself.

But Cowboy wants his sacrifice to extinguish rather than continue the John Wayne ethos. Ordering Joker to pull the squad back, Cowboy "drops his Stetson and Mr. Shortround's shotgun," and goes in with only a pistol (174). He breaks the comic pretense that defines his relationship to Joker. When Joker tries to hold him back with an appeal to that bond, "if you get yourself wasted, whose going to introduce me to your sister?" Cowboy calls the bluff, "I don't have a sister, I thought you knew that" (173). At this point, it is only the sniper who is laughing, his voice echoing through the jungle, mocking the Marines who are trapped as much by their own beliefs as by his bullets. Cowboy goes in but rather than defending his friends, he seeks to complete the cycle of violence. His legs shot out from under him and emasculated, Cowboy uses the pistol to kill his own men but has his hand shot off before he can commit suicide.

Joker is now faced with the same terrible command decision. Animal Mother and the rest are still ready to go in after Cowboy. In the face of his friend, Joker confronts the painful difficulty of giving up on John Wayne, of his own complicity in a myth he had parodied and travestied. To mimic is to remain trapped inside the limits of the discourse, even while exposing its absurdities and contradictions. John Wayne keeps getting killed and bouncing back because "Marines never leave their dead." Castrated and mutilated, Cowboy like John Wayne cannot be saved. But "the squad is going to follow Mother and commit suicide for a tradition" (177). Joker blocks Animal Mother's path, who growls, "This ain't no Hollywood movie, Joker. Stand down or I will cut you in half. . . . " (177). Animal Mother, like Gerheim, believes that violence defines reality and explodes myth. But Joker has learned that violence is often only a device to advance the plot. He takes aim and shoots Cowboy. "I NEVER LIKED YOU. I NEVER THOUGHT YOU WERE FUNNY—" Cowboy calls out as Joker takes aim, helping his friend put an end to the John Wayne joke they had shared (178). The human face is finally pulled off of war.

IF WE ARE EVER TO UNDERSTAND THE PERSISTENCE OF JOHN Wayne we cannot afford to banish him from memory as Ron Kovic seeks to do, or murder him in cold blood as Joker does. Instead, we need to return to the text of John Wayne's body of films and the metaphoric rendering of American history which sent him to Vietnam even before he made *The Green Berets* in order to explore the silences in which ideology resides. By way of demonstrating this point, I want to return to text with which I began, John Ford's elegy for the Western, *The Man Who Shot Liberty Valance*. If *Liberty Valance* foreshadows Vietnam in its depiction of violence which neither law nor self-reliance can control, it is also a proto-1960s text in its delineation of how John Wayne's self-reliant individualism is dependent on the subordination and assistance of white women and African American men, and more generally a gendered and racialized social order. In actuality, John Wayne never stands alone in *Liberty Valance*. "My boy, Pompey, there in the kitchen door," he says to Valance during their first, key stare-down, pointing out the tall, imposing figure of Woody Strode backing him up with a shotgun. When Wayne shoots down Valance from the dark alley, Pompey is there to throw him the rifle.

When Rance Stoddard (James Stewart) sets up a school to preach his American doctrine of law and democracy and tame the lawlessness of the West, he threatens the sanctity of the ideological categories on which John Wayne's freedom and power rest. Prominent among his students are Pompey and Hallie (Vera Miles), John Wayne's "girl." If Stoddard's youthful idealism already shows the corrupting influence of power and office in Stewart's decidedly aged face and patronizing manner, John Wayne understands what is at stake. As Pompey attempts to recite the "self-evident truths" of the Declaration of Independence with a portrait of Lincoln staring down on him, John Wayne bursts through the door and orders Pompey back to the ranch, to his work building the house Wayne hopes to offer Hallie. "Your schoolin's over," he shouts, as Pompey beats a hasty retreat. Wayne brings news that Valance is on the move, recruiting hired guns to defeat the small homesteaders' claims to the open range. But the threat of violence is simply a pretext for disrupting the school that would teach the dangerous lesson of democracy. "Hallie, go on back where you belong," Wayne tells Vera Miles, referring quite literally to the kitchen. "I don't want you going to school in no shooting gallery." But it is clear he does not want her going to school at all.

In *The Man Who Shot Liberty Valance*, John Wayne's individualism is defeated by the modern world of statehood, the railroad, populist democracy, and corporate interests, but it is first unmasked. John Wayne does not stand free and tall simply by means of his own "god-given" strength but by the political arrangement of power which privileges his mobility over that of others. John Wayne may be the wild cactus rose of the West, but in the film it is Pompey who plants and waters it; his labor accomplishes the transformation of the desert into the garden. To understand John Wayne in these terms is to challenge the easy invocation of his power. Here we begin to find myth "consumed to the ends built into its structure," although the ends described here are admittedly different from those privileged by John Ford's presentation. It is not only John Wayne but all our readings of his specific and generalized image which must be offered as radically contingent. Pompey's largely hat-in-hand characterization hails attention today, not only because of the revolution wrought by the Civil Rights Movement to which Ford was so cautiously alluding in 1962 but because, as I hope to show in chapter 3, of the radicalizing figuration of the black soldier in Vietnam.

To complete a reappraisal of the John Wayne myth in American culture, a reinvestigation of the historical circumstances that made him so potent a figure in Vietnam lore is needed. Richard Slotkin uses the Indian Country metaphor from Vietnam to demonstrate that habit rather than logic governs the perpetuation of ideology through myth.

> The invocation of Indian war precedents as a model for the Vietnam war was a mythological way of answering the question, *Why are we in Vietnam?* The answer implicit in the myth is, "We are there because our ancestors were heros who fought the Indians." There in no logic to the connection, only the powerful force of tradition and habits of feeling and thought.[50]

But there is in fact a logical connection between Vietnam and the Indian Wars, one which the history of the Indian fighting metaphor embodies.

Every war America has fought in Asia and the Pacific has been termed an "Indian War," beginning with the first one. In the conquest of the Philippines, the war that inspired Rudyard Kipling to write the "White Man's Burden," troops were sent from posts in the American West. John Dower recounts this significant connection in his history of race and power in the Pacific theater of World War II.

> For many Americans, the link between fighting Indians on the Western frontier and Filipinos in Asia was anything but figurative or symbolic: they personally fought both enemies, moving to the Philippines from frontier posts in the western territories of the United States.

Arthur MacArthur, the father of Douglas MacArthur, was one of the more conspicuous U.S. Indian fighters who was reposted further west in this way. That his son commanded U.S. forces in the Pacific during World War Two is as good a reminder as any of how close in time the Indian wars, the war in the Philippines, and World War Two really were. War correspondents and G.I. combatants certainly kept the analogy in mind, for jungle combat against the Japanese was often characterized as "Indian fighting."[51]

John Wayne's nostalgic embodiment of winning the West and World War II powerfully elides what came between, the imperial history of the United States' quest for hegemony in the Pacific. Ironic attacks on John Wayne's irrelevance to Vietnam ultimately serve to reinforce this ahistorical sense of the Vietnam War's difference from American history. But the obsession with John Wayne in Vietnam War literature, the need to revisit Indian Country, also points powerfully and disturbingly to the half-forgotten connections between the West, World War II, and Vietnam. It is the narrative of this forbidden memory of American imperialism that will be taken up in the next chapter.

Chapter 2

IMPERIAL ALLEGORIES
American Exceptionalism and Empire

"Pray for comfort in the certainty of your
innocence. In the purity of your own motives."
—Capt. Rhallon in *Going After Cacciato*

History is what hurts, it is what refuses desire . . .
—Fredric Jameson

M ichael Herr's *Dispatches* begins with a meditation on a map of
Vietnam that hung on the wall of Herr's Saigon apartment.

It had been left there years before by another tenant, probably a
Frenchman, since the map had been made in Paris. The paper had
buckled in its frame after years in the wet Saigon heat, laying a kind
of veil over the countries it depicted. Vietnam was divided into its older
territories of Tonkin, Annam, and Cochin China, and to the west,
past Laos and Cambodge sat Siam, a kingdom. That's old, I'd tell visitors, that's a really old map.[1]

The map is a fitting symbol to open Herr's meditation on the folly and arrogance of the American mission in Vietnam. It writes in a foreign script the
failed imperial desires of the earlier French colonial war, offering boundaries both forgotten and reinscribed on the newer American maps of North
and South Vietnam. But any particular historical lessons to be offered by
the map are quickly left behind.

It was late '67 now and even the most detailed maps didn't reveal
much anymore. Reading them was like trying to read the faces of the
Vietnamese, and that was like trying to read the wind. . . . for years
now there had been no country here but the war.[2]

43

In *Dispatches*, the fictiveness of the French imperial map gives way to the escalating scale of American violence and its own lack of meaningful boundaries. Imperialism is invoked and then dismissed as a rubric for understanding the war. Crucially, when imperialism falls out of Herr's definition of the war, so do the Vietnamese.

As the example from Herr suggests, maps are powerful symbols of imperialism, but maps of American imperialism are rare. That the map of empire is European and not American is a fundamental tenet of American exceptionalism. The changing map of Vietnam strains the logic of such distinctions. In this chapter I want to explore the question of American imperialism in Vietnam War literature as a critical example of what Fredric Jameson calls the "political unconscious."[3] Tim O'Brien's *Going After Cacciato*, Joan Didion's *Democracy*, and Maxine Hong Kingston's *China Men* are the most complex and self-conscious examples of the allegorical treatment of American imperialism in Vietnam War narratives. In many ways it should seem strange that allegory is the mode of choice. The Vietnam War occasioned many direct and incisive critiques of American imperialism both during the period of antiwar protest and as part of its revisionist legacy. By calling U.S. intervention in Vietnam an act of imperialist aggression, critics implicitly and explicitly deny the myth of American exceptionalism.

In contrast, the allegorical rendering of American imperialism by Tim O'Brien, Joan Didion, and Maxine Hong Kingston follows the logic of Roland Barthes's "dynamic" approach to myth which "consumes the myth according to the very ends built into its structure: the reader lives the myth as a story at once true and unreal."[4] In these novels the elaborate play of remembering and forgetting is plotted geographically. By following Cacciato's discarded pages of an old-world atlas, Paul Berlin tries to imagine whether it is possible to walk from Vietnam to Paris, a trip whose desired end is really to travel back in time to the glorious moment of American triumph in World War II. But as the name "Berlin" suggests, it is the divided geography of the Cold War that poses the most difficult challenges. Didion tells the story of the fall of Saigon from "the crossroads of the Pacific," Hawaii, a space crucial to the mapping of both the heyday of American imperial expansion at the turn of the century and to World War II. If the American map moves insistently from East to West, both the pragmatic needs and poetic desires of Kingston's Chinese fathers demand a more fluid and flexible mapping of the relation of East to West. The maps of Chinese immigrants do not mark borders.[5]

> The villagers unfolded their maps of the known world, which differed. Turtles and elephants supported the continents, which were islands on their backs; in other cartographies, the continents were mountains with China the middle mountain, Han Mountain or Tang Mountain or the Wah Republic, a Gold Mountain to its west on some maps and to the east on others.[6] (47)

The global maps of containment or American hegemony in the Pacific are no less fanciful than the overtly allegorical imagery of the Chinese maps. As James Corner argues, "the fictional and incomplete characteristics of maps are often masked by the appearance of measured objectivity."[7] In their fictiveness and incompleteness, each of these maps suggests, indeed demands, a narrative. In American culture the relation between map and narrative is particularly acute. The progressive narrative of American history, which few texts about the Vietnam War ever fully escape, plots a deeply mythic relation of time and place: moving from East to West, Atlantic to Pacific, beginning to glorious fulfillment of a providential vision: in other words, Manifest Destiny. The turn of the twentieth century marks a conundrum for this narrative; the frontier closes in Frederick Jackson Turner's thesis and the United States "ends."

But the naturalness of the Pacific boundary as either border or narrative can be questioned from many perspectives. Dennis Cosgrove notes that it is only from the perspective of Europe that "California and the West Coast is where the American landscape must end. 'Beyond' is no longer West but the Far East."[8] Yet, if the Far East is no longer the West, access to Asia was as M. Consuelo Leon W. reminds us, the crucial motive for westward exploration and expansion in the early years of the republic.[9] At the end of America is the Pacific, and across the Pacific, Asia and the end of American exceptionalism, the specter of imperialism. The War with Spain, the claiming of Pacific territories, and, most especially, the long war to suppress the Philippine resistance threatened not only, as the anti-imperialists charged, to violate the ideals of the American republic but to recast American history in an openly imperial mode. The imperial map of continental conquest was (and is) effectively repressed by the naturalized map of the lower 48 states and their narrative of domestic settlement.[10] The continually shifting boundaries between foreign and domestic, enacted through war and immigration, across territories and race, demand elaborate narratives of national self-definition and justification. Crucial to this project was the sanctifying rhetoric of American exceptionalism, whose terms of duty, destiny, and innocence dominated both expansionist crusades and anti-imperialist critiques.[11]

The dilemma of race and empire, of the expansive relation of the United States to the world, found its most satisfactory narration in World War II with the defeat of fascism. Michael Rogin has argued that the "grip of the good war," the compelling power of its narrative and the organization of American politics around its legacy since 1945, has "importantly to do with how it seemed to at once justify demonology and free American politics from the stigma of racism" (110). For Rogin, demonology and racism are the signs under which American imperial discourse has been organized, linking "freedom to expansion in nature rather than to social solidarity, to violent conquest of the racial other rather than to peaceful coexistence" (109). But in defeating Japan and particularly Nazi Germany, expansionist imperial powers with explicitly racist ideologies, the United States found the objective correlative for its myth of exceptionalism. World War II was "the distinctive historical moment in which the United States seemed innocent of the charges of racial and political demonology" and thus of imperial desire (Rogin, 110).

In Vietnam this innocence became increasingly impossible to maintain. The language of duty and destiny, the boundaries of the global and domestic, the relation of the Asia to the United States, the conception of the free world lost their narrative coherence. As Fredric Jameson argues, narrative works to dispel the threatening social contradictions of history. *Going After Cacciato*, *Democracy*, and *China Men* locate what Jameson calls the "logical scandal or double bind" of American history, the paradox of imperialism and exceptionalism, conquest and freedom. Their elaborate narratives mark the struggle to contain this scandal, "to square its circles and to dispel, through narrative movement, its intolerable closure."[12] The self-conscious style of each of these novels makes readable this narrative desire to avoid the imperial "end" of American history. The crossing vectors of time and place become openly fanciful, recursive, and subject to interpretation and reinterpretation. Didion's and Kingston's female narrators bring the war literally home, into the family, exposing the gendered understanding of foreign and domestic and the particular paradox of women's place in the narratives of empire and exceptionalism. In denying the nostalgic category of home to which Paul Berlin in *Going After Cacciato* so desperately clings, Didion and Kingston offer a new understanding of the American map not only as imperial but as profoundly contingent, entangled in the relations of history and geography that the myth of exceptionalism works to deny.

Friendly fire is the trope on which the narrative of imperial allegory turns. O'Brien's narrative works out from the traumatic memory of an emblematic scene of friendly fire, the fragging of an officer, into increasingly fabulous narratives of escape and confinement that cross the geography of the Cold War. Didion figures the American fall from innocence through the suggestive, if difficult to interpret, relationship between the fall of Saigon and an insane father's murder of his daughter and her lover. Kingston's genealogy of the Chinese fathers who came in search of the Gold Mountain finds its own intolerable end in "The Brother in Vietnam," a story that contains no scene of friendly fire but finds the brother trapped nevertheless in a battle with American identity predicated on the impossibility of delineating the line between home and war, past and present, United States and Asia.

GOING AFTER CACCIATO IS EXPLICITLY ABOUT LIVING A STORY that is both "true and unreal." Invoking as epigram Siegfried Sassoon's observation that "soldiers are dreamers," O'Brien tells the story of Spec 4 Paul Berlin standing watch one night in an observation post overlooking the South China Sea. As an escape from the equally powerful forces of boredom and fear, Berlin imagines the possibilities of escape from the war itself. As pretext for his tale, Berlin has Cacciato, the young, dumb, brave, and innocent member of his squad who deserted with the intention of walking from Vietnam to Paris. What if the squad pursued Cacciato? Berlin wonders. What if Cacciato led them all the way to Paris? Although *Going After Cacciato* has been read almost exclusively as a meditation on the moral dilemma of a young soldier who wants out of Vietnam, the fantastic adventures he imagines carrying him all the way to Paris are as politically and historically resonant as his name, Paul Berlin.

Paris is a logical destination, representing all that the Vietnam is not: peace, civilization, and the triumphant arrival of American soldiers in previous wars. "By God! Lunch at Maxim's! . . . My old man ate there once" (16), Paul Berlin exclaims when first imagining the possibilities of Cacciato's escape.[13] Paris is identified with World War II time and again in the novel. The squad is led by an old lieutenant who served with Eisenhower and who is literally sickened by Vietnam. Upon arrival, Paul Berlin takes an attic apartment that had not been rented since 1946 and that is more than a little reminiscent of Gene Kelly's in *An American in Paris*. Paris in 1945 symbolizes a point in history at which everything went right for Americans, the essential opposite of Vietnam in 1968. Paris denotes the desire for both absolute power and innocence.

Paul Berlin's desire to reach Paris, to leave the war, is the desire for innocence, but surprisingly, perhaps uniquely in Vietnam War fiction, not the desire for power. *Going After Cacciato* is the rare Vietnam novel in which John Wayne's name does not appear. But rather than being a sign of the novel's resistance of the typical mythologizing of World War II, this bifurcation of power and innocence is very much like Ron Kovic's recreation of a demilitarized backyard at the end of *Born on the Fourth of July*, a pledge of allegiance to an innocent America. In the chapter "The Things They Did Not Know," O'Brien writes,

> They did not know even the simple things: a sense of victory, or satisfaction, or necessary sacrifice. They did not know the feeling of taking a place and keeping it, securing a village and then raising the flag and calling it victory. No sense of order or momentum. No front, no rear, no trenches laid out in neat parallels. No Patton rushing the Rhine, no beachheads to storm and win and hold for the duration. They did not have targets. They did not have a cause. They did not know if it was a war of ideology or economics or spite. (240)

This passage is cited by both John Hellmann and Thomas Myers in their studies of Vietnam War literature as typifying the soldier's isolation from what Myers calls "historical understanding."[14] But neither critic addresses the collapse of epistemological categories at work here which is in many ways more insidious than the more commonly voiced desire to be John Wayne.

The chapter begins with the fact that the soldiers did not know the language, demonstrated through a morbidly comic incident in which Stink Harris, the squad's resident hothead, barks orders at a group of Vietnamese villagers with the aid of a Vietnamese-English dictionary. Not knowing the language, the frustrating even frightening failure to communicate with the Vietnamese, is a different thing than "raising a flag and calling it victory"—and this difference is not simply the difference between Vietnam and World War II. "Raising a flag and calling it victory" is not experiential but narrative knowledge, knowledge which comes after the event. Underpinning the sense of loss invoked in this passage is the pervasive inscription of the flag raising at Iwo Jima which is universally remembered through identification with cultural inscriptions of what happened: most prominently, Joe Rosenthal's photograph, Felix De Weldon's bronze statue at Arlington cemetery, and the John Wayne film, *Sands of Iwo Jima*. The lack felt here is a narrative one, a story that can subsume Paul Berlin's experience and restore his innocence of motive and purpose. Paris invokes the narrative Paul Berlin and his comrades "didn't know."

Paul Berlin's desire to return to the site of America's moment of apparent historical innocence seeks to recover, in the double sense of regaining and covering again, a history gone wrong. For the desire for World War II, even bereft of the direct inscription of John Wayne, is the desire for the forgetting of history in myth. In *Cacciato* and virtually every other Vietnam War narrative, World War II always slides into mythic representation because of its damning connection to Vietnam. The juxtaposition of Paris in 1945 and Vietnam in 1968 in *Going After Cacciato* ultimately draws its power not from unbridgeable discontinuity, as critics such as John Hellmann and Thomas Myers have argued, but from a logical historical relationship. Paris inevitably marks a return to the origins of the Vietnam War, the seat of the French empire which sought to reestablish its control over the land, resources, and people of Vietnam at the close of World War II. When the United States took up this colonial burden, the doctrine of American exceptionalism was strained to the breaking point.

This ideological double investment of the story's desired end offers what Fredric Jameson describes as "logical scandal or double bind, the unthinkable" which must "generate a whole more properly narrative apparatus—the text itself—to square its circles and to dispel, through narrative movement, its intolerable closure."[15] Paul Berlin's elaborate narrative, with it fanciful settings, brushes with disaster and improbable escapes, is enacted by this paradoxical desire both to achieve and to avoid the desired end. Following Althusser, Jameson suggests that ideology is that which one must believe in order to tell the story. Paul Berlin must believe in his own innocence, that he can walk away from Vietnam and reach a "Paris Peace" because he is not complicit in the war's violence. Although couched in the highly personalized terms of individual courage and cowardice, the ability to believe that the squad is pursuing a mission and not simply running away, the question of Paul Berlin's innocence is tied again and again to larger historical discourse.

For both Jameson and Paul Berlin, narrative is framed by possibility, the demands and contingencies of a given historical moment.[16] Paris represents the contradictory yet paradoxically identical poles of possibility: innocence and empire, which structure Paul Berlin's plot. He needs to do more than pretend that he's in Paris, he needs to believe that he can get there.

> . . . it wasn't dreaming—it wasn't even pretending, not in the strict sense. It was an idea. It was a working out of the possibilities. It wasn't dreaming and it wasn't pretending. It wasn't crazy. Blisters on their feet, streams to be forded and swamps to be circled, dead ends to be opened into passages west. No, it wasn't dreaming. It was a way of asking questions. (26–27)

The tools that render the possible are novelistic: realistic detail, contingency and motivation, cause and effect, in short, narrative logic. But they are not ideologically neutral. Paul Berlin's description of narrative possibilities and imperatives as "dead ends to be opened into passages west" suggests the depth of the paradox his narrative seeks to outdistance. His association of escape, freedom, and innocence with "passages West" reiterates the essence of American exceptionalism—the traditional association of territorial expansion with the extension of democratic freedom instead of colonial acquisition which Michael Rogin has argued allowed "the United States to see itself as the legitimate defender of freedom in the postcolonial Third World" (108). What this view notably represses is, in Rogin's words, the acknowledgment that "the American empire started at home . . . by expansion across the continent and by the subjugation, dispossession and extermination of the Indian tribes" (108).

Paul Berlin's narrative thus promises more than a "way of asking questions"; it inevitably entails a way of avoiding answers. Traversing the geography of the old colonial world, transformed during the 1960s into a revolutionary landscape that Vietnam typified for America all too well, the innocent image of America triumphant in World War II recedes farther and farther as imperial inscriptions become harder to avoid. In India and Iran the signs of American economic, political, and military power intrude on the tourist's panorama. Shortly after the squad's arrival in Paris, Eisenhower himself dies. But long before this symbolic loss, Paul Berlin's pursuit of history, like the pursuit of Cacciato, has become admittedly a running away. Vietnam cannot be escaped, however, because Vietnam is a metonym for history—in Jameson's words, that which "hurts," that which "refuses desire" (102).

The failure of escape is the novel's central fact. As Thomas Myers notes, Paul Berlin does not have to return to Vietnam because he never leaves.[17]

Going After Cacciato is only in part a romance of desired escape. O'Brien divides the novel's narrative between the realistic grounding in the narrative present of the "The Observation Post" chapters, the wish fulfillment of the imaginative travel chapters, and chapters that narrate past war experiences from a third-person perspective less tied to Berlin's point of view. Cautioning that "daydreaming and wish-fulfilling fantasy are by no means a simple operation," Jameson suggests that they "may have something further to tell us about the otherwise inconceivable link between wish-fulfillment and realism, between desire and history" (182). The novel's structure dramatizes these connections as the separation between narrative levels progressively breaks down. The terrifying past intrudes on an imagined future. The liberated forgetting of desired escape begins to feel the nagging self-consciousness of the novel's realism. Paul Berlin's desperate attempts to keep the past separate from his sense of future possibility resonate far beyond the personal crisis of his own fear. In the transgressions of these desired narrative boundaries, O'Brien makes readable the modalities of repression, expression, and recontainment which form historical memory.

THE NAME PAUL "BERLIN" EXEMPLIFIES THE CHARACTER'S divided sense of self and the narrative enactment of this division that allows him to be in two places at one time. But the name also centers the novel's allegorical historicizing of both personal and narrative desire in a particular moment. Unlike Paris, Berlin does not speak so much to the end of the Good War as to the institutionalization of the Cold War. Between Vietnam and Paris, between 1968 and 1945, stands the Cold War, blocking Paul Berlin's ability to unite his experience in Vietnam with the victorious mythic narrative of World War II. O'Brien locates this historical moment on his allegorical political geography in a very conspicuous place—Iran. In Iran Paul Berlin's imaginative journey goes very wrong.

Going After Cacciato was published in 1977, two years before the overthrow of the Shah of Iran. The Islamic Revolution, which was read in America primarily through the spectacle of the embassy hostages, makes it easy to forget that for most of the Cold War Iran was a conspicuously bright spot on the American geopolitical map. Iran was the shining success story in the American policy of "nation building" that was extended to South Vietnam in the early 1960s. Iran exemplified what the United States wanted South Vietnam to be: a modernized, well-armed state, intimately tied to the United States financially and politically, that would serve as a bulwark against communism.[18] Iran, along with Greece and Turkey, Paul Berlin's last two stopping points before Paris, marks the initiation point of the containment doctrine whose ultimate failure was measured in Vietnam.[19]

Containment, and the Cold War generally, insisted on defining difference, drawing lines, and essentializing oppositions, perceptions that were literalized by the Berlin Wall. In Vietnam a line was drawn at the 17th parallel but refused to hold. The insistent mutability of that boundary opened a rereading and remembering of American imperial history. The chapters devoted to Iran in *Going After Cacciato* are similarly marked by an intensifying of the self-consciousness of the narrative at all levels and by transgressions of narrative boundaries. Enactments of the trope of friendly fire intrude on the narrative at every level, forcing recognition of the links between memory and imagination, guilt and desire, past and future, public and private memory, and closing off the possibilities of escape. In imagining Iran, Paul Berlin is forced to remember the things he most wanted to leave behind—the death of Billy Boy Watkins from fear and the fragging of Lt. Sidney Martin, scenes of friendly fire whose consequences generate the journey's bleakest moment, the squad's death sentence at the hands of the infamous Iranian internal security police, the SAVAK.

Things are not quite right in Iran from the beginning. The squad arrives on Christmas and steals a spruce tree from the Shah's National Memorial Gardens, which they decorate with "medals, strings, grenades, and candles" (163). The mixing of the familiar and the foreign has marked Paul Berlin's imaginative sightseeing all along, but what had previously appeared charming, a moving closer to home, like the hotel keeper's cherished bottle of American ketchup in India, becomes undeniably and ominously paradoxical in Iran. The militarized Christmas tree all too prominently displays the war's continuing presence in ritual enactments of home and peace. Paul Berlin acknowledges the pathetic quality of their celebration but dismisses it with the observation, "It was a land of infidels anyway" (163). Such comforting attempts to blame infidelity and failure on the foreignness rather than the familiarity of the setting are immediately and violently challenged.

The narration moves abruptly to signal the change. "Then they were arrested. It happened only minutes after the beheading" (165). Out to see the sights in Tehran, the squad comes upon what Doc, the medic who prescribes a realistic attention to detail as the only cure for Paul Berlin's fear, calls "one of those true spectacles of civilization," a public beheading (165). Paul Berlin wants to leave, but Doc insists he stay, "Watch this. . . . Your fine expedition to Paris, all the spectacular spectacles along the way. Civilization. You *watch* this shit" (185). Doc's bitter imperative is a metacommentary on Paul Berlin's narration, suggesting that his imaginative observation up to this point has been limited, avoiding scenes that indict the ideological assumptions that structure his point of view and thus his narrative journey: that Paris, the West, is civilization; that civilization is the antithesis of violence and war; that he is moving away from the scene of his own fear and guilt. The narrative at first focuses on this last, most personal point when the condemned is revealed to be a soldier guilty of going AWOL. The execution quite obviously stages Paul Berlin's own fears about the consequences of running, but the crime of "being absent without leave" underscores Doc's criticism by pointing an accusing finger at Paul Berlin's imaginative escape from his observation post duties more than at the possibility of actual desertion.

The story lurches out of Paul Berlin's control, acknowledging the guilt it is intended to outdistance when "again without warning" they are arrested. Once the specter of desertion is admitted, Paul Berlin's sense of possibility is forced to recognize the squad's suspicious status. They are armed soldiers, far beyond their theater of war with no papers or orders and they are arrested. The plot recovers some of its momentum in the form of the sympathetic young SAVAK officer, Capt. Rhallon, who questions them after their arrest, accepts Doc's bizarre explanations as the honorable word of a brother soldier, and befriends them. But the bond of brother soldiers is not a comfortable one for Paul Berlin, whose travels are happiest when spent in afternoon cafes and shopping trips. Paul Berlin becomes increasing alienated within his narrative as Doc takes on a more central role, extending the metacommentary begun at the beheading. In the lively, intellectualized debate over the soldier's role and the reality of war, Doc voices Paul Berlin's own divided feelings and deepest fears. Paul Berlin silently gets drunk as the two men discuss what keeps a soldier from running, and finally walks out as Doc prepares to tell what the squad refers to as "the ultimate war story": how Billie Boy Watkins was frightened to death on the field of battle. Even within the narrative structure of his escape, Paul Berlin ends up fleeing the past.

At this point, the novel returns to the Observation Post where Paul Berlin wonders, "Why, out of all the things that might have happened, did it lead to a beheading in Tehran? Why not to pretty things? Why not a smooth, orderly arc from war to peace?" (184). The obvious answer is that the events of the past structure the possibilities of the future. Paul Berlin is forced to confront the trope of friendly fire, the narrative form for the violent return of historical memory. The death of Billie Boy Watkins, however, typifies the desire to understand history in personal, depoliticized terms. He "concentrated on the order of things, going back to the beginning. His first day of the war. How hot the day had been, and how on his very first day he had witnessed the ultimate war story" (185). The story of Billie Boy Watkins is narrated in the next chapter, "Night March," in the realistic third-person voice. The ultimate war story confirms Paul Berlin's worst fears. Billie Boy Watkins dies not from the wound inflicted by the enemy but of fright, scared to death by the sight of his own foot blown off by a land mine. The acknowledgment that he could kill himself with his own fear is made the first fact which Paul Berlin's fantastic imagination must order.

This reading accounts for why the beheading, but not why Tehran. And it is the political fact of the Shah's regime that refuses to release Berlin to happier possibilities. The story of Billie Boy now told, the novel returns briefly to the "Observation Post" where Paul Berlin seems strengthened and settled by his admission of fear.

Billy Boy Watkins, like the others, was among the dead. It was the simple truth. It was not especially terrible, or hard to think about, or even sad. It was a fact. It was the first fact, and leading from it were other facts. Now it was merely a matter of following the facts to where they ended. (196)

But this apparent sense of personal emotional control does not translate into narrative control, for the Vietnam War did not begin with Paul Berlin's first day in country and its meaning cannot be contained by his tour of duty or his personal fears and obsessions. When Berlin resumes his narrative, the squad is again arrested, this time by SAVAK officers considerably less sympathetic than Rhallon. Their necks are ominously and ceremoniously shaved each day for eight days until Rhallon brings them the official news that they have been condemned to die for espionage and desertion. Rhallon remains apologetic and sympathetic, admitting with embarrassment that it is a matter of "politics" and that it is "impolitic to talk of politics" (200). His best advice is to "pray for comfort in the certainty of your innocence. In the purity of your motives" (201). Innocence and good intentions are revealed as ironic fig leafs for a fact more unspeakable than the word "desertion"—the political fact of American imperialism as figured in an Iranian government "where internal security is paramount" (200).

Historically, this repressive Iranian dedication to internal security reflects the imperatives of the 1953 CIA-led coup which toppled the democratically elected, nationalist government of Muhammad Musaddiq in favor of the more "stable" authoritarian leadership of the Shah. With this historical legacy literally pressing on their necks, Doc attempts the classic ugly American gesture by invoking the power and prestige of the American embassy, a tactic that before Vietnam was a narrative staple for dealing with intransigent officials in foreign lands, and a gesture that in Iran, in light of the embassy hostages of 1979, takes on ever-deepening levels of historical irony. "Time for some diplomatic pressure. By Uncle Sam I mean. Time for Sammy to step in on our behalf" (204). Rhallon's answer, "your government does not know you. Or chooses not to," preempts Doc's request, suggesting that it is the SAVAK who holds the privileged link of communication with the American government. The SAVAK, which was established with the aid of American intelligence and remained a key CIA ally, functions in *Going After Cacciato* as an instrument of American historical agency. The men have no recourse because they are condemned, literally and figuratively, by American practices and beliefs; their death sentence thus becomes a scene of friendly fire. With the innocence of the American/Iranian relation thus transformed, Rhallon is replaced by his brutal "twin," a SAVAK colonel who breaks noses and scorns explanations, forcing them to confess that their so-called *mission* is nothing but a "fiction"—a "made-up story" (206).

The word "mission" is historically associated with the doubling of American imperialism and exceptionalism. In his classic (pre-Vietnam) interpretation, *Manifest Destiny and Mission in American History* (1963), historian Frederick Merk seeks to differentiate, even divorce, these terms:

> Manifest Destiny and imperialism were traps into which the nation was led in 1846 and in 1899, and from which it extricated itself as well as it could afterward.
>
> A truer expression of the national spirit was Mission. This was present from the beginning of American history, and is clearly present today. It was idealistic, self-denying, hopeful of divine favor for national aspirations, though not sure of it.[20]

To confess to the fictional quality of the squad's "mission," to be forced moreover to such a confession by SAVAK, is to declare untenable the mythohistorical distinction Merk draws. In the personalized terms of Paul Berlin's narrative, Merk's ideology of self-denial is crucial. The SAVAK officer demands they admit that their fictional mission is "an alibi to cover cowardice" (206), an apparent reference to their desertion that is revealed once again to be a displacement for deeper scenes of guilt. Mediating the personal desire to get out of Vietnam and the imperial allegory which imperils the possibilities of escape is the capital crime the squad did commit, a classic enactment of friendly fire—the fragging of Lt. Sidney Martin.

The confession is followed by two of the realistic flashback chapters that describe the fragging of Martin, who was dedicated to "mission" over "men." At issue is Martin's insistence on searching tunnels before destroying them, a by-the-book approach that challenges the informal SOP (standard operating procedure) that eschews risking men for the abstract imperatives of mission. The squad kills Martin, although it is only the ritual touching of the fragmentation grenade that is narrated. The actual act of mutiny remains suppressed within the novel, thus avoiding any direct critique. Martin's belief in mission is deemed "too clearheaded for such a lousy war" (94). Vietnam is the problem, an inappropriate field for American endeavor, and as such, the nature and implication of that endeavor remains unquestioned. There is no self-conscious return to the "The Observation Post" here as there was to deal with the memory of Billie Boy Watkins. The fragging of Lt. Sidney Martin remains conspicuously unspoken at every level of the narration.

This is not to say that the overt confrontation between the squad and Martin is over politics, history or policy; such a critique, O'Brien clearly points out, is unavailable to these men in the field. But the repression of the fragging story does effect a withdrawal in many ways from the war. It is the most immediate motivation for Cacciato to walk away. In sharing this secret the squad seems to turn inward, isolating themselves from the war through a localizing of their concern and attention. This localizing, however, means that their mutiny cannot be connected to the larger phenomenon of both violent and passive rejection of military discipline and government policy that was not limited to the antiwar movement at home but became an increasing problem in country after 1968.[21] The fact that it is Oscar, the squad's lone black soldier, who first talks about "solutions," ultimately organizes the fragging, and presumably tosses the grenade, suggests the barely suppressed politics of the confrontation, which if realized, would preclude Paul Berlin's desire for a separate peace.

"Cowardice," the crime the SAVAK sees lurking under the "alibi" of their "mission," is in fact the fear of possibility and its attendant historical inscription. Killing Martin raises the possibility that the squad is rejecting the American mission itself, which Vietnam made readable as inherently imperialist. This radical possibility is contained in the novel when the facade of mission is reclaimed in the squad's grateful acceptance of Martin's replacement, Lt. Corson, whose loathing of the Vietnam War and nostalgic association with World War II depoliticizes their action. The interrogation of the American mission is displaced once again by the mythified opposition of World War II and Vietnam and the personalized question of good officers and bad officers.

Jameson notes that when the terms of the magical narrative threaten to approximate the political contradictions registered unconsciously, "the narrative must not be allowed to press on to any decisive conclusion. Its historical reality must rather be disguised and defused by the sense of moonlight summer revels dissolving into thin air . . ." (149). In the realistic frame, Corson's arrival serves this function, but within the fantasy plot when the death sentence of the SAVAK threatens to connect Vietnam to the harsh history of American imperialism, it takes on a more suitably spectacular, even campy and literally "moonlit" form. Paul Berlin's eleventh-hour prayer for "a genuine miracle to confound natural law, a baffling reversal of the inevitable consequences," is answered (215). Cacciato appears before the window "like the moon," slides a M-16 between the bars, and whispers "go." Berlin and the squad take off amid a spectacular series of explosions which cover their escape. Condemned to death by the covert structures of modern American imperialism, the squad is rescued by the embodiment of American innocence.

In character as well as action Cacciato is everything Berlin prays for— "a baffling reversal of inevitable consequences." In his insightful reading, John Hellmann describes Cacciato as "an ultimate unresolvable mystery of contradictions" (164), a contradiction mapped on and through American myth and history.

The novel suggests that after Vietnam American consciousness can continue to follow the impulse of myth only by abandoning the logic of American history. In the anti-frontier which American history has reached in Vietnam, Cacciato is all Berlin can imagine from the mythic

trails of the American hero, an innocent and self-reliant Leatherstocking who can continue the optimistic trek westward only by dumbly
and paradoxically leaving American mission in a self-indulgent regression back to the Old World. (Hellmann 166)

For Hellmann, the crux of the journey's contradiction lies in Paris as destination, although not for the same historical reasons I have argued. Hellmann
sees Paris as European, urban, and prototypically decadent, and thus paradoxically inappropriate for an American hero who typically finds redemption in the frontier.

Hellmann's reading of the doubleness of Cacciato's character in connection with the paradoxical nature of the journey has obvious resonance
in my own. However, as I noted earlier, where he sees discontinuity between myth and history, between Vietnam and the American past, I have
argued connection, contingency, and even collapse. Hellmann preserves
history as a stable category of representation."The logic of American history" remains a positive ideology, the violation of which in Vietnam makes
myth untenable. I have argued on the other hand, that the crisis of faith
constituted by the Vietnam War actually changed history, the narrativiza-
tion of the past. In Jameson's terms, the war "shut down a certain number
of formal possibilities available before, and . . . open[ed] up determinant
new ones" for the narrative of American history (148). The fictional narrative of the Western and the historical narrative of the Indian Wars becomes one of the primary sites of this revision. But in Hellmann's reading,
the novel's insistent comparisons between Vietnam and the mythic American West works only one way, marking Vietnam as problematic without
engaging the ways in which Vietnam rewrites understanding of the West
itself.[22]

Going After Cacciato encourages both revisionist and nostalgic readings
of history. On the one hand, the novel allows the return of repressed private
and public memories, like the fragging of Sidney Martin and the encounter
with the SAVAK, that threaten to "arrest" the plot through symbolically
criminal transgressions. On the other hand, the solipsism of the trope of
friendly fire, the insistence that Vietnam was something Americans did to
each other, ultimately stabilizes the narrative boundaries between the
myth of American exceptionalism and the history of American imperialism, making escape, or at least avoidance, possible. Cacciato comes dangerously close to the squad in the jail; he risks compromising his own inviolate
innocence as he reaches though the very bars of the cell to deliver them.
And the means of this deliverance, the M-16, is anything but innocent, although the terms of the narrative effectively blur this point. Unlike the
SAVAK, which draws real blood in the largely symbolic gestures of shaving
necks and breaking noses, Cacciato's violent redemption of his comrades is
literally spectacular, marked only by brilliant flashes light and explosive
sounds, without any evident production of bodies or pain.

In the realistic frame, Cacciato was the only one to refuse to willingly join the pact to frag Martin. Paul Berlin, unable to convince him, finally wraps the boy's hand around the grenade. It is his exception from this scene of violence that causes Cacciato to leave the war and makes him Paul Berlin's embodiment of possibility, a figure which, as John Hellmann argues, follows the tradition of Emerson's Adamic American and Cooper's Leatherstocking. The jailbreak threatens to make present, even as the narrative magically moves to defuse it, the associated "structuring metaphor of the American experience" that Richard Slotkin has called "regeneration through violence."[23]

Having demonized the self he flees in the persona of the SAVAK (Stink even calls the colonel a "lousy Nazi"), Paul Berlin can now freely admit to running (205). Narrative movement is regained in hypertypical American style, the getaway car. "It was an Impala, 1964. Racing stripes sparkled on the body, sponge dice dangled from the rearview mirror. Fender skirts, mudflaps, chopped and channeled, leopard-skin upholstery. They piled in and Oscar drove" (216).

They drive out of Tehran on Eisenhower Avenue, a final ironic reminder of the collapse of World War II into the Cold War and of the American imperial imprint on the "open road." But road signs disappear as they hit open country in the moonlight. The car, an elaborate fetish of American movement, restores something of Cacciato's boyish innocence to the narrative and the squad finally reaches Paris.

IN PARIS, THE "LOGICAL SCANDAL" OF IMPERIALISM AND exceptionalism is displaced onto the character of Sarkin Aung Wan, the young Vietnamese refugee who early on joins Paul Berlin's imaginative journey. Unlike Doc, Lt. Corson, and the other members of the squad who occupy roles within the journey that are consistent with their characters in the realistic frame, Sarkin Aung Wan is clearly an expression of wish fulfillment who expands the range of narrative possibilities by her presence. She is something "that might have happened on the road to Paris" (51). The desires Sarkin Aung Wan fulfills are not surprisingly sexual, although once again the terms of the romance are oddly innocent. *Cacciato* is far removed from the hyperbolic sexualized language of Michael Herr's *Dispatches* and so much of Vietnam War literature. Sarkin Aung Wan and Paul Berlin do not "fuck"; hand holding and touching characterize their relations. The narrative suggests that intercourse does take place in Paris, but Paul Berlin's delicacy regarding the subject leaves the point as unnarrated as it would have been in a Hays Office-era Hollywood film.

This nostalgic innocence is exactly the idea Paul Berlin seeks to establish through Sarkin Aung Wan. By falling in love, Paul Berlin, like Hemingway's Frederick Henry, seeks to declare his separation from the war. He is no longer an alien presence, a soldier, an embodiment of a national and imperial identity, but a lover, a man, an individual. Yet, in spite of the scrupulous avoidance of the traditional signs of domination in sex and Sarkin's vocal expression of her dreams of life in Paris, her character always verges on the idealized, transnational, and transhistorical Western fantasy of the Asian woman as supreme servant, the "geisha." In two resonant and representative gestures, Sarkin licks Berlin's wounds and washes his feet, "chipping away at the war" with nail clippers (103). As refugee she should represent what the war has done to the Vietnamese, but this crucial point is ultimately displaced by Paul Berlin's need for her to recognize what the war has done to him, to cleanse and heal his symbolically wounded body.

Sarkin Aung Wan's ministrations to Paul Berlin's body invert the memory which offers her as a narrative possibility. Significantly, her avatar is remembered in the flashback chapter already discussed, "The Things They Did Not Know," which describes the failure of Vietnam to be World War II. In a paragraph which runs nearly two pages, Paul Berlin confronts the "nagging question": "Who were these skinny, blank-eyed people? What did they want?" (233). "These people" become personified by a "little girl with gold hoops in her ears and ugly scabs on her brow" to whom Paul Berlin addresses the questions which torture him about his presence in Vietnam.

> did she feel, as he did, goodness and warmth and poignancy when he helped Doc dab iodine on her sores? Beyond that, though, did the girl *like* him? Lord knows, he had no villainy in his heart, no motive but kindness. He wanted health for her, and happiness. Did she know this? Did she sense his compassion? When she smiled, was it more than a token? And . . . and what *did* she want? Any of them, what did they long for? Did they have secret hopes? His hopes? Could this little girl—her eyes squinting as Doc brushed the scabs with iodine, her lips sucked in, her nose puckering at the smell—could she somehow separate him from the war? Even for an instant? Did she see him as just a scared-silly boy from Iowa? Could she feel sympathy? In it together, trapped, you and me, all of us: Did she feel that? Could she understand his fear matching it with her own? (233)

The solipsism of this passage is profound. Paul Berlin wants to be credited for feeling healing compassion without admitting any complicity in the impoverished circumstances to which her diseased body testifies. She is at most an indirect victim of the war, sick not wounded. Even more striking is the desire of the American soldier to be seen as a victim equal to the Vietnamese child whose home is torn apart by war, a gesture which, as Susan Jeffords has demonstrated, echoes throughout Vietnam war literature.[24] Jeffords argues that the inscription of the Vietnam soldier and veteran as victim enabled a displacement of the Civil Rights and Women's Movements, which in turn allowed a revitalization of traditional patriarchal and capitalist values. If *Going After Cacciato* is atypical of what Jeffords calls "remasculinization" in its rejection of spectacles of violence and masculine display, it nonetheless effects the same sort of conservative return. Although Paul Berlin asks questions rarely articulated in American novels about the war, the logical sequence that moves from his pain to that of the Vietnamese again ensures that these questions will never be answered.

This evasion is explicit at the end of the section about the little girl. The section closes with one of the most direct considerations of the Vietnamese in an American novel.

> What did she *aim* for? If a wish were to be granted by the war's winning army—any wish—what would she choose? Yes! If LBJ and Ho were to rub their magic lanterns at war's end, saying, "Here is what it was good for, here is the fruit," what would Quang Ngai demand? Justice? What sort? Reparations? What kind? Answers? What were the questions: What did Quang Ngai want to know? (235)

But a few lines before this, Paul Berlin has assured that his investigation will never reach Quang Ngai. His journey quite literally is figured as an escape from the site where such questions can be asked.

> He would ask her to see the matter his way. What would *she* have done? What would *anyone* have done, not knowing? And then he would ask the girl questions. What did she want? How did she see the war? (235)

By insisting that she see things "his way" first and positing an "anyone," a universalized self in whom the American soldier's position is made the same as the Vietnamese woman's, Paul Berlin assures that "how she sees the war" will never be known. The one thing he wishes he could tell the people is that "he was no tyrant, no pig, no Yankee killer. He was innocent. Yes, he was. He was innocent" (234). The unspeakable come close being spoken at this point. "Tyrant," "pig," "Yankee killer" all invoke the stereotypes of communist propaganda whose key term, "imperialist," is conspicuously absent. He must avoid finally asking "how she sees the war" because he does not want to ask if the Vietnamese see him as an imperialist, collapsing personal and historical frames of understanding. He dares not invoke America's exceptional status, so he instead begs them to recognize his innocence, to make an exception for him, to "separate him from the war, just for a minute."

If Sarkin Aung Wan does not constitute a Vietnamese subjectivity, she does challenge Paul Berlin's solipsistic desire to be a victim. In the novel's most striking scene, Paul Berlin and Sarkin Aung Wan enact the Paris peace talks. In a public room, across a large table, they "state their positions." Sarkin reminds Berlin that

> Even the refugee must do more than flee, He must arrive. He must return at last to a world as it is, however much in conflict with his

hopes, and he must then do what he can to edge reality toward what he has dreamed, to change what he can change. . . . Spec Four Paul Berlin, I urge you to act. (284)

Sarkin here demands that Paul Berlin recognize the radical potential of his passive rejection of the war, to act on what he feels, to resist "false obligation," to build a new world rather than avoiding a critique of the old one. But Paul refuses. "I confess that what dominates is the fear of abandoning all I hold dear" (286). He is "afraid of exile" and loves his home, his father, his town. Although the discussion once again takes place in intensely personal terms, the politicized stage suggests the way in which the personal covers the political, both disguising and involving it. "We all want peace," Paul Berlin proclaims, but not as much as he wants to return home to Fort Dodge. Once again, home is named with allegorical suggestiveness. If to reject Vietnam is to rethink American history, to reconsider the costs of "dead ends to be opened into passages west," to risk rejecting a vision of the past on which his identity is built, then the price is too high. Sarkin Aung Wan walks away; the possibility Paul Berlin's mind can articulate must ultimately be rejected in a profoundly conservative desire to return to the status quo antebellum. *Going After Cacciato* thus demonstrates how close to private and public consciousness Vietnam bought the repressed narrative of imperialism in American history whose contradictions had traditionally been suspended in the myth of exceptionalism. But even more crucially, *Cacciato* shows how powerful is the desire to forget, a desire deeply embedded in the structures of everyday life.

LIKE *GOING AFTER CACCIATO*, JOAN DIDION'S *DEMOCRACY* features an allegorically named protagonist, Inez Christian Victor, and plots the doubled narrative of empire and exceptionalism across a resonant political geography, the Pacific. Like Paul Berlin's Paris, the Hawaii of *Democracy* anchors a history in which the triumph of World War II seeks to cover over the troubled legacy of imperialism. Both novels feature highly self-conscious narratives which foreground their own conditions of possibility and impossibility; both turn to the figure of the refugee to voice the outside of an increasingly untenable narrative of American exceptionalism. But there are also conspicuous differences. *Going After Cacciato* is a novel obsessed with the possibility of an ending, not simply the romantic happy ending but the practical one of returning home. *Democracy*, in contrast, is written out of the moment of *the* ending, the fall of Saigon, a story that Didion tells us she has "no unequivocal way of beginning."[25] If *Going After Cacciato* in the end affirms the desire to return home, *Democracy* refuses the American desire to be "exempted from the general movement. Just because they believed they had a home to call. Just because they were Americans" (208). These differences are mapped most profoundly through gender, as attention turns from the fate of the American son to that of the daughter. This filial emphasis is inextricably linked to the novel's deeply self-conscious narrative style.

Didion's lack of an "unequivocal way of beginning" is, as I have suggested, symptomatic of these relationships. Edward Said has argued that the classical novelistic beginning can be understood as an act of "fathering."[26] In *Beginnings* Said traces the decline of the "novel's paternal role—to author, father, procreate a rival reality" that he finds so powerful in the eighteenth and nineteenth centuries. Textual unity and integrity are "maintained by a series of genealogical connections: author-text, beginning-middle-end, text-meaning, reader-interpretation," which are undergirded by "the imagery of succession, of paternity, of hierarchy."[27] In Modernism, Said argues, the dynastic "familial analogy [of] fathers and sons" gives way to the "brother," the figure of "complementarity and adjacency."[28] Such beginnings do not descend from and succeed a revered and authorized origin, but stand next to other beginnings, other possibilities. In *Democracy*, Didion's decidedly equivocal beginning stands quite literally next to another beginning, now set aside: "'Imagine my mother dancing,' that novel began" (21). This abandoned beginning suggests the limits of Said's critique of paternity that allows for no figurative mothers and daughters, no sisters. Said's filial model of narrative has a political analogue in the deeply gendered conceptions of the relation of foreign to domestic and the relegation of women to the realm of the home and the private, an association that was particularly acute during the Cold War.[29] In *Democracy*, it is the daughter's role in the family and history that exemplifies the radically contingent and circumstantial response Didion offers to the failure of another form "of succession, of paternity, of hierarchy," the American "involvement" in Vietnam. "Adjacency" is precisely the model of narrative possibility Didion enacts. The presence of Inez or her sister Janet or daughter Jessie at historically significant places and times is quite literally "besides the point." They are not in Jakarta or Saigon or Kuala Lumpur to shape events the way their husbands and lovers and fathers seek to. But neither is their presence purely coincidental. It is the adjacency of events, the fact that Janet's murder and Jessie's "disappearance" makes headlines alongside the fall of Saigon, that Didion forces to our attention. The perversity of these events frustrates our novelistic desire for cause and effect even as it challenges us to imagine the meaning of their relation.

When Joan Didion introduces herself to the reader at the beginning of chapter 2, "Call me the author," she denaturalizes a set of textual relations that are inextricably bound to the possibilities and impossibilities of narrating the story of American democracy and imperialism. She began the novel she tells us, at a time at which she "lacked certainty" in personality, narrative, beginnings, ego, memory, the past. But, like Inez at the end of the novel, Didion takes "the long view" that is, perhaps not coincidentally, the (grand)daughter's view.

as the granddaughter of a geologist I learned early to anticipate the absolute mutability of hills and waterfalls and even islands. When a hill slumps into the ocean I see the order in it. . . . A hill is a transitional accommodation to stress, and ego may be a similar accommodation. A waterfall is a self-correcting maladjustment of stream to structure, and so, for all I know, is technique. The very island to which Inez Victor returned in the spring of 1975—Oahu, an emergent post-erosional land mass along the Hawaiian Ridge—is a temporary feature, and every rainfall or tremor along the Pacific plates alters its shape and shortens its tenure as Crossroads of the Pacific. In this light it is difficult to maintain definite convictions about what happened down there in the spring of 1975, or before. (18)

In insisting on the mutability of hills, Didion literally undermines one of the oldest and most resonant images of the role of the United States in the world: "we shall be as a city on a hill, the eyes of all people upon us," John Winthrop declared aboard the Arabella in 1630. In the secularized history of the republic, the city on the hill comes to represents not Winthrop's city of God but the equally utopic city of man, democracy. The Vietnam War marks a profoundly distopic moment, refiguring the leader of the free world as a corrupt imperial power.[30] But Didion's critique gives up more than the corrupt city, which one might still hope to redeem as ideal; it gives up the hill, the very ground on which the city stands in its exemplary and exceptional power. This exceptional identity of America and Americans is one of the things the novel in the end most forcefully rejects: the belief that Americans should be exempt from "the general movement," immune from the violent convulsions of history.

Didion's geologically derived principle of "absolute mutability" is significantly emplotted through female characters. If Paul Berlin seeks desperately to reunite his story to that of his father, "Inez Victor (who was born Inez Christian)" figures a more openly ironic and disjunctive sense of history (13). Inez's maiden and married names together define post–World War II identity as surely as John Wayne—Christian suggesting the secularized righteousness of an American history traced back to the Puritans, and Victor invoking the American triumph of World War II, the moment of unchallenged global supremacy and absolute innocence. As daughter and wife Inez figures a very different set of social relations from those of Paul Berlin's deeply conservative desire to return to his father, to meet paternal expectations. The family in *Cacciato* is figured nostalgically, separate from the war. But in *Democracy*, family, politics, business, and empire are intimately related. Inez's matrimonial change of names, "Victor born Christian," figures the naturalized connections of American myth and history. The symbolic and material stress placed on Inez's marital bond suggests that women play a particular role in the accommodation of form and meaning. "Victor born Christian" is like a waterfall, the naturalized, spectacularized jump which affirms social order, national narratives, and economic privilege. When Inez leaves her husband by walking out of her uncle's home, she ruptures the fictional coherence of that order.

Democracy begins with an openly nostalgic inscription of the islands Didion characterizes as "transitional."

> The light at dawn during those Pacific tests was something to see.
> Something to behold.
> Something that could almost make you think you saw God, he said.
> He said to her.
> Jack Lovett said to Inez Victor.
> Inez Victor who was born Inez Christian. (11)

In a novel in which Didion, as narrator, tells us she had no "unequivocal way of beginning," the image and the memory of atomic tests serve to introduce the central characters, Jack and Inez, the novel's competing tones of irony and elegiac romance, and its central concern with the presence and absence of American imperialism. For it is not simply the power of the bomb or the privilege of having been so near to these gestures of power that marks the opening as imperial but the specificity of the Pacific as a site for the exercise of American power. "Nobody had pleasurable feelings about Nevada," Jack tells her. And "you would never recall an Aleutian event with any nostalgia . . . big deal for the civilians, but zero interest" (13). The power of the Pacific lies in its remoteness, its dawn's early light— "Where America's Day Begins" proclaims the newspaper Inez later buys in Guam; its unspoken history of an American empire. "They were just atolls, most of them. Sand Spits, actually." Just enough land to carry the imprint of American military power: "Two Quonsets and one of those landing strips they roll down, you know, the matting, just roll it down like a goddamn bathmat" (11).

So "He said to her. Jack Lovett said to Inez Victor who was born Inez Christian." These lines repeat throughout the chapter, accruing novelistic details of background and context and, most important, underlining Inez's role as the audience for this nostalgic message of power. In *Democracy* Inez's body serves, like those Pacific atolls claimed by the U.S. military, as a transfer point for relations of power governed by presence and absence, by hot war and cold war, by imperial desire and narratives of democracy. But unlike atomic bombs named for female icons such as Wonder Woman or Gilda, Inez does not serve primarily as a point of projected and transferred sexual fantasies of domination. Rather, she marks the center of a set of incestuous social relations that embody, even as they privatize and disguise, the workings of an American empire. As daughter, wife, lover, mother, sister, niece, and granddaughter Inez locates the conflicting, violent, and romantic history of American adventures in the Pacific; all these relations come to a crisis in the spring of 1975. As the daughter of the wealthy Christians of Hawaii, a family "in which the colonial impulse had marked every member," Inez's inheritance is literally the expansionist triumphs of the 1890s (26). But Hawaii, with its belated admission to statehood, also quiets anti-imperial criticism, particularly after the bombing of Pearl Harbor renarrates the islands as domestic American space. The family business, Chriscorp Development, compresses the unholy alliance of missionaries and Pacific traders that made Hawaii the center of the debate over an American empire at the turn of the century. In the narrative present, Chriscorp, although not part of the defense industry per se, is heavily invested in bases and developments in Vietnam, contemplating bidding on a complete overhaul at Cam Ranh Bay even as the NVA is marching on Saigon.

Didion tells us early on that she had set out to write a very different novel, "a study in provincial manners, in the acute tyrannies of class and privilege with which people assert themselves against the tropics"; in short, an expose of American colonialism (22). Shards of this novel are visible in the montage of *Democracy*. Inez's sister Janet in particular embodies this narrative, with her 14 pink dresses ("'I thought pink was the navy blue of the Indies,' Janet had said in the Cathay Pacific Lounge at Hong Kong," paraphrasing *Vogue* editor Diane Vreeland [93]); her confusion of India and the Indies as "same look, *n'est-ce pas?*" (93); her romantic admiration for "hill stations," and her insistence on teaching the house servant how to make coconut punches while waiting out the rioting in Jakarta in 1969 (101–102). Janet's story would appear to be a fairly simple study in irony—a deflation of the myth by which fatuous, privileged Americans drape themselves in the mantle of democracy. But not even Janet's narrative is in the end very simple.

The end of chapter 1 suggests Didion's more complex strategy when Inez, Jack, and the descriptions of those "sweet" "events in the Pacific" of 1952 and 1953 are finally anchored in a specific time and place:

> "Oh shit, Inez," Jack Lovett said one night in the spring of 1975, one night outside Honolulu in the spring of 1975, one night in the spring of 1975 when the C-130's and the C-141's were already shuttling between Honolulu and Anderson and Clark and Saigon all night long, thirty-minute turnaround at Tan Son Nhut, touching down and loading and taxiing out on flight idle, bringing out the dependents, bringing out the dealers, bringing out the money, bringing out the pet dogs and sponsored bar girls and the porcelain elephants: "Oh shit, Inez," Jack Lovett said to Inez Victor, "Harry Victor's wife." (14–15)

As the "American assistance effort" in Saigon unravels, a process Didion represents with a withering selection of factual detail throughout the novel, Jack Lovett, himself a key player in that effort, saves his irony for the fact that Inez is Harry Victor's wife. Sen. Harry Victor, a Kennedy-esque politician with a youthful, media-savvy image, opposes the war but, whether in

Washington, Jakarta, or Saigon, ultimately cannot see anything beyond the machinations of the political machine he hopes in vain to ride to the presidency. As his wife, Inez has lived in the camera's eye, an object of public obsession similar to Jackie Kennedy. Jack Lovett is the shadow in her blindingly public life. The army officer with whom she had an affair at 17, Lovett sends her a wedding present that perfectly captures the novel's doubling of the domestic and the political, the ironic and romantic: a cigarette box inscribed in French with the imprint of the residence of the governor of Indochina, a token Lovett had won in a Saigon poker game.

The specificities of Lovett's role remain pointedly unnamed in the novel; "Exactly what Jack Lovett did was tacitly understood by most people who knew him, but not discussed" (40). His resume is first given in the text through his wives' descriptions: from 1945–1952, "army officer"—his first wife made a "convincing army wife"; from 1962–1964, he was, according to his second wife, "an aircraft executive"; his 1975 visa names him generically a businessman. His wives' normalizing descriptions serve as an alibi for a life marked by "what intelligence people call 'interest' . . . odd overlapping dates, unusual post at unusual times"—like Saigon in 1955 (40). Lovett is, if not CIA, then CIA connected—a conduit for the transfer and interception of information, resources, and goods, but a conduit, unlike Inez, that remains insistently beyond public visibility or definition. The narrator believes that Jack Lovett is one of the fuzzy figures in the background of the *Newsweek* cover of the American ambassador leaving Phnom Penh in the spring of 1975, but she cannot be sure—he was supposed to have been somewhere else.

Jack's wives provide the necessary alibi, the normalizing gloss that allows Jack to move through society without attracting undue attention. Jack's romance with Inez brings what Michael Rogin has described as the twin components of postmodern American imperial power into direct relation: media spectacle and covert operation. For 20-odd years, from the mid-1950s to the spring of 1975, Jack and Inez "do not touch," but they do look for each other in remote places, as Jakarta in 1969. As Alan Nadel has discussed, this flirtation marks not coincidentally the years of an entrenched cold war and an American foreign policy of containment that is both global and interventionist.[31] Inez leaves Harry, or, more correctly, leaves with Jack, at exactly the moment marking the failure of this policy—the fall of Saigon. When Inez walks out the door of her uncle's house on Manoa Road with Jack Lovett, he is at a loss as to where to go. "I used to think I could always take you to Saigon. Drink citron presse and watch the tennis. Scratch that" (167). Vietnam has functioned for Jack most openly, but really for all the characters, like the Western frontier, as a place of romantic possibility offering escape from social, economic, and political limitations and, more profoundly, from what Jameson would call the contradictions of history that are repressed in and through narrative.

When South Vietnam falls, narrative becomes impossible. In 1955, as a student at Berkeley, Didion tells us she first noticed what she calls the "quickening of time." "In 1975 time was no longer just quickening but collapsing, falling in on itself, the way a disintegrating star contracts into a black hole" (72). Reading the dispatches from Southeast Asia, she finds "in those falling capitals a graphic instance of the black hole effect" (73). In the face of her students' language of "liberation," Didion "modified 'falling' to 'closing down'" (73). This semantic struggle is essentially one of point of view, whose side one takes. "Closing down" refers specifically to what the Americans were doing in those capitals of Southeast Asia in the spring of 1975, but in Didion's narrative, much more selfconsciously than in virtually any other American narrative of the Vietnam War, so does falling. The chaotic withdrawal of the United States from Vietnam and Cambodia marks the U.S. fall from innocence—the collapse of the myth of exceptionalism.

Didion plots the narrative impossibility of this fallen world through two inexplicable events: the murder of Inez's sister Janet by their father and Inez's daughter Jessie's trip to Vietnam to find a "cinchy job," both of which occur during Easter week of 1975. It is these two events that place Jack and Inez in the off-limits Happy Talk Lounge across from Schofield Barracks where Jack tells Inez of pink dawn of the atomic tests in the Pacific and, when words fail, exclaims, "Oh shit, Inez. Harry Victor's wife." Crisis is too mild a word for the state of the Christian and Victor families at this point; sister, daughter, wife, mother— all these roles are suddenly and violently made untenable.

It is all but impossible to render these events into critical coherence, except to say that Paul Christian was insane when he shot Janet. But this is an evasion, not an explanation. As Didion says when she offers the police report of the murders, it is a way of "resisting narrative" (113). Paul's increasingly erratic behavior had been visible for some time and takes two key forms: presenting himself as disinherited, bemoaning an imaginary impoverishment signified by his room at the "Y," and through his public demands that the board of directors of Chriscorp "explain themselves," promising that he was "gathering together certain papers that would constitute an indictment of the family's history in the islands" (131). Paul's acts of violence take the place of this indictment. The papers gathered in the wake of the murders are quite literally an indictment, but one that offers little in the way of a direct answer to the immediate source of guilt being identified in the Christian family.

When Paul shifts his scene of action from stockholders' meetings and the corporate offices to Janet's home, he is also asserting his position as father over that of son and brother, the relations that define his place in Chriscorp. The significance of paternal authority is underscored by the fact that it is not just Janet he kills but her presumed lover, Wendall Omura. Omura emblematizes a counterhistory to the Christians' colonial presence. A Nisei congressman who went to law school on the GI Bill after serving in World War II with the famous Japanese-American unit the 442nd,

Omura's career represents a substantive and symbolic challenge to the authority of the Christians. Paul's violence is fueled in part by racism, but his cryptic statements afterward present Omura as a symptom, not the cause of his rage at his family. Nor is Omura a perfect foil for the Christian's corruption; he is himself a player in many of their business and political dealings, which is another source of Paul's violent antipathy. In Paul's construction of a family at war with itself, he sides with Janet's less-than-successful businessman husband, suggestively at least shoring up a patrilineal relation threatened both by the daughter's infidelity and by Omura's racialized position as interloper in the genealogical order. In his madness, Paul incoherently asserts a tangled set of familial, historical, racial, political, and business relations and marks violence as their only public representation. These relations are mirrored in the contemporaneous collapse of Cambodia and South Vietnam, a connection cynically made in the newspaper headline that catches Didion's eye: "CONGRESSIONAL FOE OF VIET CONFLICT SHOT IN HONOLULU" (74).

It is Janet's death even more than Omura's which symbolizes the collapse of the American cause in Southeast Asia. While Omura dies instantly, Janet hovers on life support for two days, her doctor refusing to say whether she's alive or dead. Janet's displacement, her adultery and her body's indeterminacy, figures the family's loss of a firm anchorage in the Pacific and in history as Saigon falls. The "certain gray area" between life and death (150), the "technical death" the doctor tries to explain to Inez at Janet's bedside (151), mimics the presence and absence of the United States in Vietnam in the spring of 1975, losing a war that is "technically" over. Janet's fate is linked to that of Vietnam over and over again in the novel. Harry Victor's typically vague and qualified press release could apply equally to the shooting of his sister-in law and a congressional colleague or to the collapse of South Vietnam: "expressing not only his sympathy and deep concern but his conviction that this occasion of sadness for all Americans could be an occasion of resolve as well . . . resolve to overcome the divisions and differences tragically brought to mind today by this incident in the distant Pacific" (156–157). As Alan Nadel suggests, Hawaii is not distant but home in many senses to Inez if not Harry. Although Harry implicitly "others" Janet, Omura, Paul, and Hawaii with this statement, the "differences" shared by "all Americans" would necessarily have to refer to the Vietnam War in order to have the kind of public resonance required by political rhetoric. In the bankrupt terms of Harry Victor's liberal politics, terms hardly more coherent than Paul's delusions, Janet's and Omura's deaths become the occasion, albeit somewhat premature, for putting Vietnam behind us.

Rather than leave Vietnam behind, the action of the novel moves insistently west, toward Vietnam. Janet's death sets in motion a series of trips across the Pacific: from the mainland to Hawaii, but also to and from Guam, Hong Kong, Saigon, Johnson Island, Jakarta, Subic Bay, Manila, Phnom

Penh, Vientiane, and Kuala Lumpur. The familiarity of these routes to many characters in the novel contradicts the sense of foreignness and self-protective distance Harry's comments attempt to establish. In the novel Hawaii is situated not as the far edge of United States but as the "crossroads of the Pacific," the center of a network of nearly indistinguishable military and commercial interests. All the main characters travel these routes. The failure of Janet's husband, Dick Ziegler, as businessman and patriarch is best seen in the contempt he earns when he has difficulties getting off of Guam during an airline strike after the shootings. It is Jack Lovett who most effectively travels between these destinations, not simply because his military contacts have primacy over those businessmen but because he is one of the few who "understand war itself as a specifically commercial enterprise" (159). But this understanding cannot ultimately overcome the historical convulsions which as surely as any earthquake are altering the map of imperial power centered by Hawaii.

Didion presses this point by making Harry and Inez's daughter Jesse rather than Jack Lovett the literal point of connection between the Christian and Victor families and the collapse of South Vietnam. Jessie, Didion tells us, is "the crazy eight in this narrative," the sign that as narrator, she, like Jack Lovett shuttling across the Pacific, no longer has "time for the playing out" (164). The day after Janet is shot, 18-year-old Jesse checks herself out of a drug rehabilitation program in Seattle, talks her way onto a transport flight and then through customs in Saigon with a driver's licence and a fake press card, looking for one of the "cinchy jobs" a guy from Boeing had told her about. She finds one at the American Legion club. Jessie's plot is even more difficult than Paul's murder of Janet and Omura to assimilate into novelistic structures of cause and effect. As "crazy eight" Jessie figures the peculiar randomness of the American evacuation from Saigon, a randomness which resulted from an entrenched disbelief that it would happen. But the logic of the Seattle/Boeing/Vietnam connection is anything but random. Jessie is attaching herself to a very real "trade route." This is part of the reason that Jessie's perverse escapade is not figured with the same dismissive irony as her twin brother Adlai's "vigil for peace." There is a certain respect in the novel for Jessie's radical disengagement from her family and the world's preoccupations. The trip to Vietnam is motivated by a "convergence of yearning and rumor and isolation" (176). But the novel's end finds Jessie living in Mexico City writing a novel, a historical romance about Maximilian and Carlotta, suggesting a deepening appreciation on Jessie's part of her own disengagement. Like Inez and the narrating Didion, Jessie has begun to actively interrogate historical memory and national boundaries.

It is the combined effect of Janet's death and Jessie's excursion which prompts Inez's own radical disengagement from her family and from "the American exemption." The two events are and are not meaningfully connected. Jessie goes to Vietnam instead of going to Janet's funeral, but she does not go to Vietnam because Janet was shot. The relation between these events is neither causal nor simply coincidental. It is, as Didion maintains all human behavior to be, "circumstantial" (186)—confined by the possibilities of time and place, in other words, subject to history. Inez comes to understand this in Hong Kong while waiting for Jack Lovett to find Jessie and bring her out of Saigon during the first week of April 1975. It is an understanding "that Inez's experience had tended to deny. She had spent her childhood immersed in the local conviction that the comfortable entrepreneurial life of an American colony in a tropic without rot represented a record of individual triumphs over a hostile environment. She had spent her adult life immersed in Harry Victor's conviction that he could be president" (211). Removed from the Christians and the Victors, Inez comes to recognize "the convulsions of a world largely unaffected by the individual efforts of anyone in it" (211).

In the reception room of the American embassy in Hong Kong, Inez reads news stories "about Harry Victor's relatives."

> In the *South China Morning Post* she read that Harry Victor's wife had not been present at the funeral of Harry Victor's sister-in-law, a private service in Honolulu after which Senator Victor declined to speak to reporters. In the Asian edition of the *International Herald-Tribune* she read that Harry Victor's father-in-law had required treatment at the Honolulu City and County Jail for superficial wounds inflicted during an apparent suicide attempt with a Bic razor. In the international editions of both *Time* and *Newsweek* she read that Harry Victor's daughter was ironically or mysteriously missing in Vietnam.
>
> "Ironically" was the word used by *Time*, and "mysteriously" by *Newsweek*. (191–192)

At stake is not simply the insufficient rational for Jessie's actions but the presumption that Harry Victor's daughter should not be part of the "playing out" of American policy in Vietnam, a policy Harry both failed to significantly shape and capitalized on in his career as a politician. In the U.S.-centered view of the media, it is "ironic" or "mysterious," that is completely unexpected, that Jessie should be subject to "the convulsions of history" in Southeast Asia. The stories presume that Jessie and her mother should be at her father's side. But as Janet's fate suggests, the father is no guarantee of safe haven. As daughter, Jessie marks this immersion in history more powerfully than, for example, a differently plotted novel might have done by making her twin brother, Adlai, subject to the draft. Jessie's plot is less about the hypocrisy of politicians who either waged or allowed a war in which privilege disproportionately exempted their own children than about the more fundamental presumption of a home that is not subject to imperatives beyond individual, and specifically the father's, control.

Inez becomes increasingly detached from her family while reading about them in the third person from Hong Kong. Gender is crucial to appreciating the hollowness of Harry Victor's claim to centrality, but so is geography. From Asia, Harry and his presidential aspirations to lead the free world appear increasingly irrelevant as a context for rendering events meaningful. It is when Inez hears the final evacuation message from Saigon, the playing of "White Christmas" and the message to phone home, that she comes to the "long view of history," the realization that none of the people in her family should "be exempted from the general movement. Just because they believed they had a home to call. Just because they were Americans" (208). This conviction is not abstractly political but is centered by her loss of compelling interest in the members of her immediate family. "They were definitely connected to her but she could no longer grasp her own or their uniqueness, her own or their difference, genius, special claim" which should differentiate them from the rest of the world which on that night "was full of people flying from place to place and fading in and out" (208). The loss of the "special claim" of family and nation erodes the naturalized assumptions of an "us" and a "them" on which the logic of war, empire, and racism all crucially depend.

Didion's dilemma as novelist is her dependence on narrative, and particularly on character's privileged relation to plot.

> When novelists speak of the unpredictability of human behavior they usually mean not unpredictability at all but a higher predictability, a more complex pattern discernable only after the fact. Examine the picture. find the beast in the jungle, the figure in the carpet. Context clues. The reason why. (215)

But "after the fact" of the fall of Saigon, the novel's final chapters are marked by all the things Didion as narrator could not figure out in retrospect. Even a simple chronology of events is hopelessly muddled, not just by faulty or motivated memories but by the international date line which is crossed and recrossed during these plot lines. Time and space, the founding vectors of history and its narratives, are, in this globalized context, radically relative. Didion finally must fly to Kuala Lumpur, where Inez is working in a refuge camp to find out what has happened. The first thing Didion discovers is that Jack Lovett is dead, having suffered a heart attack in the same swimming pool in Jakarta where Jesse and Adlai had played Marco Polo in 1969. These and other "correspondences," as Inez calls them, suggest the presence of narrative to her, a pattern she could not have suspected while living her life. Didion as narrator is less sure. But for Didion the author and for the reader, these correspondences across the Pacific are, at the very least, markers of imperialism not "democracy," significations of immense power normalized, historicized, and not fully metaphorized as family relations. It is not the innocence of the child's voice that finally echoes from Jakarta but the discoverer's name, "Marco Polo."

Inez's response is to "give up the American exemption" and move to Kuala Lumpur where she goes to work as director of a refugee camp. Inez and the novel end in a space that "existed only as the flotsam of some territorial imperative," a space at best tangentially connected to the maps and plots of the United States (228). The overlapping sense of narrative and political containment that Inez exceeds with this move is quite literal. She is inaccessible to Didion's attempts to bring her into the story. Kuala Lumpur

> seemed to [rule] out any pretense of casual access. I could call Dwight Christian and say that I just happened to be in Honolulu, but I could not call Inez and say that I just happened to be in Kuala Lumpur. No one "happens to be" in Kuala Lumpur, no on "passes through" en route somewhere else: Kuala Lumpur is en route nowhere. . . . (215–216)

Geography, more than character determines narrative in *Democracy*, the plausibility of being in a given place at a given time. Like Jessie's trip to Vietnam or Paul's murderous visit to Janet's lanai, from a certain familiar perspective, it is both ironic and mysterious that "a woman who had once thought of living in the White House was flicking termites from her teacup and telling me about landing on a series of coral atolls in a seven-passenger plane with a man in a body bag" (228). That events in the White House can effect the dislocations of hundreds of thousands of people in Southeast Asia is a commonplace acknowledgment. Didion's strategy of using a privileged American woman to make that connection is not.

There are no "real" refugees in *Democracy*: no depictions of displaced Vietnamese, or Cambodians, or Montagnards, or Hmong. Didion's strategy is thus the opposite of O'Brien's, which self-consciously enacts the desire to humanize the refugee's plight by imagining the individual, Sarkin, representative of unimaginable numbers: 1.5 million Southeast Asian refugees over 20 years.[32] Didion eschews this liberal gesture, presenting instead the structural accommodation of mass displacement: refugee camps situated "en route nowhere" worthy only of the occasional sidebar news item. Indeed, it is Inez rather than the plight of the refugees which brings Didion as narrator and character to Kuala Lumpur to search out the end of the story. Although Inez is described as "having many of the traits of a successful refugee," she does not stand in for the displaced peoples of Southeast Asia. Rather, Inez's self-exile marks war and empire as narratives and realities which exceed the domesticated patterns of American lives. Inez remains a figure of privilege, but she has recentered that privilege within the global realities of "having and not having" rather than in the self-satisfied presumption of American dominion (211).

In its refusal to affirm the privileges of "home," *Democracy*'s ending is radically different from most other Vietnam War novels, for example, Ron Kovic's return to a mythified backyard in *Born on the Fourth of July* or Paul

Berlin's desire to return home to Fort Dodge. For all those novels' powers of critique, their conservative returns end up containing Vietnam as a limited episode long ago and far away, enabling the return of all American boys and proper sons in a still-centered narrative of American history and social relations. Didion resists this closure. As daughter, wife, and mother, Inez defects, and it is this defection that makes visible the significant absence of imperialism in the American narrative of democracy.

MAXINE HONG KINGSTON'S ELEGANT GENEALOGY OF THE Chinese fathers who came to various "Americas," *China Men*, complicates notions of home even more profoundly than does *Democracy*. Moving from China to Hawaii, Alaska, New York, and California, the fathers of *China Men* reverse the trajectory of American imperialism in the Pacific. But *China Men* ends with a reversal of this reversal. The final chapter, "The Brother in Vietnam," tells the story of the narrator's brother's perverse "return" to Asia as a sailor in the U.S. Navy during the Vietnam War. Lisa Lowe has argued that "the material legacy of the repressed history of U.S. imperialism in Asia is borne out in the 'return' of Asian immigrants to the imperial center" (16).[33] Lowe places "return" in scare quotes, challenging through her ironic echo both racist and nostalgic presumptions about the "return" of American-born children of Asian descent to the mother country. It is precisely this irony that is central to the style and structure of *China Men*. Kingston plays upon not only the impossible demand to return to a place one has never been but also the insistent return of the repressed history of the Chinese in the United States.

As Lowe suggests, the act of immigrating from Asia to the United States entails profoundly complicated material and symbolic relations of before and after, here and there. Kingston's narrative defies definitions of memoir, novel, and history, exceeding the categories of fiction and nonfiction, past and present, public and private in its pursuit of familial, cultural, and national genealogy. Once again, the Vietnam War marks the paradoxical end of history, the loss of a meaningful relation of time and place. Even more clearly than *Democracy*, *China Men* insists that the Vietnam War was not a unique moment in history. Both the mythical Land of Women accidentally discovered in the book's opening allegory and the historical Gold Mountain to which the various Chinese fathers journey are said to be characterized by the absence of war; yet, the narrative of *China Men* is saturated from beginning to end with the immediate presence of war and its legacy. Nor is it simply war but wars fought by the United States in Asia that forge the terms of history under which the narrator grows up and against which, in significant part, she composes her genealogy: World War II, the Communist Revolution in China, Korea, Vietnam—and hardly remembered but symbolically present, the earliest war in the Philippines.

As the narrator surmises at the beginning of the chapter on "the Brother in Vietnam," "[t]here was always a war whether I knew it or not" (264).

The narrator pronounces this fact while rehearsing her earliest memories, beginning with her panicked confusion as a young child at a war movie. It is hardly surprising that "The Brother in Vietnam" begins with the spectacle of World War II movies—many if not most memoirs of the Vietnam war begin figuratively or literally with them. But unlike the memoirs of Ron Kovic or Philip Caputo, for Kingston World War II movies are not the ideological opposite of Vietnam but its violent and senseless prefiguration. This is not simply a pacifist rejection of all war but an historical understanding of Vietnam as literally continuous with World War II, a concept absolutely untenable to most narratives of either war.

It is telling that not only the last chapter on "The Brother in Vietnam," but the first, "The Father from China," begins with memories of World War II.[34] "Father," she begins, "I have seen you lighthearted." These opening memories are taken from the summers of "The War" (capital T, capital W) when the father amused his children by turning captured dragonflies into airplanes and killing "Hitler moths"—games played on a front porch reached after walking through the Chinatown of Stockton, California, past "the Japanese's house, nobody home for years, and the Filipino Lodge" (12). Kingston's memory of playing war games echoes even as it recasts the nostalgic glow of World War II in the Cold War childhoods described by Kovic and Caputo. For Kingston and her father, however, killing Hitler does not offer the same promise of an identity centered in a moral and global order. At the beginning of the book, Kingston renarrates World War II as a story of fathers and daughters enacted within a neighborhood in which the geography of American military and economic hegemony in the Pacific is carried home—a history powerfully suppressed by the narrative of killing Hitler and one that needs to be remembered in relation to Vietnam.

This choice of a beginning, the when and where that will lead to the brother in Vietnam, is critical. *China Men* offers a deeply canny counter-text, in both form and substance, to the progressive, westward moving narrative of American history. Just as the China men move backward across the geography of American history, traveling east to the American West, so Kingston insistently challenges the naturalized relation of events across time. The popular American narrative of "killing Hitler" begins and ends in the Pacific, moving from Pearl Harbor to Hiroshima, but the centrality of Asia is curiously displaced by the spectacular evil of Nazism that emblematizes the fascism held to be the cause of World War II. In *China Men*, however, the war in Asia never ends. "'The War,' I wrote in a composition, which the teacher corrected, 'Which war?' There was more than one" (276).

"The War" in *China Men* is continuous across space as well as time. The "home front" quite literally crosses the Pacific. The narrator's VJ-day souvenir photo of the atomic bomb is juxtaposed with the return of the "one family of AJA's, Americans of Japanese ancestry, on our block" (273). The narrator and her siblings suspect the family of hidden crimes, like those of wartime propaganda, but understand her parents' acts of generosity toward them: "[W]e would want them to be nice to us when the time came for us Chinese to be the ones in camps" (274). Stated in the terms of childish misunderstanding, Kingston here marks the schizophrenic terms in which the narrator is made to understand her difference from and connection to other Asians. That this sense of connection derives equally from racist coercion and the communal bonds of experience only intensifies the paradoxical place Kingston narrates through irony. Growing up as a Chinese-American girl during the Cold War, the narrator becomes increasingly aware of the fraught relation of public and private, us and them, here and there.

> For the Korean War, we wore dog tags . . . our dog tags had *O* for religion and *O* for race because neither black nor white. Mine also had *O* for blood type. Some kids said *O* was for "Oriental," but I knew it was for "Other," because the Filipinos, the Gypsies, and the Hawaiian boy were *O*'s. Zero was also the name of the Japanese fighter plane, so we had better watch our step. (276)

As the Cold War "comes home," the coercive categories of American identity continue to reinforce the alienated status of Asian Americans. This is particulary ironic in that the "communist threat" is quite literal to the narrator's family, who receive letter after letter from relatives in China detailing "reeducation," death, and torture at the hands of the communist regime. But the dog tags given out at school in no way resist this violence. Rather, they are yet another aspect of the same overwhelming presence of war that surrounds the narrator.

The Vietnam War is introduced in this very particular context:

> Before the letter writers stopped complaining about the Communists, the Vietnam war had begun. The government said that Viet Cong weapons came from China. We ought to bomb China into the Stone Age, the generals said. Soon the war would be Chinese Americans against Chinese. And my brothers old enough to be drafted. (276–277)

For the narrator and her brother, the Vietnam War is nothing but "friendly fire," the violent coming together of radically different understandings of self, identity, and history. But if friendly fire typically makes the Vietnam War plottable, offering, as in *Going After Cacciato*, the revealed secret at the heart of the war, or, as in *Democracy*, the perverse trope of delusion and solipsism, this understanding of the war leaves the brother devoid of possibilities, with nowhere to go and nothing to do. In the terms of both Cold War ideology and family history, it is the "loss of China" which is refought in Vietnam. The war becomes the occasion for the brother to "return" to a home he has never known, again reinforcing his status as alien in "the only country he had ever lived in" (283). Public sentiment deems that "'Orientals'

belonged over there in Asia fighting among their own kind" (277). The high
school students he teaches dismiss his criticisms of the war and America as
"his being gookish" (279). But his mother's parting words reinforce the
racial connection from another direction: "Bring a wife home. Look for a
Chinese girl, but the Japanese are okay too, Koreans are okay. Just as long
as she has a soft smile" (285). The mother leaves out Vietnamese in her catalogue of potential brides, eliding with them the immediate circumstance
of the war as the occasion for the brother's departure. The categories of race
and war, immigration and imperialism, family and nation are so deeply intertwined as to resist the brother's rational disentanglement. Already placed
"over there" in the Asia of American Orientalism, the brother finds it increasingly difficult to avoid the war.

Ironically, the antiwar movement's critique of the imperial nature of
American economic as well as military power works to further shrink the
possibilities of the brother's world.

> In a country that operates on a war economy, there isn't much differ-
> ence between being in the Navy and being a civilian. When we ate a
> candy bar, drank grape juice, bought bread (ITT makes Wonder
> bread), wrapped food in plastic, made a phone call, put money in the
> bank, cleaned the oven, washed with soap, turned on electricity, re-
> frigerated food, cooked it, ran a computer, drove a car, rode an air-
> plane, sprayed with insecticide, we were supporting the corporations
> that made tanks and bombers, napalm, defoliants, and bombs. For
> the carpet bombing. Everything was connected to everything else
> and to war. (284)

As both an American and the child of Chinese immigrants, the brother's
life is always already connected to the war in Vietnam. Burdened by this
recognition that the war is everywhere and everything, the brother joins
the Navy, retracing the routes of immigration and war, making port in the
Philippines, Korea, Taiwan, and Hong Kong. The brother maps with heavy
heart the imperial history that binds him to his impossibly compromised
place. His story becomes one of deferrment and denial, resolutions about
what he will not do rather than what he will. "He would not shoot a
human being; he would not press the last button that dropped the bomb"
(285). He rationalizes that in Navy he was "only coming a few miles physically closer to Vietnam, and his job of flipping switches and connecting cir-
cuits and typing was the same as on land, the numbers and letters were almost the same" (296).

The brother avoids as much as possible actually crossing the last distance to Vietnam. "On the ocean, he would not have his heart broken at the
sight of Vietnamese grandmothers and babies" (284). The exclusion of the
Vietnamese from the brother's frame of vision and the narrative as a whole
is not, however, the same as the typical gesture of relegating the Vietnamese

to the background of American narratives. It is precisely because of the brother's fear that he will see the Vietnamese both as individuals and as a people with whom he shares certain familial and historical resemblances that he seeks to avoid them. He draws his moral line at shooting "another human being" (285). He thus refuses to accept the designations of friend and enemy that are ironically played out in the trope of friendly fire. The irony of his place in Asia haunts the brother even though he avoids confronting his likeness to and difference from the Vietnamese. In Taiwan he shrinks from the old man hired as "houseboy," fearing both failure in the proper enactment of Chinese customs and reproof for "being in the Navy, for living with a gang of white devils, for going out with girls, for drinking, for coming in late, for smoking dope, for the invasion and colonization of Asia" (295). The fear and very possibly the desire here is both personal and political. The old man is cast as both Chinese father and the Asian victim of American imperialism. But the anticipated rebuke never comes. In Taiwan, as earlier in Korea, when the brother is called on to answer the question "What are you?" the designation "Chinese American" is met not with derision or criticism but with the simple response, "Lucky" (296). This response is less a sign of having internalized ideas of American superiority than an appreciation of having successfully completed the immigrant act. Traveling across the Pacific the terms of self and other, American and Asian retain the same shifting complexity experienced in the United States.

The brother's weak resistance to service in Vietnam stands in ironic opposition to his father's experience in World War II. The story of saving BaBa from the draft is vividly told in the brother's chapter. After cataloging the violent and drastic self-mutilations performed in Chinatown to avoid military service, Baba is arbitrarily excused by his draft board as too skinny. This story must be told in the Vietnam chapter and not the American father's chapter. Vietnam radically recontextualizes the significance of avoiding service in World War II which is all but sinful, which is to say un-American, in the progressive narrative of American history.[35] But Baba's avoidance of the World War II draft, no less than the brother's service in the Vietnam War, is a moment that confounds easy designations of Chinese and American, there and here, then and now. "Freedom from the draft was the reason for leaving China in the first place. The Gold Mountain does not make war, is not invaded, and has no draft" (269). The father and his peers have internalized a crucial part of the myth of exceptionalism, that the United States "does not make war." But they are also acting out a deeply immediate relation to the war; for China is where the battle is fought, across the bodies and on the backs of their relatives: the grandfather bayoneted by a Japanese soldier (21), the mother another of the "natives" who builds the roads (69) which the "foolhardy" cousins who serve in the army drive down in tanks (272–273).

The father and son war stories of *China Men* stand in openly ironic relation to most American narratives of World War II and Vietnam. The father can actively avoid service in World War II because of his familial and communal understanding of the war as something other than a unique moment in history that began without warning at Pearl Harbor. The brother cannot avoid the Vietnam War and go to Sweden or Canada for precisely the same reason: his profoundly personal knowledge that the United States is already in Asia and Asia in the United States. Neither war is particularly "special" in Kingston's account. In this sense it is crucial to remember the larger scope of *China Men*, which does not confine itself to the generations of World War II and Vietnam but looks back to grandfathers who earlier transformed the relation of East and West, in both global and continental frames of reference, by building the railroads and clearing the rainforests of Hawaii. No less than the brother, these men occupied a paradoxical and contested place in the history of American imperialism.[36] Both in the material effects of their labor and in their silenced place in history, the grandfathers become literal and figurative markers of the importance of Asia, and in particular China, as the constitutive far horizon of the American expansion across place and time.

History in *China Men* quite literally repeats itself. Kingston resists the coercive logic of American imperialism which, in moving from East to West, beginning to end, both appropriates and silences the labor and narratives of the China men. Her genealogy is insistently antilinear, marked by the failure of sequence, by impossible relations of space and time, by repetition and contradiction. The father's story in particular marks this formal necessity. His story is told and retold, as "the Father from China" (chapter 1) and "the American Father" (chapter 5); the immigrant and the citizen; illegal and legal; arriving in New York and San Francisco, past Ellis Island and through Angel Island. The father's story becomes one of Jameson's magical narratives which fantastically displays even as it disguises the contradictions of history. But in Vietnam the magic of both American and Chinese narratives seems to have been exhausted. The brother lacks the father's power to have multiple lives. Instead of the "Chinese son" and "the American Son," there is only "the brother in Vietnam" who is unable to claim the exceptionalist justifications of duty, destiny, and innocence.

But in naming the last of the China men "brother" rather than "son," Kingston works another kind of narrative magic, bringing the concept of genealogy to a critical rather than coercive end. Like Didion, Kingston presses the "adjacent" place of the sister and daughter in relation to family and history. If war and immigration are deeply intertwined as the ground and effect of the relation of the United States to Asia, both are likewise violently gendered. The text of *China Men* begins as the narrator's response to her father's angry silence and his "wordless male screams" (13), but in the end of the book her relationship to her brother is also structured across a gulf of gendered silence. The chapter "the brother in Vietnam" breaks in halves between the sister's narrative of their childhood in which one war gives way to another (World War II, the communist revolution in China,

Korea, Vietnam) and the brother's silent struggle with the draft and service. The narrator's "I" totally disappears from the chapter once she drops brother off for induction. He literally will not let his sister go with him. War thus recapitulates the gendered history of immigration that likewise sought to deny Chinese women entry.

The narrator is both understanding and critical, I believe, of her brother's plight and place. The complex interconnection of past and present, Asia and the United States, war and everyday life is one of the fundamental lessons of *China Men*. While this understanding of the imperial nature of American society as radically diffuse should involve the brother and sister equally, it does not. The brother is literally conscripted into his impossible place in history. The narrator's dispassionate account of her brother's internal struggles both respects the particularity of his place and subtlety marks his failure to either voice or enact his opposition to the war. But more important, the narrator does not write herself back into the war story. She does not describe her place on the "home front": writing letters, following the news, supporting her family or any of the other typical duties of women during war. Again, like Didion, Kingston refuses to place women in the recuperative place of home which gives meaningful shape to both war and empire. In *Democracy* Inez steps beyond her naturalized place in the family and the nation. In *China Men*, however, the "unnaturalized" relation of family and nation tremendously complicates the ability to locate the boundaries of the American empire, even as the history of exclusion and citizenship, immigration and war becomes the narrative's recurrent text and context.

When the brother decides not to avoid the draft by going to Canada or Sweden, he resolves that "the United States was the only country he had ever lived in. He would not be driven out" (283). The brother does not connect this version of the "driving out" to the earlier one experienced by his grandfather, Ah Goong, following the completion of the railroads, but the sister's narrative pointedly sets up this historical echo (148). The draft forces a choice on the brother which recapitulates the debate in Asian-American studies over the efficacy of "claiming America" or following diasporic models of culture, identity, and history.[37] The brother's negative choice—to "not be driven out"—suggests the difficulty, if not the impossibility of enacting such choices. At the end of *Going After Cacciato*, Sarkin urges Paul Berlin "to act," presenting the fantasy (*his* fantasy) that he may choose to be a part of the war or walk away from it. Paul Berlin's failure to leave the war is figured as a personal, if understandably human, failure of courage—"the fear of abandoning all I hold dear." The brother's negative resistance to the war is likewise haunted by the specter of cowardice, the failure to stand up for his belief that the war was wrong. But like Didion, Kingston ultimately insists on "the long view . . . the convulsions of a world largely unaffected by the individual efforts of anyone in it" (Didion 211). This is not, in any sense, a nihilistic understanding of history. The brother must struggle to find his place in history, even if he cannot make history conform to his desire. Much in the same way, the sister seeks to write a narrative of war and the daughter the narrative of immigration in spite or because of being barred from an acknowledged place within those histories.

China Men's closing allegory, "On Listening," seems to leave the war in Vietnam behind. The narrator's "I" returns to the narrative. She describes a party where a Filipino scholar tells her a fantastic tale of Chinese travelers tricking the Spanish in the Philippines. This story begets others, as a group of young Chinese Americans join in with stories of Mandarins in Mexico and Chinese villages in California. These final fairy tales remember the geography and time lines of American imperialism far better than any map or history. The narrator, however, becomes confused, unable to hear the details as the young men interrupt each other. The narrator is relieved when the Filipino scholar offers to write it down and send it to her. "Good. Now I could watch the young men who listen" (308). The openness of this, the book's final line, challenges the rationalization of history into a unified narrative which marches with imperial force across continents and time. Her resistence is gendered, as well. The young men offer competing tales of discovery and exploration. By taking herself out of the competition, the narrator is free to mark the overlap and repetition within the stories and, more important, to observe the active engagement of these young men in the act of telling their tales. "On Listening" thus tropes Kingston's relation to the book as a whole, both recording the "lighthearted" moments of the free telling of tales (1) and entering the void of the "wordless male screams" (13). As the gendered outsider to the narrative of war and its narration of empire, immigration, and the meaning of crossing the Pacific, Kingston attends to history rather than trying to make it. Instead of justifying one man's place in the war, Kingston pays heed to the Vietnam War for its magical recapitulations of times and places which may be long ago and far away but are decidedly not bathed in the nostalgia of an innocent America.

Chapter 3

"BETWEEN THE DEVIL AND THE DEEP BLUE"
Black Historical Authority and the Vietnam War

We have been, for the most part, talking about
contemporary realities. We have not been talking
about a return to some glorious African past.
But we recognize the past—the total past. Many
of us refuse to accept a truncated Negro history
which cuts us off completely from our African
ancestry. To do so is to accept the very racist
assumptions we abhor. Rather we want to
comprehend history totally, and understand the
manifold ways in which contemporary
problems are affected by it.
— Larry Neal, "And Shine Swam On"

If you know your history,
Then you'd know where you're coming from,
Then you wouldn't have to ask me,
Who the hell I think I am.
I'm just a buffalo soldier,
Dredlock rasta.
Said I am a buffalo soldier,
In the war for America.
And I had to fight on arrival,
Fighting for survival.
—Bob Marley

We black men here are so much
between the Devil and the Deep Blue.
—Sgt. Major J.W. Galloway
To the editor of the *Richmond Planet*
from the Philippines Sept. 30, 1899

Near the end of Ralph Ellison's *Invisible Man*, the protagonist worries about the fate of black Americans living outside the patterns of recorded history, "too distant from the centers of historical decision, to sign or even to applaud the signers of historical documents[.] We who write no novels, histories, or other books. What about us?"[1] In Vietnam War texts by African American writers, this exclusion from recorded history occasions the trope of friendly fire. The image of Americans killing Americans in these works is distinguished from those considered in previous chapters by the overt ideological critique made possible by an articulate black nationalist consciousness. Such scenes of violent confrontation, however, are not a new feature of African American war narratives.

In increasingly self-conscious and aggressive form since the Civil War, African Americans have viewed military service as a way to place themselves within the mainstream of American history. One thinks of Richard Wright's account in *Black Boy* of his grandfather's painstaking attempts to document his service in the Union army in order to claim his rightful pension. The trials of Richard Wilson, rechristened "Vinson" by a white officer's careless inscription, all too vividly captures the frustrating reality of service in Jim Crow institutions. The regimental histories of segregated units such as the 54th and 55th Massachusetts Volunteers in the Civil War or the "Buffalo Soldiers" of the 9th and 10th cavalry in the West and the Spanish-American War became curiosities of military history, just as the soldiers themselves had been relegated to the most obscure and distant posts.

The injustice of being called to serve in a segregated army was further compounded by the imperialist nature of American wars in the twentieth century. Sgt. Major J. W. Galloway's observation that black men in the Philippines were "so much between the Devil and the Deep Blue" expresses the black soldier's quandary in fighting a war against "goo-goos" and "niggers." Letter after letter from black soldiers published in Negro newspapers around the country during the Spanish-American War confronted the question of split allegiance between the American flag and the perceived "sable brethren," whether, like Galloway, to agonize over it or to dismiss it.[2]

The emergent black nationalism of the 1960s confronted this double bind, one form of the "double-consciousness" W. E. B. Du Bois formulated as the 9th Cavalry fought the Philippine insurgence, by privileging the separatist position of African Americans. In the words of Larry Neal, the black nationalism first "synthesized" by Malcolm X "was the truth as only the oppressed, and those whose lives have somehow been 'outside of history,' could know it."[3] Vietnam War novels by black writers seek to make sense of the war from this place "outside of history." But the act of recentering not only one's relation to history but history itself is more complex, more dangerous, than Neal's recontextualizing of Ellison's complaint as empowering difference might at first appear. As Neal makes clear, with the sense of being separate comes "a concomitant sense of being 'at war.'"[4] No figure better embodies this identity, "separate" and "at war," and exemplifies its dangers than does the black soldier.

In "And Shine Swam On," Neal argues that this state of being at war is both a "pressing historical reality" and an attack on history itself; "history weighs down on all of this literature. Every black writer in America has to react to this history, either to make peace with it, or to make war on it."[5] For Neal, "the answer" was to be found "outside of historical materialism," in the cultural construction of meaning. Western cultural configurations "lead to certain ideas of what art is, what life is . . ." (648). One should add "what history is" as well. As the afterward to the anthology *Black Fire*, one of the founding texts of the Black Arts Movement, "And Shine Swam On" stands as a cultural manifesto, both calling for and enacting a redefinition not simply of the black artist's place in history but of history itself.[6]

Neal's move to the "outside" of American history is a move away from the reified Western conception of history as narrative, especially linear, written, professional narrative. Ellison's invisible man fears that by leaving the Brotherhood's scientific conception of history he will be outside history itself. Yet beyond the Brotherhood's agenda, embodiments of the past surround him. To cite but one example, Brother Tarp's violently scarred iron link represents, and thus makes available for interpretation, more "sensuous human activity" than all the Brotherhood's policies, formulations, and analysis. Tarp's link records the continuing history of individual black action through which slavery gave way to freedom, a history buried under the narrative in which "Lincoln freed the slaves." But where Ellison suggests that such unwritten texts are destined to remain invisible, unavailable to be read, Larry Neal and the Black Arts Movement sought to move the site of cultural interpretation away from the text as written document and toward performance, thus enabling new conceptions of art and meaning.[7]

This renunciation of the conventions of Western historiography has obvious analogues in the Vietnam narratives considered in previous chapters. And while the trope of friendly fire is once again the central figuration of this textual battle, in the novels by African American writers to be considered in this chapter this violence is conditioned by the ideological terms of Black Power. The emotional force and coherence of Black Power's definition of black America as a separate nation enabled a powerful critical position "outside of history," but the experiences of black soldiers who fought in Vietnam demonstrate many of the conflicts incumbent to the stance. It is crucial to note that the separatism of the 1960's black nationalism does not per se constitute the trope of friendly fire, although at least one text to be considered here, John A. Williams' *Captain Blackman*, ends in a global declaration of war between black and white Americans.[8]

Rather, friendly fire is the trope that marks what Hayden White calls the "swerve" away from "literal, conventional, or 'proper' language use" in discourse, "a deviation *from* one possible, proper meaning, but also a deviation *towards* another meaning. . . ."[9] The trope of friendly fire as figured by

African American authors marks the move away from the traditional, "proper" discourse of American history and identity, not simply toward a discourse of disillusionment but toward a discourse of black consciousness which is primarily tropic, recorded in the figures, gestures, and rituals that have existed in the New World for 300 years in the fragmented reality of the African diaspora. The violence of friendly fire comes to reflect the continuing material oppression of African Americans, most notable during the Vietnam era in the systemic inequality that placed black men at a continual disadvantage when confronting the realities of service, the draft, combat, and, especially, military justice.[10] But it responds, as well, to the dominant discourse's appropriation and use of the figure of the black soldier in representations of the war.

The ubiquitous presence of the black soldier is the feature that most prominently distinguishes the cultural and historical record of Vietnam from past American wars. But like rock-and-roll sound tracks, helicopters, and water buffalos, the black soldier is primarily placed as a prop of realism, even in the most surreal representations of the war. Black soldiers are "in" *Apocalypse Now* or *Going After Cacciato* because they were "in" Vietnam. They assure the viewer or reader that this is "how it was," but such appropriations rarely consider what the black soldier's presence "means." The black soldier does not in these works represent the tropics of American history, the point at which a discourse acknowledges the possibility that it could have been written another way[11]; he serves instead as little more than local color. "Tropic," Hayden White tells us, "is the shadow from which all realistic discourse tries to flee."[12] The black soldier is such a tropic "shadow" in American discourse; one whose transformative expressive possibility is evaded through the limiting gesture of realistic representation in its crudest form, the stereotype.

C. D. B. Bryant neatly summarizes the ancillary role of the black soldier in his description of the "Generic Vietnam War Narrative." Bryant includes in his imaginary platoon a character named "Juice," "the cool black dude who can smell booby traps and ambushes," and thus one surmises always walks point, like Alice in *The Short-Timers*.[13] Bryant enumerates the roles open to Juice: fragging the psychotic company commander (see Roger in *Going After Cacciato*), saving the good sergeant (see almost any episode of the television show *Tour of Duty*), and as the one who survives the final firefight along with the college educated narrator (see *Platoon*). The radical possibility of the black soldier's alienation is covertly acknowledged in the plot options of fragging the company commander or saving the good sergeant, but, as Clyde Taylor notes about *Platoon*, such actions take place "short of the foreground." Taylor, in fact, describes the black soldiers in *Platoon* as "shadows," reflecting the moral conflict between the white characters at center stage.[14] Because these black shadows never confront each other, reference can be made to black radicalism without having to engage the implications of its critique.[15]

In the jungles of Vietnam the geographic and figurative meanings of tropic intersected. In the excessive heat and luxuriant growth of the Vietnamese landscape, the discourse of modern American power discovered its turning point, the limit and boundary of its extension. The American push West ended in Vietnam. And if the narrative of American history did not extend everywhere, then one could be outside American history and still be somewhere. In the 1960s, Africa came to name this somewhere else. Vietnam brought into acute focus the need to understand the "nation" of black America in relation to the past and present of Africa, but it also demonstrated the enormous difficulty of realizing this connection.

The necessity of mapping an alternative world geography became only too clear to many black American soldiers in Vietnam. The uprising at the U.S. Army Stockade at Long Binh, 18 miles north of Saigon, on August 29, 1968, is emblematic of the extension of a radically separatist vision to the rank and file. LBJ, as the stockade was commonly and "unaffectionately" known ("for 'Long Binh jail' Army officers carefully explained" to *Newsweek*), was "overcrowded (719 men crammed into a space reserved for 502), had no indoor plumbing, and was staffed by inexperienced, overworked guards."[16] When MPs moved in to break up a fight among prisoners, they were overpowered and stripped of their keys. "Led by a group of blacks," the prisoners unlocked the maximum security cellblock and burned the administration and other buildings to the ground.[17] An all-out attack by MPs using "fixed bayonets" and tear gas left 87 wounded and 1 inmate dead. Here is how *Newsweek* presented what followed:

> **Blankets:** When order was restored, the MP's sorted the prisoners into "cooperatives" and "uncooperatives." The 220 uncooperatives, all black save for three Puerto Ricans, were locked into an enclosed part of the stockade—and with that the prison officials assumed the rebellion was over. But this, as it turned out was a highly premature conclusion. Secure in the knowledge that their records had been destroyed with the administration building, the black militants gave false names and serial numbers. Even more provocatively, many of them proceeded to shed their uniforms and to don white kerchiefs and African-style robes which they made out of Army blankets. "Some of them were running around naked or wearing bits of clothing as loincloths," reported one shaken Army officer. "Others were beating out jungle sounds on oil drums."

The forms of both the rebellion at LBJ and *Newsweek*'s coverage are illustrative of the violent confrontations between the "inside" and "outside" of history. The paradox of a military prison, especially LBJ as the war in Vietnam became increasingly unpopular, is that it uses the coercive structure of the prison not to exclude individuals from society but to keep soldiers in the army. Many of the prisoners were there for having been AWOL, and Army psychologists claimed that "most of them just wanted out of the army and out of Vietnam."[18] Throughout the war, black soldiers "received punishments at double the white rate for such arbitrary offenses as disrespect and provoking gestures."[19] In 1967, one college-educated black enlisted man was reported serving time at LBJ for having been caught reading H. Rap Brown.[20]

Unable to reach the outside, in August 1968 the men turned the logic of LBJ around, locking themselves in and creating a revolutionary "cell" beyond the army's jurisdiction. In a small and enclosed space, surrounded without but free within, this group of black men proceeded to redefine themselves, symbolically "shedding" the American identity formed by uniform, name, rank, and serial number and enacting an alternative identity that gestured toward Africa.

This gesture clearly shares the ideological perspective of Black Power and the Black Arts Movement. The black soldier/prisoners of LBJ vividly acknowledged their status as "separate" and "at war." They recognized that the destruction of the documents that constituted the narrative of their identity within the Army and, by extension, within American society had placed them, for a time, outside the system. In place of this American identity, the prisoners declared what David Cortright has called "a kind of liberated African State."[21] And however crudely reported, the revolutionary suggestion of the African gesture is recoverable; in an act of emotional self-determination, the soldiers were claiming an alternative history for themselves and placing Vietnam and their presence there in a new political geography, one defined by revolutionary struggle rather than the Cold War.

But as the ridiculing tone of the *Newsweek* article makes clear, any radical significance in the soldiers' turn to Africa is easily circumvented by a very unsubtle turn toward stereotype. There is no mention of black American leaders' increasing insistence that the civil rights struggle in the United States, the war in Vietnam, and revolutionary struggles in Africa were inherently connected issues.[22] No connection to black militarism in the United States or urban riots was ventured at all. The fundamentally political nature of the prisoners' form of rebellion was denied on all sides. Instead, what *Newsweek* offered was the specter of black "militants," "hardcore insurgents" and "rebels" descending into naked, drumming savagery once removed from the system's discipline. The image was all too familiar: when the governor of New Jersey called out the National Guard to suppress rioting in Newark in the summer of 1966, he had declared, "The line between the jungle and the law might as well be drawn here as anyplace in America." But in Newark, there was also the powerful voice of LeRoi Jones (Amiri Baraka) to insist on the political nature of the Newark uprising, to declare that these were not "riots" or "criminal actions" but acts of "rebellion."[23] The prisoners at LBJ had little more than a column and a half in *Newsweek.*

The *Newsweek* story ends much less provocatively, recounting the Army's "incredibly permissive" decision to wait the "holdouts" out (the last ones surrendered a little over a month later) and giving a capsule history of the Army's "just pride" in the opportunities afforded the black soldier since desegregation, lamely concluding that "the vaunted egalitarianism of the Army cannot, by itself, erase the ingrained tensions that unfortunately exist between white and black Americans." In essence, the report coerces the rebellious black soldier back into his approved role in the narrative of American history—loyal, patient, grateful for the opportunity to prove his worth. The *Newsweek* Long Binh story is accompanied on the same page by a report on the promotion of Col. Fredric Ellis Davison to brigadier general, "the third Negro in history to be made a general in the Armed Forces," in what was described as a "routine army affair." American readers horrified by the description of events at LBJ were no doubt reassured by the photograph of the very soldierly Davison receiving his star. The possibility of a radical alternative is dismissed through the use of familiar sterotypes, while, Davison's story is reinforced as the "real" story, the one which had been and would continue to be told. No interviews were conducted inside LDJ, no follow-up stories filed on the six inmates tried for murder. And if *Newsweek*'s story could not be called objective, it was at least filed. The *New York Times* was the only other major media source to report on the events at LBJ— a suspiciously quiet response to an event that happened 18 miles from what was probably the largest concentration of reporters in the world at that time.

What the events at LBJ meant to the participants cannot be discerned from such sources. But the desperation and idealism of the revolutionary gesture performed there express the complex struggle for black historical authority during the Vietnam War. They suggest the transformative possibilities of a cultural and political identification with Africa to challenge established American authorities even as they define the overwhelming power of the army and the media to encircle and outwait such transgressions, to control bodies and expression. As gesture, the soldiers' Africanized liberation, like the flag raising on Iwo Jima or the Last Stand, transforms history into an image that gains its power through historical amnesia. But as a gesture offered from the outside of history, it serves to reveal rather than erase this loss of history. The gesture is self-consciously tropic, inviting the question, "Why have you forgotten Africa?" The answer demands a different telling of history: a remembering of the Middle Passage as a story not only of slavery and oppression but of cultural continuity and accomplishment. If this story gains utterance and black Americans move inside their own history, the history of America itself would have to be fundamentally revised.[24] American discourse protects its hegemony by offering its own crude answer to the question: "You have forgotten Africa because it is a place of savagery; only as Americans do you have culture and history."

But perhaps the most salient characteristic of the revolutionary gesture at LBJ is its idealism, a fundamental characteristic it shared with the larger Black Power movement. Houston Baker has described at length the degree to which the black nationalist movements of the 1960s resided "in an isolated context constituted by desire alone," a description certainly appropriate to a revolution contained within a stockade.[25] Baker's reading of Larry Neal's essay, "The Black Arts Movement," defines terms that not only bear directly on LBJ but structure the central challenge to black novelists writing about the Vietnam War.

> "Desire," "proposes," "perform," "radical reordering" are terms [from Neal's essay] which mark what I call the conative mode. They communicate Neal's desire to alter existing structures to accord with the wishes of black America. . . . Neal's statements are characterized by the absence of words that point to specific agents, events, or strategies. The phrase, "Black Arts Movement," occupies the stage alone— proposing, preforming, speaking and so on. Its words do not point to any tangible referent. . . .[26]

These terms aptly define the soldier/prisoners' appropriation of Africa. The desire of those men to radically reorder the system holding them is certainly understandable. But their proposal and performance of an alternative African identity is indeed "without tangible referent." What, where, when, and/or who is meant by "Africa" is discernible only in broad outline.

This lack of specificity centers key questions regarding the nature and status of history. As an invocation of a point of origin, "Africa" denotes a collapse of time and space in much the same way that "Vietnam" has come to define more a time, "the Vietnam era," than an identifiable place with its own complex history in American discourse. Both terms, "Africa" and "Vietnam," suggest a radical decentering of American history, but the sleight-of-hand that endows the past with the apparently stable and material weight of a continent or country evades the crucial question of the form of history itself. It is this question of form that will be of central concern in discussing the novels to be considered here, John A. Williams's *Captain Blackman* (1971) and A. R. Flowers's *DeMojo Blues* (1985).

IN JOHN A. WILLIAMS'S *CAPTAIN BLACKMAN* VIETNAM IS presented as the battleground that reveals the nature of an age-old American war. Following a "battle" described in the muted but relentlessly familiar iconography of the Vietnam War, "screams dying, the huts burning," the novel's protagonist, Captain Abraham Blackman, comes to understand the true configuration of the war he is fighting.

> This, Blackman thought, this My Suc was not about black and white against the brown, not really. The blacks and whites wanted to kill

each other, not the Vietnamese, and only the fact that there *were* Vietnamese to kill prevented them, most times, from doing so to each other.[27]

There are no Vietnam fraggings in *Captain Blackman*; when Blackman is wounded it is by enemy fire. But Blackman's conviction that the war in Vietnam was a substitute for the mortal struggle between black and white Americans sends him literally back in time to place the black soldier's experience in Vietnam into historical perspective. This history is structured by past scenes of friendly fire, of black soldiers betrayed, coerced, and murdered by the military as an institution and by individual white soldiers. Knowledge of this past and present "reality" becomes a matter of global, racial, and personal survival. Blackman begins teaching black military history to his men in the hope that "those legs with their mushrooming Afros and off-duty dashikis" will learn "that they were not the first black soldiers to do what they were doing," and thus would not risk their lives unnecessarily (14).

The conceit of the novel enacts Blackman's historical syllabus. Wounded in the battle, Blackman becomes a time traveler, refighting each of America's wars, recording for history the valor and frustrations of the black soldier, reestablishing the "sense of continuity that," Blackman knows, "everyone had tried to keep from [his men], from kindergarten up" (15). Williams proceeds like a triumphantly literate version of Richard Wright's grandfather, producing the documents that authenticate his service and write (and right) his history. At various points, as epigrams to chapter openings and as interchapters titled "Drumtaps," Williams provides quotes from Teddy Roosevelt and W. E. B. Du Bois, congressional hearings and soldiers' memoirs, newspaper reports, and military orders which testify to the factual basis of his fictive recreation of the black soldier's experience from Bunker Hill to Vietnam. This long view of the black soldier's history is critically vital to any analysis of the black soldier's role in Vietnam.[28]

Williams, however, wants to do more than recontextualize the present; ultimately the purpose of establishing this "sense of continuity" is to reject it completely. Blackman's recovery of history serves not only to establish and valorize the central role blacks have played in American wars but, simultaneously, to reveal the essentially racist and imperialist nature of American history. The black soldier is only allowed to step inside American history so that he may choose to leap back out. This leap takes the form of an apocalyptic dream at novel's end in which Blackman is able to disarm the American nuclear capacity from a base in Africa by mobilizing a secret army of light-skinned spies within the American military.

That the novel ends inside Blackman's head is key. The novel is about a coming to radical black consciousness. Blackman finally wakes up from the nightmare of history, and with one leg amputated from his battle wound, recognizes the unalterable violence wrecked upon him by white America. The global revolution he dreams in response signifies his transformed vision of his own identity. Like the prisoners at LBJ, he declares himself "separate" and "at war" through a gesture toward Africa.

Ultimately, *Captain Blackman* ends up hung by the paradox that Houston Baker describes in the black nationalist moment of late 1960s and early 1970s.

> It was paradoxical that those who had so recently come into contact with the writhing history of the West felt compelled to reject it. It was as though possession of what Richard Wright called "a vocabulary of history" gave blacks precisely the terms they needed to protect themselves, to knock the serpent of Western historical aberrations into the street. Or, to state this another way, it was as though blacks after a long pilgrimage had arrived at the Western city only to find it stricken with plague, or caught in the lurid flames of its destruction.[29]

A study of the past thus enables not a vision of the future but a literally devastating critique of the present. The possibility for change then moves into the realm of desire. *Captain Blackman* ends with a leap into utopia, an act of pure wish fulfillment clearly signified by the "incredible smile" on Blackman's sleeping face which the doctor attributes not to visions of global revolution but to dreams of the voluptuous Mimosa Rogers. This turn away from history and toward dream, however, suggests not an escape from history but, rather, Williams's continuing enslavement to its "Western aberrations."

When Abraham Blackman ceases teaching history and begins to live the past, critical distinctions dissolve. In the collapse of history with the past, narratives with events, "history" emerges as an "it," an objectified, autonomous reality. The novel's time-travel conceit once again confuses time with place, transforming the past into a place Blackman can literally visit. This reification of history is further supported by the novel's form. Despite the fantastic shifts in time, broadly satiric interchapters, and the allegorical suggestion of the title, *Captain Blackman* is essentially constructed as a realistic novel. The novel asserts the meaningfulness of chronology, emphasizes narrative continuity, and, most important, uses the consciousness of an individual to register social reality. Two hundred years of black history are telescoped into the consciousness of Abraham Blackman who is both participant and witness. He speaks from the authority of experience demanded by the realistic novel, "I was there, let me tell you how it was." Neither perception nor articulation are troubled by the ambiguities of subjectivity. And here is where the novel critically undermines its attempt to liberate black history from obscurity and oppression.

The totality of history in *Captain Blackman* is a function of Williams's grandly paranoid vision. Like Ishmael Reed, Ken Kesey, Norman Mailer, and Thomas Pynchon, John A. Williams writes of a world in which every event, even the most apparently quotidian, is imbued with conspiratorial significance. In *Captain Blackman* the source of the conspiracy is clearly identifiable; it is white, capitalist, imperialist power, personified in the bankers, presidents, generals, and industrialists depicted in the "Cadences" interchapters which grow more broadly satiric as the novel progresses. Blackman's first dream after being wounded is of white men in powdered wigs planning a revolt against the Crown to increase their profits and pursue a global empire. "Knew it all the time, Blackman thought. Chuck ain't shit. Talk about the *Devil!*" (17). Blackman's trip through time, his visions of the crude power of the white capitalists, do not teach him anything new. Williams carefully establishes the objective sources for this knowledge in his account of Blackman's research into the history of the black soldier. This objective knowledge is brought to life and made to confirm Blackman's subjective knowledge of the nature and intentions of white America.

This subjective knowledge holds out the possibility of another way of knowing the past, a different historiography. The light-skinned slaves who "crept around the room" unnoticed by the men in powdered wigs are positioned as the unacknowledged witnesses to the centers of historical decision (16). Williams does not detail the forms through which this "unofficial" knowledge was passed down, although the novel is filled with marching songs and black folk recitations. The toasts "The Titanic" and "The Signifying Monkey" are quoted at length but seem to function simply as much needed escape and entertainment for black soldiers in a hostile system. The "Signifying Monkey" ends a chapter without any description of its effect or reception, and "Shine" makes the men laugh until they cry, distracting them from imminent departure for a French battlefield in World War I. There is no suggestion of the tropic power such critics as Henry Louis Gates or Larry Neal discovered in their forms.

Only once does a folk form take on the status of historical document, challenging the authority of the verifiable historical sources quoted in the "Drumtaps" interchapters. In the chapter devoted to World War II, Williams tells of the U.S. Army's intentional massacre of some 200 black American deserters who had taken refuge in a swamp near Tombolo, Italy. The action is masked as a move against a German SS division with orders to take no prisoners. Blackman bitterly acknowledges that "no battle order would ever be discovered that would read: Commenced attack on two hundred niggers holed up in Tombolo" (267). The "Drumtaps" section which closes the chapter has only the enigmatic refrain of a marching song to quote:

> There is a place called Tombolo
> Where Swamps are said the deepest;
> There is a place called Tombolo
> And buried there are secrets.

But this fragment of memory does not challenge white power's stranglehold on history because its survival has been decreed by the white general in charge. Blackman, in his role as World War II morale officer for a black unit, is made privy to the plan and ordered to witness its effect. "Because . . . somebody's got to know," the general explains to a less savvy white officer. "Somebody on their side, understand, because one day the shit's really going to hit the fan, and if we don't have a point or two on our side, forget it . . ."(268). The general sees America headed for a race war, one which only force and the threat of force will control. And if the song's enigmatic secret certainly seems to suggest meanings other than the general's threat, it is prevented from questioning the totality of historical discourse itself. Its tropic possibilities are contained within the white man's hegemonic power.

Blackman's entrapment within the emplotments of white power is, not surprisingly, demonstrated most clearly during the Civil War. Recovering from wounds suffered when his advancing all-black unit is attacked by retreating white Union soldiers, Blackman finds himself enacting "the white man's nightmare." When Blackman's lover is raped by a white union officer, Blackman takes his revenge, surprising the officer and his lover, a white Southern belle, in bed, tying the officer to a chair and raping the woman in his presence. Blackman relishes thoughts of how his action will restructure the white man's sense of power and control.

> [The officer] would think of nights like this and grow uneasy about his women, uneasy about himself, and would nightmarishly over and over again imagine the sheer audacious horror of it, a black man barreling through centuries of monumental and ritualized taboo to revenge himself. (87)

Ultimately this attack on the white man's dominance garners Blackman himself no power or autonomy. His act attains significance only within the white man's perspective. He enjoys the white officer's shock at waking up "inside the white man's nightmare," but by enacting this psychodrama, Blackman only demonstrates his own position within that nightmare rather than escaping from it (88). His revenge does not yield a black subjectivity, a position that would enable a truly different telling of history. Instead, it recapitulates the oppressive violence of race, class, and most especially gender distinctions on which nationalism is all too often based.

On the one hand, this failure to achieve a black subjectivity is clearly the failure of that particular historical moment. That Blackman's enemy is a Union officer suggests the North's betrayal of Reconstruction. But the image of "a black man barrelling through centuries" is too much like the structure of the novel itself to be limited to a single moment in time. Blackman's envisioned move to Africa at novel's end recapitulates the terms of his revenge on the white officer, just as the rape of a white woman suggests Eldridge Cleaver's obnoxious brand of 1960s black nationalism.[30] Blackman moves his army of vets to Africa, "where sky surveillance is almost nonexistent," suggestively beyond the white man's perspective, but uses it only as a place to plan his attack on white America (328). And although Blackman says to his lover Mimosa, "teach me how to say I love you in something African . . . I don't want to use their language for that anymore," he does not leave the discourse of white American history behind (321).

The novel's final section, part of Blackman's own dream of future triumph, is told from the point of view of General Whittman, Blackman's nemesis through the ages. Whittman has known something odd was happening in Africa, something connected to Blackman, but tellingly "somehow he'd always felt that Africa was a diversion" (333). As the novel ends, Whittman is trapped on a jet piloted by an officer who didn't "look colored" but is now clownishly crooning "Swanee River" over the loud speaker. Africa remains a diversion. Even in triumph (Whittman knows that he's "just lost a war to the niggers") the black soldier remains trapped within the plot of the white man's nightmare. The idea of a national identity encoded in the name "Blackman" ends up naming the continuing hegemony of white America. History fails to bring the black soldier home in *Captain Blackman*; Africa remains literally nothing more than a place on a map—a mythic elsewhere where the contradictions of history can be resolved.

A. R. FLOWERS'S *DEMOJO BLUES* SHARES WITH *CAPTAIN Blackman* the vision of Vietnam as a crisis that demands a radical redefinition of the black soldier's identity and a new vision of black history. Unlike Williams, however, Flowers does not seek to speak through the conventions of Western historiography which have traditionally suppressed black history. The very names of the novels' main characters suggest the configuration of this distinction. Against Williams's Blackman, Flowers presents Tucept Highjohn. Both names suggest nationalist identifications, implicit narratives of history and identity. Both are befitting soldiers: Blackman in its militancy; Highjohn in its implicit appositive, "the conqueror." Blackman denotes the Adamic assertions of Black Power, the insistence upon an affirming, identifying black difference enacted, to return to Houston Baker's phrase, in "the conative mode." "Highjohn" literally roots this difference in the rituals and practices of black folk culture.[31]

DeMojo Blues is very much a work of the Black Aesthetic; Flowers's novel seems to stand in relation to Larry Neal's "And Shine Swam On," much in the way Walt Whitman has been seen as fulfilling Emerson's call for a truly American artist in "The Poet." *DeMojo Blues* begins and ends with an epigraph from the African American toast which gives Neal's essay its title, "The Titanic." Neal glosses "The Titanic" as emblematic of the African American's relation to America in the late 1960s: the ship is sinking, the powers-on-the-way-down are offering to share their riches, if only Shine will save them. But the black man rejects their offers and saves himself. The toast's resonance for Neal and Flowers is readily apparent, embodying a postcolonial vision of a declining West (a vision greatly enabled by the persistent Vietnamese resistance) and a self-determined, self-responsible black man. Writing at the moment of turning away from a corrupt American dream, Larry Neal quotes the section of the Titanic in which Shine turns down the Captain's offer of money and the "lily-white" daughter's offer of sex.

Flowers's novel, written more than a decade later, opens with the shark's warning, "Shine, Shine, you doing fine, but if you miss one stroke your ass is mine" and ends with Shine's determination that "ain't none of these fish gonna outswim me," suggesting the author's concern with the dangers which exist away from the devil and out in the deep blue. *DeMojo Blues* engages the rhetoric and reality of the radical black nationalist moment of the late 1960s and early 1970s, but from the longer perspective of the decline of Black Power in the 1970s and the consolidation of a conservative political agenda in the 1980s. As Houston Baker has noted,

> "Black Power" as a motivating philosophy for the Black Aesthetic was deemed an ideological failure by the mid-seventies; no sovereign Afro-American state within the United States was even vaguely to be hoped for. Hence, those who adopted fundamental postulates of the Black Aesthetic as givens, did so without a corresponding acceptance of its initial philosophical buttresses.[32]

DeMojo Blues is situated in exactly the cultural, political, and historical moment Baker describes. The conception of Black Power which demanded a political definition of the black self, particularly the black soldier, in relation to an identifiable black nation is neither denied nor revised in *DeMojo Blues* but historicized. If, as Baker suggests, the dream of "a sovereign Afro-American state" had died in the 1970s, Flowers presents the experience of black soldiers in Vietnam, especially after 1968, as realizing a separatist union within the U.S. Army, one constituted not as political shadow but as cultural difference.

The novel opens with three black soldiers climbing off the "freedom bird" in handcuffs. Tucept, Mike, and Willie D. leave Vietnam bonded not so much by the experience of combat as by the rituals and realities of "black Vietnam." The dap, giving Power, Soul Alley, The Ghetto, the vow to never let a brother go down are self-styled transformations of the political reality embodied in the handcuffs they wear home. As Welch, the 22-year-old "oldman of The Ghetto," the unit's only all-black tent, tells Tucept upon his arrival in Vietnam, "Bloods here is blackenized. . . . you aint gon find this nowhere else in the world, not even in New York New York."[33] The uniqueness of Vietnam as a site of black self-empowerment is a function of the extremity of the danger, the vulnerability of black soldiers to both the violence of war and the injustices of the system that sent them to Vietnam. With their backs to the wall, black soldiers declare allegiance to each other, creating in effect an alternative nationalist identity.

The metaphor of "backs to the wall" repeats throughout the novel, but in his description of the most recognizable vestige of black Vietnam, the dap, Flowers moves from metaphor to performance.

> a long line of Blacks and Bloods stood leaning up against one of the walls. The dapline. Jethro, Mike, Willie D., Welch and Prester John started with the first man on the line and dapped their way down, fists slapping the intricate Firebase Sin Loi version of the dap—two fist slaps, the backhand slap, the grasp, the thumb hook, handshake, wrist grip, and the handshake grasp. Thick brass Montagnard bracelets on their wrists clink to the beat. (123)

The dapline formalizes the ritual structures of the dap and significantly alters its more familiar Hollywood form. In movies such as *Hamburger Hill* and *Platoon*, the "Black to Black salute" comes to signify the solidarity of the "grunts." In these movies black and white men are seen dapping out in the field, demonstrating the famous "foxhole brotherhood" which Wallace Terry and the rest of the American media found so pervasive, especially before 1969.[34] But in *DeMojo Blues* the dap is performed off duty in the enlisted men's club. Even in the earliest years of the war, when the black soldier was the great success story of an integrating society, the habit of "self-segregation" off duty, the early rise of "Soul Alley" in Saigon, was noted with some discomfort. Often this "habit" was explained as reflecting different "tastes" in music or other forms of "entertainment," suggesting that this segregation was cultural and not a threat to the political achievement of integration on the battlefield.[35]

But in doing the dap, a space is created in which the limits of one narrative of history, identity, and allegiance are demarcated and an alternative narrative enabled. This boundary is thrown into relief by the main character Tucept's original resistance to going down the dapline. Tucept feels a "surge of fraternal affection" watching the others dap but insists on viewing the ritual from the outside: "Fuck it, it was jive, he didn't have to do digital acrobatics to be Black. It had become a big show they put on for the white troops . . ."(126). Tucept is looking at the dapline from the wrong side, emphasizing, as do Hollywood films, an external audience unacknowledged by the structure of the line and ignoring the wall which gives it shape and meaning. With their backs to the wall, the black soldiers see only each other, face to face, the structure of the dapline encoding their solidarity and their jeopardy. Their performance off duty is no more "for" the sake of a white audience than their performance on the field is "for" the sake of their officers and the military and civilian authority they represent.

The reality of this distinction is brought home to Tucept in a paradigmatic enactment of the trope of friendly fire. Out on patrol, Prester John has gone in to investigate a tunnel when the unit draws fire. The careerist white Lt. Kicks moves to call in an air strike which would bury Prester John. Jethro "accidentally" shoots out the radio, but Kicks recognizes the insubordination of Jethro's action and points his M16 at the black soldier. Tucept points his gun at Kicks.

> Tucept's focus narrowed down to Jethro and Kicks, to the nose of the pig centered on Kick's guts, to the faintest trigger finger twitch on Kicks' M16. The firefight raged around their little frozen tableau, an oasis in chaos. . . . (134)

At this moment, Tucept sees clearly the structure of his war. Everything outside the black soldiers' commitment to each other disappears from view. Self-affirmation crosses over into mutiny when the threat comes from the American officer. But the clarity of this vision is dependent on its static, temporary quality. One cannot remain "frozen" while under fire. The soldiers, black and white, turn back to fight their parallel wars, as Tucept moves to pull Prester John out of the tunnel and Kicks to break the ambush. But the illusion that the black soldiers in Kicks's command were fighting "for" him has been replaced by the incipient violence of Kicks's and Jethro's showdown.

The men remain vulnerable, however, even in their empowering dedication to self-protection. Prester John is killed in combat trying to bring out another wounded soldier, a victim of the dangers faced by any soldier in any war. Jethro, however, is ordered by Lt. Kicks to walk point day after day as punishment for his overt insubordination until finally Jethro walks into the bamboo forest where he dies. When Tucept returns to base he goes down the dapline, his position within its matrix of danger and commitment having been revealed to him in all its horror and necessity. The dapline allows the places of the dead and the missing to be marked and the solidarity of the group to be renewed through performance.

Afterward, Tucept, Mike, and Willie D. plot in drunken grief to kill Kicks, but it is Welch who actually tosses the fragmentation grenade into Kicks's tent in a textbook example of fragging. Yet unlike most fragging plots, Welch's actions are explicitly political in both intention and effect. In *Going After Cacciato*, for example, the fragging of the Lieutenant, while organized and executed by the unit's only black soldier, is motivated by the most basic desire of the soldiers to live and remains unspoken and unspeakable, a guilty secret to be repressed and not an act seeking the redress of unjust power relations.

When Welch shows up at The Ghetto that night he has been officially listed as a deserter. From the beginning, Welch serves as the arbitrator between the inside and the outside of the system. The one to "blackenize" Jethro and Tucept upon their arrival in Vietnam, Welch is on his second tour and keeps an apartment on Soul Alley where he lives with a Cambodian woman. This apartment is more than an escape from the army and the war; it is the center for another life. Welch is a major player in the black market, trading money, PX cards, drugs, liquor—"you name it" (125).

"Serious about the rituals of black Vietnam," Welch ultimately realizes their separatist vision (124). He tells the others that killing Kicks will only get them from LBJ to Leavenworth—"you'll never get home" (210).

But Welch can kill Kicks with impunity because he is already home, having deserted America along with the army. He "plunges outside of history," to borrow Ralph Ellison's phrase, but unlike Tod Clifton in *Invisible Man* he discovers far more on the outside than a grotesque parody of his own identity.[36] The black market, the underground economy that was in many ways more real in Saigon than the officially "democratic" South Vietnamese government, comes to symbolize the rich "somewhere" which exists outside of the American discourse of power. Welch's highly planned and premeditated move out of U.S. jurisdiction suggest the decentering of global politics and history that was key to what Larry Neal called "Black Power in the International Context." The Third World, which is usually represented by the West as a site of lack defined by the need for development on Western models, is radically refigured by the direct interaction of previously marginalized subjects, like the Vietnamese and African Americans, without any intermediate reference to the power of the United States. Welch is not heard from again in the novel, but his absence signals discovery more than loss.

SO FAR I HAVE CONSIDERED WHAT HAPPENED IN VIETNAM, but *DeMojo Blues* is fundamentally a novel of coming home. Time moves forward in the novel; 10 years pass following Tucept, Mike, and Willie D.'s dishonorable discharge in 1970. It has become cliche to note that in this period, America experienced a "collective amnesia" regarding the Vietnam War. For the veterans of "black Vietnam" this denial was coupled with the active repression of black nationalism in the early 1970s which yielded what Houston Baker has called the "eerie silence from the black nationalist camp" just a decade after its brave pronouncements.[37] The defining contexts of the black soldier's experience thus fell out of American discourse, making it difficult at best for the veteran to give voice to memory, let alone to write history. *DeMojo Blues* both describes and embodies the search for a form which would not only preserve the memory of the black soldier's experience in Vietnam but would enable and elaborate the continuing performance of the power and solidarity discovered there.

Willie D. makes the most conscious attempt to remember his experiences in Vietnam. Years later, he is "still a believer . . . serious about being a vet" (84). At the New York City welfare office for Vietnam veterans where Willie regularly hangs out, "vetting it," the legacy of Vietnam becomes as accommodating as the well-worn fieldjackets and boonie hats that the mostly black and Hispanic men continue to wear. But the comfort of this shared identity melts away one afternoon when a black vet starts screaming for his "mule" and his "forty fucking acres." At first Willie and his friends enjoy the performance, taking the man's rage for the "Vietvet

Freakout Show" "all of them had put on . . . once or twice to break the check free" (141). But when the man rips open his shirt to "show a throbbing gouge carved out of his chest" the distance between the role "Vietnam Vet" and the painful legacy of the war inscribed on the man's body shatters their mutual satisfaction.

Standing in the benefits office, waving the Purple Heart, which all too literally symbolizes the "dues" he has paid to America, the angry vet's demand for his "mule" asserts the iconography of a terribly familiar narrative of African American history. Drawing a line from Reconstruction to Vietnam, this veteran, like Ellison's mad vets at the Golden Day or Shadrack in Toni Morrison's *Sula*, represents the physical fact of black labor on behalf of American society and the cruel denial of its benefits. The veteran in essence tells the same story John A. Williams tells in *Captain Blackman*. In affirming this narrative, the achievement of black power in Vietnam falls out of history. The radical difference of black Vietnam is lost.

This loss of power is literalized in the present. When the police come to take the man away, Willie and the other vets find that all they can do is "beg" them to set the man free. They cannot stand up to the authority that threatens one of their own, much less stand it off, as Jethro did with Kicks. "Roscoe said what they were all thinking. When we were in the war we could have helped that brother, he paused, somehow" (145). The profound disjunction between the welfare office as the site of performance and the rituals of commitment and identity carried from Vietnam measures what Willie has refused to: the drastic change in the times. Ritual has become habit as memory yields to nostalgia; the vets are "junkies skinpopping a memory" (146). Willie wakes up from the false sense of well-being that habit brings with a disorienting look at where he is now. "[T]hey hadn't been able to help the brother. They hadn't the heart or the muscle. It wasn't Nam, it was New York and it was 1975 already" (146). Nostalgia is the attempt to live in the past, a denial of the past's connection to the present, and thus a refusal to write history. In the absence structured by this denial, Willie's experiences in the war become subject to the already written narrative of the black veteran, a story formed by loss, betrayal, and oppression.

Flowers discovers a model for a more radical, resistive historiography in the veteran's flashback. For John A. Williams, who is not himself a veteran of the Vietnam War, the union of personal and historical memory can be achieved without trauma. In *Captain Blackman*, Williams proposes that the title character can quite literally gain access to the past, can speak the history others have kept from his men and in so doing change the world. In *DeMojo Blues*, a veteran's text, history is personal and giving voice to the past is painful, even dangerous. The novel is structured by an intricate series of flashbacks, the first of which is not simply a literary or narrative one but the violent, involuntary memory of a combat veteran. Attending a party when first back in the world, Tucept feels an alienation hardly unusual for returning soldiers.

He watched the party with a strange sense of distance, as if standing off and watching himself watch the others. His distance surprised him. His contempt. Plastic people with plastic concerns. He grew suddenly angry. His eyes misted and Jethro's green fatigued back walked slowly through the jungle foliage. A gold bamboo forest loomed in front of them. . . . (15)

Unlike nostalgia, the flashback is an acknowledgement of the profound disjunction between where Tucept has been and where he is now, refusing the solace of comraderie Willie D. experiences. Jethro dies in the bamboo forest. Tucept relives this moment of profound loss and alienation until called back to the present by his fellow survivors, Mike and Willie D.

By writing the novel out of this moment of loss, Flowers enacts the tropic heart of black folk culture, commanding its potential as an alterative historical discourse. The persistent memory of Jethro's death has its objective correlative in the small leather satchel Jethro always wore around his neck, the mojo bag he gives to Tucept the night before he dies. "Take the bones," Jethro tells his friend, but it takes three years for Tucept to open the bag and actually see the "little pieces of bone" inside. Opening the bag marks the first step in Tucept's quest to interpret rather than to simply relive his loss and thus to write history. As the originating site of historical interpretation, the bones, like Brother Tarp's iron link or the juxtaposition of the angry vet's scar and his purple heart, are persistent invocations of the material conditions of black American lives. The mojo bones are the "bearable" form of the physical horror of Jethro's broken body, of the "blood and bone fragments" which clung to Tucept's uniform after the body bag was carried away (16).

When dropped on the floor, the bones fall "in a circular, symmetrical pattern. The shouldered cross" (72). This figure was one of the central codings of the African circle rituals which Sterling Stuckey has argued literally formed a common ground for Africans of different tribal identities enslaved in the New World.[38] Signifying "the meaning of life as a process shared with the dead below the river or sea—the real sources of earthly power or prestige," the shouldered cross transforms Tucept's obsessive identification with Jethro from a veteran's pathology, the flashback, into a revolutionary recalling of the past.[39] Unlike the African gesture performed by the prisoners of LBJ, the shouldered cross asserts a particular and recoverable connection to Africa. Jethro's loss recapitulates the original loss of community. His bones invoke the bones of those "beneath the sea," those lost in the Middle Passage.

Staring at the pattern, Tucept has a vision. "He saw a people marching. Tired and worn lean by survival's demands, yet still they marched, even danced, an elegant graceful dance of survival" (72). Surviving Vietnam becomes the trope for the pattern of crisis and survival which defines Afro-American history. Flowers thus removes the black soldier from his typically

marginal or "dishonorably discharged" position in American history, placing him instead at the formal center of an already constituted African
American history. Although this vision is clearly born of the war and although the power promised by the mojo bag and the shouldered circle are
clearly continuous with the rituals of "giving Power" in Vietnam, Tucept's
war experience does not directly enable him to read the text of history revealed to him. Tucept must train himself first in the vernacular tradition of
conjure, fulfilling the vocation inscribed in his family name— "Highjohn."

As the comfortably middle-class son of a doctor, Tucept does not feel his
estrangement from American history in material terms until he goes to
Vietnam. It is Jethro, the blues-singing son of a dirt farmer from Taproot,
Mississippi, who calls the Highjohn name to issue. The class split Flowers
investigates here is not a simple story of estrangement or cooptation. When
Jethro asks how he got such a name, Tucept shrugs, "According to my fam-
ily, my great-grans chose it after the Civil War, the Surrender my granma
calls it when telling the tale. Named after some root. Some Highjohn de
Conqueror root" (67–68). The Highjohn name represents the ability of
Tucept's family successfully to negotiate critical trials of American history.
In contrast to the post-Civil War historical erasures experienced by Richard
Wright's grandfather or Toni Morrison's Macon Dead, Tucept's forebears
were able to encode their autonomy at the moment of freedom and to preserve the black historical perspective defined by the word "Surrender." His
father's profession suggests another successful negotiation of the limited
opportunities afforded blacks in American history.

But in Vietnam the protections of those achievements are unavailable.
Jethro's death forces Tucept to realize that his own back is to the wall. A
clear symbol of oppression, the wall is also the figure for the tropics of history, the boundary and turning point which sends Tucept actively looking
for an alternative, revolutionary discourse. He begins to remember more
about Vietnam than simply the bamboo forest. The flashbacks become functions of narrative structure rather than a veteran's anger and alienation.
The narrative enacts Tucept's reinterpretation of the past, contextualizing
flashbacks to Vietnam within the ongoing present, in effect training the
reader along with Tucept to read the significations of these memories. The
knowledge Tucept needs to read the past is written in the "Lost Book of
Hoodoo," the book in which Jethro tells him, the story of Highjohn the
Conqueror is written. In Vietnam, Tucept was not ready to listen, comically
asking who published the "Lost Book." But the vision induced by the shouldered circle forces him to interpret Jethro's "riddling" answer, "Go back to
where the blues was born."

From this point on, Tucept's search for the "Lost Book of Hoodoo," the
"black book of power," returns him time and again to the already familiar.
Raised in Memphis, Tucept goes to Beale Street, and open for a sign, re-
ceives one from an old man sitting in W. C. Handy Park. The old man tells

him if he wants to read the Lost Book to go see Mike and Willie D., enforcing the fact that blacks are their own source of historical authority. Tucept enters what Houston Baker calls "the blues matrix . . . the multiplex enabling *script* in which Afro-American cultural discourse is inscribed."[40]

The visits to Mike and Willie D. are filled with memories of Vietnam. But the significant act of remembering is formed by the seemingly coincidental points of convergence in the increasingly different present lives of the old buddies. Tucept is living his hermit's existence studying Hoodoo in Memphis. Mike goes to law school, gets a corporate job in D.C., drives a Mercedes, and considers running for office. Willie D. becomes a community activist, first rebuilding tenements in the South Bronx and then organizing grass-roots action in Harlem. But the dredlocks on Willie's head are linked to Bob Marley, whose performance Tucept sees with Mike. Marley's fingernails are cut in triangles, as were Jethro's, as are the old man's, as were those on the Nigerian sculpture of an African sorcerer Tucept saw at the Met with Willie D. The museum's information plaque informs Tucept that "nails [are] delta cut in the tradition of some African sorcerers before recorded history" (85). In his encore, Marley sings "Redemption Song," and when Tucept hears the line, "We've got to fulfill the book," he realizes that he has found his way into the center of a web of significance and signification. "The Lost Book" is not lost at all but is in continual performance all around him. The reading of history becomes literally an act of revision, seeing anew what was always already there.

THIS REVISION MARKS THE TURNING AWAY FROM REIFIED narrative, in both form and content, which marks the tropics of history. The end of the novel moves to literalize the transformative possibilities of the tropics, as Tucept puts out the call for the people to rise. Rather than analyze the ways in which this call both shares and resists the romantic self-assertions of the uprising at LBJ or the close of *Captain Blackman*, I would like instead to return to image of foxhole brotherhood and to reimagine the confrontations of black and white which Vietnam War narratives so often feature. By way of demonstration, let me turn briefly to one of the least comforting passages in what is undoubtedly the most well-known and often taught text of the black soldier's experience in Vietnam, Wallace Terry's collection of oral histories, *Bloods*. Gene Woodley is out on a long-range reconnaissance patrol (LRRP).

We recon this area, and we came across this fella, a white guy, who was staked to the ground. His arms and legs tied down to stakes. And he had a leather band around his neck that's staked in the ground so he couldn't move his head to the left or right.

He had numerous scars on his face where he might have been beaten and mutilated. And he was peeled from his upper part of his chest to down to his waist. Skinned. Like they slit your skin with a knife. And they take a pair of pliers or a instrument similar, and they just peel the skin off your body and expose it to the elements. . . .

The man had maggots in his armpits and maggots in his throat and maggots in his stomach. You can actually see in the open wounds parts of his intestines and parts of his inner workings bein' exposed to the weather. . . .

It was a situation where it had to be remove him from his bondage or remove him from his suffering. Movin' him from his bondage was unfeasible. It would have put him in more pain than he had ever endured. There wasn't even no use talkin' 'bout tryin' and takin' him back, because there was nothing left of him. It was that or kill the brother, and I use the term "brother" because in a war circumstance, we all brothers (241–242).

Woodley puts his M16 to the GI's temple and shoots him. This scene can be read in *Platoon*-like ways as identifying the terrible moral ambiguity of war in which action preempts discussions of right and wrong. But this "universalist" reading would in turn preempt the question of race. Inevitably my students will tell me, race is not at issue here.

The first thing Woodley tells us, however, is that the soldier is white: "we came across this fella, a white guy, who was staked to the ground." He comes to the conclusion that they are brothers, but this identification is revealed by the literal peeling away of skin, the key signifier of race in American culture. Beneath the skin, Woodley and the white GI can become brothers, but it is not a lifeaffirming identification. Both men know that the white GI is going to die. To be comforted by the stories of "foxhole brotherhood" which abound in *Bloods* and which LBJ (as in President Johnson) found to be the only good news coming out of Vietnam in 1967,[41] risks denying the terrible violence which shapes and surrounds both foxholes and narratives of American race relations.

Back in the world, Gene Woodley has nightmares.

> I see me in the nightmare. I see me staked out. I see me in
>   the circumstances where I have to be man enough to
>   ask someone to end my suffering as he did.
> I can't see the face of the person pointing the gun.
> I ask him to pull the trigger. I ask him over and over.
> He won't pull the trigger.
> I wake up.
> Every time. (257)

The reversal which structures Gene Woodley's nightmare speaks painfully of the material circumstances of his homecoming: sporadic employment, a decaying neighborhood, and no enactable hope for the future. But it also speaks to the American tradition of seeing racism's inscription only on black bodies. Returned to the structures of American society, and to his oppressed position within it, Gene Woodley cannot sustain the image of the terrible power he held in Vietnam; the responsibility to judge even with compassion, the viability of the white body. Whites have made such judgments about blacks since the days of the Middle Passage, when the sailors' duties included throwing the dead or soon-to-be-dead overboard.

To cite an example from classic American literature, *Letters to an American Farmer*, when Crevecoeur encounters the slave suspended in a cage, alive but with eyes and flesh eaten away by birds and insects, he thinks the greater kindness would be to "mercifully with one blow end this scene of torture." Finding himself without a weapon, Crevecoeur offers the "living specter" a drink of water instead.[42] "Muster[ing] strength enough to walk away," Crevecoeur continues on to the house where he was to dine. Letter IX ends,

> They told me that the laws of self-preservation rendered such executions necessary, and supported the doctrine of slavery with arguments generally made use of to justify the practice, with the repetition of which I shall not trouble you at present. Adieu. (179)

Crevecoeur's silence reflects his discomfort; he does not wish to "trouble" the reader further. In the abstract, as in the opening of Letter IX, Crevecoeur condemns the baroque wealth of Charleston whose beneficiaries "neither see, hear, nor feel for the woes of their poor slaves, from whose painful labours all their wealth proceeds" (168). Crevecoeur does see, hear, and feel the slave's torture, but when confronting the source of this violence, the planter who is his host, he falls into silence. The comforts of decorum forbid his passing necessary judgment on the bodily comforts and wealth which are so ruthlessly being "preserved." The desire for violent action only associates itself with the specter of marked black bodies and not with comfortable white ones.

The iconography of the black man with the gun, key to the self-representation of the Black Panthers and other militant black nationalist movements of the Vietnam era, worked to reopen the space of that silence, explicitly questioning the comfort of white bodies and rejecting the abjection of black ones. Resonating behind this image, giving it shape and substance, was the figure of the black soldier fighting in Vietnam.[43] The historicity of the black soldier's image has the power to shape narratives well beyond those of Black Power or the Vietnam War. It offers a place to reopen the vexing overdetermination of crossing the color line in American culture, to move beyond silence whether enforced by violence or decorum and reimagine the parameters of power, authority, and voice that continue to unequally shape American memory.

Foxhole brotherhood, black and white men bound by blood on the battlefield, is one of the most popular images of the Vietnam War. By permission of the Bettmann Archive for UPI. Photograph by Steve Northrup. 3/16/1966.

Chapter 4

GRUNTS

The Vernacular of Postmodernism

But once in a while you'd
hear something fresh,
and a couple of times you'd
even hear something high,
like the corpsman at Khe Sahn who
said, "It it ain't the fucking incoming
it's the fucking outgoing.
Only difference is who
gets the fucking grease,
and that ain't no fucking difference at all."
—Michael Herr, *Dispatches*

One wonders if the last war of
them all will be between
the blacks and the whites,
or between the women and
the men, or between the beautiful
and the ugly, the pillagers and the managers,
or the rebels and the regulators.
—Norman Mailer, "The White Negro"

"Fuck'em if they can't take
a joke": A catchphrase
often used when some dreadful
military tragedy is revealed. During the
Vietnam War it was most frequently
used when friendly positions were
accidently bombed or shelled by our own troops.
—Colonel John R. Elting,
A Dictionary of Soldier Talk

The story of the Vietnam War has been most often told from the "grunt's" point of view. In privileging the foot soldier's perspective, representations of the war have been violent and profane to an unprecedented degree. The boundaries of the grunt's narrative become quite literally the boundaries of the body and its obscene violation. This bodily narrative centers a deep tension in Vietnam War literature between realism and postmodernism, or, perhaps, within postmodernism itself. As Elaine Scarry argues, the need to claim the "incontestable reality of the body" is fundamental to the structure of war (62).[1] In the face of the profound loss of public faith in the government and the media during Vietnam, the veteran alone has become charged with the responsibility to tell us "what the war was really like." Bodily dismemberment and atrocities serve as markers of realism, evidence that the narrator has "been there." At the same time, however, the self-conscious turn in Vietnam War literature to what critics most commonly call "American myth" suggests an ideological crisis, that the American "imagined relation to the real" was ultimately the war's crucial scene of battle.

Susan Jeffords, Tania Modleski, and Kaja Silverman, have all argued that it is the ideology of masculinity, more than the physical body, which is represented as violated and in need of healing after war.[2] But the American body is as deeply invested in race as it is in gender. As Richard Dyer has argued, "[r]epresentations of black people are one of the key places in which the 'problem' of the body is worked through."[3] Like Scarry, Dyer argues that "how we use and organize the capacities of our bodies *is* how we produce and reproduce life itself."[4] But in his insistence on the "problem of the body," Dyer foregrounds what Scarry tends to elide, the systematic appropriation of the body and its labor which ideology works to deny. The burden of exploitation, past and present, is particularly acute for black bodies. "Blacks thus become the most vivid reminders of the human body as labour in a society busily denying it. Representations of blacks then function as the site of *remembering* and *denying* the inescapability of the body in the economy."[5] The Vietnam War, particularly the terrible class inequalities of the draft, politicizes the body in precisely these terms. As Elaine Scarry notes, war is "the most unceasingly radical and rigorous form of work" (82). In Vietnam War literature remembering the body is figured as an instinctively resistive act. Black soldiers are consistently represented as those who "know" what the body knows and can speak "its" language.

Michael Herr's *Dispatches* and two of David Rabe's plays, *The Basic Training of Pavlo Hummel* and *Streamers*, are works which are particularly dependent on the body and voice of the black soldier to make sense of the American presence in Vietnam. The encounter of black and white men in Vietnam is a crucial structuring trope of the war's representation—one with classic American resonances. In these works black soldiers emerge as the masculine ideal capable of speaking out of and thus beyond the "historical trauma" of the Vietnam War. The critical relationship of race and masculinity is fraught with conservative and subversive potential. Before turning to a discussion of the works of Herr and Rabe, it is important to revisit the claim to black vernacular power made by Norman Mailer in his notorious 1957 essay, "The White Negro." Both Herr and Rabe are inheritors of Mailer in their interest in masculinity, race, and war. Their turn to the black soldier's signifying difference continues in part the appropriative tradition renewed by Mailer.

But Vietnam in 1968 is a very different place and time than Greenwich Village in the mid-1950s. For Mailer, the soldier and "the Negro" are mutually exclusive categories, separate but equal in the ability to speak from the body. When Michael Herr and David Rabe turn to the black soldier for a language to voice the "historical trauma" of the war, they are drawing on more than Mailer's sensuality and instinct; they are seeking the radical possibilities of the black soldier's transformative place "outside" of American history described in chapter 3. But even here, the project of turning to the defiant black soldier to shore up white American masculinity is ultimately profoundly conservative. The greater challenge, visible only intermittently in *Dispatches* but powerfully realized in the dramatic denouement of *Streamers*, is to understand the naturalized boundaries of body, race, masculinity, and nation as coercive fictions and to accept the impossibility of preserving their integrity.

"The White Negro" is explicitly framed as a response to what Kaja Silverman has termed the "historical trauma" suffered by masculinity in World War II.

> Probably, we will never be able to determine the psychic havoc of the concentration camps and the atom bomb upon the unconscious mind of almost everyone alive in these years. . . . We have been forced to live with the suppressed knowledge that . . . we might . . . be doomed to die as a cipher in some vast statistical operation in which our teeth would be counted, and our hair saved, but our death itself would be unknown, unhonored, and unremarked, a death which would not follow with dignity as a possible consequence to serious actions we had chosen, but rather a death by *deus ex machina* in a gas chamber or a radioactive city. . . . (338)[6]

As the essay makes aggressively clear, this violence is specifically aimed at masculine identities, bodies, and narratives. Silverman argues that, "the normative male ego is necessarily fortified against any knowledge of the void upon which it rests, and—as its insistence upon an unimpaired bodily 'envelope' would suggest—fiercely protective of its coherence" (61).[7] The systematic unmaking of bodies in the extermination camps and the atomic bombings destroys this coherence and denies any possibility of self-protection. The terribly familiar Holocaust image of piled body parts testifies to a form of dismemberment far more debilitating than the trauma any single body can sustain. The very idea of the body's wholeness is subsumed by the operations of the bureaucratic nation state and its technologies of power in their most obscene form. The loss of hair and teeth simultaneously invokes a more familiar and mundane fear of the male body's dissolution through aging, just as the security of economic expansion, consumerism, suburbanism, and the nuclear family comes to seem threatening to masculine identity in the postwar era. World War II opens this void and the Cold War refuses to allow it closure.

Mailer's answer to this unmanning spectacle of historical trauma is "the Negro." "Knowing in the cells of his existence that life was war, nothing but war," Mailer's "Negro" claims bodily instinct and expression from a society which offers "a life of constant humiliation or ever-threatening danger" (341). Without rehearsing the full, breathtaking scale of Mailer's racist presumptions in the essay, I want to focus on the charged relationships he establishes between language, race, sexuality, and war. These connections have profound implications for the literature of the Vietnam War and its distinctive vernacular.

> Add to this, the cunning of their [Negro] language, the abstract ambiguous alternatives in which from the danger of their oppression they learned to speak . . ., add even more the profound sensitivity of the Negro jazzman who was the cultural mentor of a people, and it is not too difficult to believe that the language of Hip which evolved was an artful language, tested and shaped by an intense experience and therefore different in kind from white slang, as different as the special obscenity of the soldier, which in its emphasis upon "ass" as the soul and "shit" as circumstance, was able to express the existential states of the enlisted man. (348)

Mailer differentiates the "cunning" language of "the Negro" from the "special obscenity" of the GI, but links them in their qualitative difference, earned through oppression, from dominant language. The language of Hip cannot be taught because it is tied to body. This claim of embodied experiential authenticity is at the heart of Mailer's racism: "the Negro" is primitive not civilized, expresses feeling not intellect, is a creature of the body not the mind. The sign of this embodiment is Mailer's completely unexamined acceptance of the myth of black sexual prowess. Sexuality and danger are, in turn, the connections to the soldier's obscenity. Mailer has never been black, but he has been to war and this claim to his body having been "there," placed in material jeopardy, "with his ass on the line," so to speak, underwrites his authority as a Hipster in the same way that his literary career was founded on the success of his war novel, *The Naked and the Dead*.

In "The White Negro" Mailer leaves out the most conspicuous and fraught term of the soldier's "special obscenity" as featured in *The Naked and the Dead*—"fugging," the compromised, publishable rendering of "fucking." The absence of "fugging/fucking" coincides with Mailer's strangely transcendent reading of "ass as the soul." In *The Naked and the Dead*, the reliance on obscene language to express the body's vulnerability raises the specter of homosexual panic; the assumption of heterosexuality is always on the verge of coming undone as men "get fugged up" in war. This panic is suppressed in the "homosexual villain," Mailer's own term for the character General Cummings. Although in a later essay he comes to see the artistic, even moral, failure of making Cummings a villain because of his homosexuality, Mailer never admits the ideological necessity of Cummings as scapegoat to shore up heterosexuality and, thus, masculinity's dominion.[8]

The language of the Hipster is not the language of the soldier or even of "the Negro" per se but "the child" produced through a "wedding of the white and the black" in which "the Negro . . . brought the cultural dowry" (340). This use of the marriage metaphor is strikingly odd. Mailer will claim but three sentences later, "[t]he cameos of security for the average white: mother and the home, job and the family, are not even a mockery to millions of Negroes; they are impossible." It is in fact this impossibility Mailer values, "the Negro's" exclusion from the normalizing and domesticating of the male body that he dreads. The appeal of the marriage metaphor, thus, lies not it its legitimizing of the language of the Hipster but in its illegitimacy, the specter of miscegenation which Mailer asserts with inflammatory insistence is the inevitable meaning of desegregation.

The sexual crossing of the boundaries of race is Mailer's paradigm for the revolutionary undoing of social restriction, a paradigm whose unacknowledged analogue is crossing the boundary between heterosexuality and homosexuality. Miscegenation violates the American norms of domesticity so profoundly that the marriage of black and white is destined to end not in divorce but in war.

> One can well wonder if the last war of them all will be between the blacks and the whites, or between the women and the men, or between the beautiful and the ugly, the pillagers and managers, or the rebels and the regulators. (357)

What begins as a language of cultural synthesis ultimately reveals the long deferred promise of the Cold War, the spectacle of total war. But instead of a nuclear war between superpowers, Mailer imagines Americans at war with each other—or with Otherness at home—an apocalyptic vision of friendly fire.

The Vietnam War would prove the most compelling site for representing this violent spectacle of the undoing of American cultural coherence. Mailer's literary forays into the war, *Why Are We in Vietnam?* (1967) and *Armies of the Night* (1968), textualize as postmodern schizophrenia this interiorized battleground. Mailer's Vietnam is typical, even prototypical, of American representations, offering once again a study in the violence

Americans are doing to each other rather than to the Vietnamese. Standing at the steps of the Pentagon in *Armies of the Night*, Mailer fights the apocalyptic war between "the pillagers and managers . . . the rebels and the regulators." In *Why Are We in Vietnam?* this schizophrenia becomes most deeply and, to many critics, obscurely associated with race. The narrative voice is decidedly "hip," but rather than signifying the miscegenated offspring of the "marriage of the white and the black," the voice presents a puzzle; it belongs either to D.J., the privileged son of Dallas or "a black-ass cripple Spade . . . sending from Harlem."[9] "Which D.J.," we are asked in the novel's closing lines, "white or black could possibly be the worse genius if Harlem or Dallas is guiding the other, and who knows which?"[10] "Who is the voice of America?" black or white, is the novel's last question, the ironized battle point from which to approach Vietnam.

Mailer's turn to "the Negro" as the articulate response to the traumatic question, "Why are we in Vietnam?" underscores, perhaps unconsciously, what Kobena Mercer calls "the privileged metaphor of race" in the periodizing of politics and identity in the postmodern era (292).[11] Mercer invokes the same points of historical trauma cited by Mailer, the Holocaust and Hiroshima, foregrounding what Mailer elides: the central place of "the representation and signification of race" in the "historical rupture or break from a classical to modern regime of truth" (297). Typically, however, readings of Vietnam's postmodernity have eschewed race entirely in their rush to document the war and its literature's complete break with the past.[12] Fredric Jameson's often quoted reading of *Dispatches* is representative.

> The extraordinary linguistic innovations of this work may still be considered postmodern in the eclectic way in which its language impersonally fuses a whole range of contemporary collective idiolects, most notably rock language and Black language: but the fusion is dictated by problems of content. This first terrible postmodernist war cannot be told in any of the traditional paradigms of the war novel or movie—indeed that breakdown of all previous narrative paradigms is, along with the breakdown of any shared language through which a veteran might convey such experience, among the principal subjects of the book and may be said to open up the place of a whole new reflexivity.[13]

Susan Jeffords has powerfully demonstrated the degree to which meaning in *Dispatches* is structured by the most traditional paradigm of the war novel—initiation into a masculine collectivity.[14] But Jameson's identification of "rock language and black language" as constitutive "idiolects" of Herr's style begins to suggest the crucial role played by race as well as gender in upholding meaning where it seems to have been lost. It is striking that the "whole range of contemporary idiolects" invoked by Jameson is represented only by these two examples, because the language of rock and roll is a conspicuous inheritor of black vernacular language and style. The American language of the Vietnam War is conspicuously sexual, but it is also racially inflected.

A significant body of work has emerged which seeks to rethink the constitutive place of race and, in particular, of African American cultural forms in U.S. postmodernism.[15] One result of this project with deep significance for understanding the Vietnam War has been to claim a postmodern sense of history, to see the "loss" of masternarratives not nostalgically but as opening a space in which other, contested histories emerge along the ideological fault lines formed by race in American culture. In *Dispatches*, for example, Michael Herr describes the sacred relics and good-luck charms soldiers would carry in the war, including "pictures of John Kennedy, Lyndon Johnson, Martin Luther King, Huey Newton, the Pope, Che Guevara, the Beatles, Jimi Hendrix" (57).[16] On the one hand, this list marks the flattening of categories of social value representative of postmodernism, a feature often criticized as apolitical. On the other hand, it suggests how profoundly African Americans forced themselves into the cultural imaginary of Americaness in the 1960s, challenging white political leadership and cultural domination. Herr's integrated host of secular saints resonates with Philip Harper's suggestion, echoed in the works of Kobena Mercer, Whaneema Lubiano, Cornel West, and bell hooks, that "marginalized groups' experience of decenteredness is itself a largely unacknowledged factor in the 'general' postmodern condition."[17]

The postmodernity of *Dispatches*, *The Basic Training of Pavlo Hummel*, and *Streamers* is informed by race at every level: language, form, and content. The different stagings of friendly fire in each work underscores this relation. In *Dispatches*, friendly fire is an ironic trope testifying to a crisis in American identity that places inordinate pressure on vernacular lnaguage and meaningful connections between black and white men. *The Basic Training of Pavlo Hummel* is written out of the moment of Hummel's death at the hands of another white soldier in a fight over a Vietnamese prostitute. This scene of violence conjures the spectral black soldier, Ardell, who attempts, and ultimately fails, to bring Hummel to some understanding of the circumstances of his life and death. In *Streamers* a black soldier kills two white soldiers in an act that crosses lines of class, sexuality, and generation, as well as race. *Streamers* thus marks the violent fictions of American masculinity and, at play's end, renounces them. In this renunciation, *Streamers* moves beyond the black and white dynamic charted by Mailer and allows the return of the repressed Asian presence against which this American drama has been played.

MICHAEL HERR'S *DISPATCHES* IS LITTERED WITH STORIES OF friendly fire. A grenade-rigged latrine kills a Marine at Khe Sanh and becomes "another one of those stories that moved across the DMZ, making people laugh and shake their heads and look knowingly at each other, but shocking no one" (58). "There were always plenty of stories about . . . Marines ambushing Marines, artillery and airstrikes called in on our own positions, all in the course of routine Search-and-Destroy operations" (102). "The stories from that time became part of the worst Marine legends; the story of one Marine putting a wounded buddy away with a pistol shot because medical help was impossible, or the story of what they did to the NVA prisoner taken beyond the wire—stories like that. Some of them may even have been true" (122). Friendly fire is part of the texture of the war, a terrifying possibility but also a self-conscious trope. It is the story grunts tell themselves about themselves, the ironic figuring of what it means to be an American in Vietnam.

These stories "may even be true" but Herr, like Roland Barthes's mythologist, is "no longer concerned with facts except inasmuch as they are endowed with significance."[18] In *Dispatches*, friendly fire is already a myth in Barthes's terms, a secondary language "*in which* one speaks about the first."[19] In myth fact becomes form, and thus Herr's invocation of friendly fire as a story, not to designate falsehood but to locate his interest in it as a formal structure. In *Born on the Fourth of July*, *Going After Cacciato*, and even *The Short-Timers*, friendly fire is the revealed secret at the heart of war, the mark of authenticity which organizes these narratives and makes the plot move.

Herr's narrative, in contrast, is famously fragmented and self-reflexive, the key feature of its critically noted and usually celebrated postmodernism. John Limon begins his book, *Writing After War: American War Fiction from Realism to Postmodernism*, with an extended reading of the infamous "hermetic tale" Herr tells early on in *Dispatches*: "Patrol went up the mountain. One man came back. He died before he could tell us what happened" (6). In Limon's commentary, as in most, the tale is emblematic of the inside of war, the soldier's experience which we seek in reading about war but are by definition barred from, if we are not veterans. The story is about the gap between experience and representation which carries the mark of authenticity. In this context, Herr's postmodern style is seen as oddly mimetic. Limon concludes, "Just as Herr tenders this opaque anecdote as an illumination of Vietnam, he bombards us with unsorted information (technical terms, slang, acronyms) in imitation, perhaps, of the unmeaning bombardment of Khe Sanh. You had to be there—you are."[20]

Dispatches, more than any other text, has served as the reference guide for the proliferation of "grunt" speak in U.S. popular culture. The cultural work performed by the plot of friendly fire in other texts is borne by the vernacular in *Dispatches*. It is in the vernacular that the war comes home, which is a very different claim than to say that the vernacular takes you "there," to that "place of a whole new reflexivity," the mysterious Other of Vietnam.

[O]nce in a while you'd hear something fresh, and a couple of times you'd even hear something high, like the corpsman at Khe Sanh who said, "If it ain't the fucking incoming it's the fucking outgoing. Only difference is who gets the fucking grease, and that ain't no fucking difference at all." (30)

Herr offers this quote as exemplary of the expressive possibilities of the war. It is certainly emblematic of the reflexivity Jameson sees in Herr's account, but rather than being beyond narrative paradigms or shared language, the quote epitomizes both the trope of friendly fire and the "special obscenity of the enlisted man," which is itself a conspicuous literary tradition of the twentieth century.[21] "Us" and "them" breaks down in this quote; incoming artillery should be "theirs" and outgoing "ours," but because it all means somebody is dying, it is all the same at the bodily level that the use of "fucking" as an intensifier claims. Because the paradigmatic example of friendly fire is the possibility that the incoming may be "ours" anyway, the distinctions cannot hold. *A Dictionary of Soldier's Talk* defines the term, "fuck 'em if they can't take a joke," in terms that underline the deep relationship between friendly fire, rhetorical obscenity, and reflexivity: "A catchphrase often used when some dreadful military tragedy is revealed. During the Vietnam War it was most frequently used when friendly positions were accidentally bombed or shelled by our own troops."[22]

The relationship between the vernacular and the body is made explicit in Herr's gloss of what is probably the quintessential vernacular expression of the Vietnam War:

There it is, the grunts said, like this: sitting by a road with some infantry when a deuce-and-a-half rattled past with four dead in the back. The tailgate was half lowered as a platform to hold their legs and the boots that seemed to weigh a hundred pounds apiece now. Everyone was completely quiet as the truck hit a bad bump and the legs jerked up high and landed on the gate. "How about that shit," someone said, and "Just like the motherfucker," and "There it is." Pure essence of Vietnam, not even stepped on once . . . the moment of initiation where you get down and bite off the tongue of a corpse. "Good for your work," Flynn would say. (254)

The rhetoric of "there it is" is again inherently reflexive, constructed on pronouns without defined referents. But in this passage, the "it" does invoke a range of understandable meanings: the cruel casualness with which the dead are treated; the terrible physicality of a dead body, the commonness of death's presence. "There it is" points to the gap Elaine Scarry sees at the heart of the structure of war: "the laying edge to edge of injured bodies and unanchored issues" (108). After war, in the cultural act of memorialization, "the body in pain, the body maimed, the body dead and hard to dispose of" is put to use substantiating the national identity for which it suffered injury; if, that is, the soldiers died for the victor (Scarry 62). But losing the Vietnam War failed to provide American bodies with a national narrative that would become the referent for "it" and subsume the interiority of the bodies opened in war. Lacking a legitimizing national memorial narrative, like the flag raising at Iwo Jima, Herr holds close to the body itself and to the language produced under the bodily circumstances in country. The language of the war remains like the wound, imminent, always referring back to the body and to the nontranscendent, embodied characteristics suppressed in national identity: gender, sexuality, race, and class.

The fact that "shit" and "motherfucker" are synonyms for "it" is particularly telling. The suppression of the soldier's characteristic obscenity is a traditional feature of demobilization, a way of marking a "return" to prewar social mores. The failure to purge the soldier's obscenity from the literature of the Vietnam War marks the change wrought in social standards during the contemporaneous period of rapid social and demographic change (the sexual revolution, youth and counterculture, etc.), but it also keeps the language of the war current in a way that the literature of World War I and World War II, for example, did not. In *A Farewell to Arms*, "They'll shell the———out of us"[23]; in *The Naked and the Dead*, from beginning, "Even *they* can't fug me this time," to end, "mother-fuggin sonofabitch," wartime obscenity presses the limits of postwar toleration.[24] In both cases, what would have been said in war cannot be printed afterward. The censoring of language becomes like burying the bodies, a way of moving beyond imminence.

Postmodernist readings of Herr, like Limon's or Jameson's, argue that the war and the text of *Dispatches* are moving (or being pushed) beyond known meaning and language even as such readings reify the absoluteness of the soldier's experience. Death in this passage from Herr, and throughout the book, certainly marks an experiential and representational point of crisis. Herr writes that after a while "even the dead started telling me stories . . . their story was always the same: it went, 'Put yourself in my place'" (31). In Herr's commentary on "there it is" and to a large degree in Scarry's discussion, the dead body is conceived as "pure essence"; the social and political meanings, habits, and identities of life are assumed to be utterly "deconstructed" through violence.

Once again, however, as Jeffords has argued, the limits demarcated here are less those of language or meaning per se than of masculinity. These bodies remain insistently male, in fact, as soldiers, and in Herr's narration. Moreover, because Herr cannot put himself in the place of the dead, he has to settle for proximity in the war and textually; he metaphorically presses his own body, his own mouth up against the dead: "the moment of initiation where you get down and bite off the tongue of a corpse." The altruistic vision of the reporter who speaks for those who can no longer tell their own story is undercut by Herr's invocation of the sexually parasitic qualities of his role. The use of "you" rather than "I" drags the reader down with Herr, supporting the sense that the sexual is primarily a metaphor for Herr's writerly and our readerly desire to know war.

But the invocation of Sean Flynn, ("'Good for your work,' Flynn would say"), who is both the true connoisseur of the war and an "incredibly beautiful" movie star fantasy figure, presses homoerotic possibilities, the suppression of which constitutes a key narrative boundary of traditional war stories. Homoeroticism both symbolizes and brings to a crisis the relation of body to language Herr seeks to establish, throwing into relief the treacherous relation between experience and expression. Flynn, perhaps more than anyone in the book, literally embodies the knowledge Herr goes to Vietnam to claim. "After three years he'd turned into the thing he came to photograph" (253). Herr is drawn to Flynn, whose physically seductive presence figures his authoritative knowledge of the war.

> Sean Flynn could look more incredibly beautiful than even his father, Errol, had thirty years before as Captain Blood, but sometimes he looked more like Artaud coming out of some heavy heart-of-darkness trip, overloaded on the information, the input! The input! He'd give off a bad sweat and sit for hours, combing his mustache through the saw blade of his Swiss Army knife. (8)

The desire for what Flynn knows attaches itself to his body, because, as the photographer who quit taking pictures, that is the only story that Flynn, like the dead, offers. Sexuality is the key signifier of the radical proximity Herr seeks, representing as it does a violation of the boundaries of expression and bodies.

The question of just how embodied Herr's eroticized metaphors might be is ultimately deferred when Flynn disappears into Cambodia, "MIA to say the least" (254). Flynn's bodily absence at the end of *Dispatches* marks the limits of how far Herr was willing to go to be with Flynn. Once again, the boundaries of writerly experience are overlaid with sexual suggestion. In one sense homoerotic desire in *Dispatches* and much of war literature is like Scarry's description of pain—"the moment it is lifted out of the iron-clad privacy of the body into speech, it immediately falls back in" (60). Homosexuality "opens" the male body in ways that threaten the naturalized narratives of identity and nation. But this "opening" is foreclosed by the assumption that it is the pleasure of the text not the body which is at stake. The boundaries of the body, which are metaphorically presented as the boundaries of what can be said ("Get down and bite the tongue off a corpse"), depend on a heterosexual presumption which obtains even after death, working to stabilize meaning and referentiality in a familiar, unspoken way.

If the presumption of masculinity and heterosexuality remains for the most part securely unnamed in *Dispatches*, racial inscriptions of the body are open to question and interrogation far more directly. The very excessiveness that marks obscenity in war, the use of "fucking" as an all-purpose intensifier after every noun in a sentence, for example, reinforces the assumption that the meaning is not literal. "Motherfucker" is the best example of this, for it can mean anything—friend or foe, good or ill—except its incestuous denotation.[25] But at the same time that "motherfucker" lays claim to the status of an empty sign as the bodily "ground zero" of the soldier's obscenity, it also carries a barely suppressed racialized history. In a 1956 article which continues to be widely cited in dictionaries of slang, Arthur Norman argues that "motherfucker" emerged as the privileged "obscenity symbol" for American English from African American vernacular following desegregation of the military.[26] Norman's evidence is at best anecdotal. And while dictionaries of African American vernacular include "motherfucker," the term is clearly visible even in the censored texts of white veterans of World War II. *The Naked and the Dead*, for example, published before desegregation, uses "motherfugger" and "motherfuggin" numerous times, as in the example cited previously. As J. L. Dillard notes, "terms like *motherfucker*, which have been around in General [*sic*] American 'obscene' usage for a long time, are much more easily observed in and elicited [by linguists] from Blacks." [27]

Even Norman admits that the term was not unknown to white soldiers, and although his argument is ostensibly about general usage, it rapidly takes on a moral dimension. According to Norman, the "word is so forcefully repugnant that it suffices to use the first two syllables, however illogically, in calling a man a name, in describing the state of the weather, or the like."[28] Norman's vilification of "motherfucker" and particularly "mofo" as both "repugnant" and "illogical" stands in contrast to his reading of the traditional (and, in his article, unnamed) obscenity symbol, "fuck," which entered common usage following World War II. Works such as *Catcher in the Rye* are said to represent a "progress toward . . . a 'cleansing' of the taboo" whose "gradual rehabilitation" Norman "credits" to the U.S. military.[29] Obscenity issuing from the World War II army ceases to be obscene. The new obscenity comes from the newly desegregated army—an obscenity marked as clearly foreign to "human," that is, his own, white middle-class sensibilities. In arguing that the army cleansed the obscenity symbol, Norman is in effect cleansing the army, a project crucial to both the memorialization of World War II and the nature of the Cold War. To do this he needs a new obscenity symbol which he locates in, and by extension as, black America. Norman is the square obverse of Mailer's "white Negro," scapegoating black vernacular rather than celebrating its appropriation.

THE ASSOCIATION OF THE CULTURAL SIGN OF BLACKNESS WITH the army and obscenity, the body and vernacular is very much at stake in *Dispatches*. In a book that was first published with a brown paper jacket, black soldiers become the models for speaking from the gap between the body and the nation. Herr's first encounter with a black soldier underlines the significance of language.

> a black paratrooper with the 101st who glided by and said, "I been *scaled* man, I'm *smooth* now," and went on, into my past and I hope his future, leaving me to wonder not what he meant (that was easy), but where he'd been to get his language. (28)

The relation of meaning to location is crucial here. By saying that the meaning of soldier's words is "easy," is Herr assuming the reader shares his understanding, or pushing the reader out, as in the tale of "patrol went up a mountain," disdaining to explain an "in country" joke? But because Herr is left wondering "where he'd been to get his language" the "in country" bond would seem insufficient. Has the soldier been to some remote place or experience within the war, or has his language been carried from "the world"—from Detroit, or Memphis, or Watts, from, in other words, somewhere in black America? But even this reading is unsettled by Herr's locution of "where the soldier had been" rather than where he was "from" and even more so by the temporal relation set up—"into my past and his future." In "The White Negro," the history of black oppression voices a future white liberation. In Herr's account, the black soldier's future is distinctly different from the white writer's past and thus the text of *Dispatches*, but Vietnam is the literal and significantly figurative crossroads: the point of intersection for different trajectories through time and space, different American languages and histories, which throw into relief the contested borders of national identity.

   The ambiguity at the heart of this encounter is paradigmatic of Herr's relations to black soldiers and their authorizing presence in his text. In interviews Herr has consistently emphasized both the fictive qualities of *Dispatches* and soldiers' speech as the locus of veracity in the text. Herr describes constructing characters out of phrases, expressions, and stories he heard in Vietnam and inventing language "out of a voice that I heard so often and that made such penetration into my head."[30] But the signal presence of black soldiers in his text belies the singularity of the grunt voice described here and crucially marks Herr's sometimes masked inassimilable difference from the soldiers. Moreover, his insistence on the fictive quality of the stories in *Dispatches* highlights the structuring of his most significant encounters with black soldiers that are figured around Jimi Hendrix, the Black Panthers, and the assassination of Martin Luther King. The association of each of these figures with the war is historically demonstrable and as such their presence in *Dispatches* marks a kind of realism of milieu, the local color described in chapter 3. But in many ways these figures become more crucial if we take Herr's fictiveness seriously—that he may have invented or elaborated such encounters because they enact certain cultural truths at stake in Vietnam.

This possibility is most apparent in a section from "Illumination Rounds" which begins as the story of the first time Herr was in a rice paddy and ends as the story of another, ultimately more crucial, first experience.

> I was thinking, Oh man, so this is a rice paddy, yes, wow! when I suddenly heard an electric guitar shooting right up in my ear and a mean, rapturous black voice singing, coaxing, "Now c'mon baby, stop actin' so crazy," and when I got it all together I turned to see a grinning black corporal hunched over a cassette recorder. "Might's well," he said. "We ain' goin' *no*where till them gunships come."
>
> That's the story of the first time I ever heard Jimi Hendrix, but in a war where a lot of people talked about Aretha's "Satisfaction" the way other people speak of Brahms Fourth, it was more than a story; it was Credentials. "Say, that Jimi Hendrix is my main man," someone would say. "He has *definitely* got his shit together!" Hendrix had once been in the 101st Airborne, and the Airborne in Vietnam was full of wiggy-brilliant spades like him, really mean and really good, guys who always took care of you when things got bad. That music meant a lot to them. I never once heard it played over the Armed Forces Radio Network. (181–182)

The reality of the rice paddy is displaced by the Jimi Hendrix soundtrack in a gesture not unlike that of *Apocalypse Now* or other Vietnam movies. The landscape of Vietnam is inscribed with an overpowering American cultural presence, although a significantly ambivalent one divided between Herr's "I" and the "they" of the black soldiers. Like most of Herr's encounters with black soldiers, this scene is uncomfortably double in its effect. On the one hand "wiggy-brilliant spades" is the unchallenged language of the white hipster which, in trying to talk itself past racism, ends up reinscribing it. But at the same time the passage denotes the historically specific position of the black soldier within the army and the war and, somewhat more remarkably, of rock icon Jimi Hendrix within black music. In specifying the black soldier's position, though, Herr lays claim to his own "Credentials." Herr's ironic attitude toward his official affiliation with *Esquire* suggests that this is not an empty gesture of authorization. What kind of credentials, then, is Herr claiming?

David James's perceptive reading of rock and roll as the stylistic and structuring conceit of *Dispatches* offers one possible answer. James notes the similarities between the formal ruptures in Herr's language and those of rock lyrics, but more importantly argues that "at its most characteristic moments [*Dispatches*] reaches for the phenomenal intensity and pansensual overload that rock and roll epitomizes."[31] Herr's writing becomes at key points "the verbal equivalent of a guitar solo" (85). Jimi Hendrix is the obviously perfect model, the virtuoso guitarist who poses the question that stands behind Herr's credentials: "Are you experienced?" The immediacy of

Hendrix's musical invocations of the war, seen, for example, in "Purple Haze" (the image taken from the colored smoke used to mark landing zones), "Machine Gun," or his retort that lighting his guitar on fire was "no more of a stunt than dropping napalm,"[32] mark the potentially radical use of rock and roll to represent the war. Hendrix's service with the 101st Airborne deepens this connection. The high percentage of black casualties at the beginning of the war was in significant part a function of the relatively high number of black enlistees, like Hendrix, who volunteered for the higher pay and prestige of the Airborne, a history the black soldiers cited by Herr clearly recognize.[33] As such, Hendrix speaks critically from inside the soldier's position, as Herr wants to, and not from a position of externalized rejection.

Moreover, Hendrix's career reasserted black performance into the foreground of rock and roll. In connecting Hendrix here to Aretha Franklin's "cover" of the Rolling Stones and at other points to the Rolling Stones and the Mothers of Invention, Herr suggests different if synchronic listening communities, such as the black soldiers and his own white correspondent friends. This multiple positioning maneuvers around the implicit assumption that Hendrix has either "transcended" or "sold out" his position as a black musician or that black music is either the margins or the pure essence of rock and roll. In this way Hendrix offers a radically richer model than the appropriative absurdities of "The White Negro" for making present the constitutive place of black expression in American culture—an expression Herr suggests is as crucial to the war's meaning as it is to rock and roll.

The flip side of Herr hearing Hendrix under fire in Vietnam is Hendrix's performance of "The Star Spangled Banner" at Woodstock. The performance references the war in Vietnam in multiple ways. Most obvious are the long breaks of improvisation launched following "the rockets red glare" and then again after "the bombs bursting in air." Just when the melody seems utterly abandoned in the aggressively electronic guitar riffs, suggestive of the technological sublime Herr so often notes in the war, Hendrix returns to the melody to discover that "the flag was still there." If this intercession also returns the national anthem to its own wartime scene of composition, Hendrix's eerie blues-inflected playing of taps in the next moment makes present another part of the Woodstock generation, the soldiers dying in Vietnam. The performance becomes a signal moment in the memory of the 1960s because it animates not only the conflict but also the overlap between the crucial cultural and material oppositions that structure that fraught historical moment: the escalation of the war and the summer of love, soldiers and hippies, orthodoxy and the counterculture, black America and white America, black music and rock and roll.[34] Instead of Mailer's "last war of them all," Hendrix offers a radically inclusive performance on an insistently national, if not nationalistic, stage.[35]

Rewriting national identifications from a radically different direction during and within the war in Vietnam were the Black Panthers and other black nationalist movements. Just before the story of hearing Hendrix and claiming credentials in "Illumination Rounds" Herr tells the story of his encounter with a black soldier who tests Herr with various invocations of black nationalism.

> He was a really big spade, rough-looking even when he smiled, and he wore a gold nose-bead fastened through his left nostril. I told him that the nose-bead blew my mind, and he said that was all right, it blew everybody's mind. . . . after we'd talked for an hour he laid a joint on me and we smoked. (180)

The language is among the most dated in the book, "blew my mind," "laid it on me," and the continually vexing problem of "spade" in the text. The encounter echoes the cliche-ridden embrace of the Black Panthers by New York society so mercilessly parodied by Tom Wolfe in *Radical Chic*. Herr is talking himself into the cool world, but the black soldier tests Herr's ability to play along.

> he told me that in his company alone there were more than a dozen Black Panthers and that he was one of them. I didn't say anything, and then he said that he wasn't just a Panther; he was an agent for the Panthers sent over here to recruit. I asked him what kind of luck he'd been having, and he said fine, real fine. . . .
> "Hey, baby," he said, "that was just some shit I tol' you. Shit, I ain't no Panther. I was just fuckin' with you, see what you'd say."
> "But the Panthers have guys over here. I've met some."
> "Tha' could be," he said, and he laughed. (180)

What saves the scene from being simply a projected fantasy of coolness (which it certainly is) is the soldier's laughter. The soldier plays with Herr's assumptions about race. As though reading Herr's reading of him as a "rough-looking spade," the soldier tries to shock Herr with the danger the image represents to whites—militant black nationalism. When he discovers Herr all too willing to accept such an image, the soldier "turns the joke and slips the yoke" of Herr's definitions. If Herr is not naive enough to discount the possibility of black militancy then he can be shown too ready to believe, suggesting that old stereotypes have simply been replaced with new ones.

Even when Herr claims firsthand knowledge of the Panthers in Vietnam (and it seems odd that he doesn't tell the story of this encounter in the book), the soldier keeps the ambiguity of meaning in play, signifying on Herr's experience and understanding.[36] His laughter attests to the possibility that there is always something Herr doesn't know or understand, some part of the joke that Herr doesn't get. The soldier flies off in a helicopter, leaving Herr literally and figuratively behind: "as it rose from the strip he leaned out and laughed, bringing his arm up and bending it back toward him, palm out and the fist clenched tightly in the Sign" (180–81). Within the text, the clenched-fist sign of Black Power, like the invocation of the Black Panthers, remains a gesture rather than a radical challenge to established meanings and identities, but, like the black paratrooper who had been "scaled," this soldier moves off into his own future, one separate from Herr's text.

The radical moment of crisis in national and personal identification evaded in the confrontation with black nationalism comes with the assassination of Martin Luther King. Herr writes, "The death of Martin Luther King intruded on the war in a way that no other outside event had ever done" (158), echoing the decisive and dividing statement that echoes through many of the oral histories in *Bloods*, "And then they shot King."[37] Herr notes the scattered riots in country and the official denial of them, but also the uncanny version of friendly fire experienced when listening "to the sound of automatic-weapons fire being broadcast from a number of American cities" (158). The assassination intrudes on Herr's experience of the war when "a black staff sergeant in the Cav who had taken me over to his outfit for dinner the night before cut me dead on the day that we heard the news" (158). But even before being excluded by the black soldier, Herr's sympathies are claimed by a white officer. "A southern colonel on the general's staff told me it was a shame, a damn shame, but I had to admit (didn't I?) that he'd been a long time asking for it" (158). If Jimi Hendrix provides the credentials for Herr's ecstatic rushes of language, the assassination of Martin Luther King strips him of language. Implicated by white assumptions of common sympathy and denied previous friendly association with African Americans, Herr self-consciously "shows his color" and falls silent.

The black sergeant later returns and tells Herr that "it shouldn't happen that way," but what exactly is "it"—King's murder or its racially polarizing effect? The self-reflexive language of the Vietnam war ("there it is") has become the self-reflexive language of the "American problem," slavery's legacy of racism and segregation.

He was from Alabama and he had all but decided on a career in the Army. Even before King's murder he had seen what this might someday mean, but he'd always hoped to get around it somehow.

"Now what am I going to do?" he said.

"I'm a great one to ask."

"But dig it. Am I gonna take 'n' turn them guns aroun' on my own people? Shit!"

That was it, there was hardly a black NCO anywhere who wasn't having to deal with that. We sat in the dark, and he told me that when he'd walked by me that afternoon it had made him sick. He couldn't help it.

"Shit, I can't do no twenty in this Army. They ain' no way. All's I hope is I can hang back when push comes t' shove. An' then I think, Well, fuck it, why should I? Man, home's jus' gonna be a hassle."

   . . . the man was crying, trying to look away while I tried not to look.

   "It's just a bad night for it," I said. "What can I tell you?"

   He stood up, looked at the hill and then started to leave. "Oh, man," he said. "This war gets old." (159)

Herr's side of the conversation is marked by his acknowledgment that he cannot speak from or to the experience of this black soldier—"What can I tell you?" The crisis of identification posed by the assassination affects the black soldier far more deeply and complexly than Herr. The use of troops to suppress the urban uprisings that followed the assassination marks the violent threshold of DuBoisinan double consciousness, ever feeling one's "twoness, an American and a Negro."[38]

But if the story is more significantly about the black sergeant's impossible position than about Herr's, Herr's response is still very much at stake. At other points Herr tries to gloss over or talk his way past the historically and materially conditioned differences between black and white men, strategies which inevitably rebound with racist registers. Here Herr's narration is marked by denial and omission, things not said and not seen. The presence of Herr's silence is very different, however, from the example of Crevecoeur noted at the end of chapter 3 (this volume). Whereas Crevecoeur's silence regarding the horror of the tortured slave disturbs neither the operations of slavery nor his own status as guest in the master's house, Herr's silence is a conspicuous rupture in his text and the reader's experience of it. Nothing else puts Herr at a loss for words, not death, or fear, or institutional hypocrisy, or the loss of friends. There are no ecstatic bursts of metaphor and allusion to point out the gap opened between himself and the sergeant. His silence exactly marks what usually goes without saying—the privilege of his whiteness.

The question of race, social privilege, and narrative possibility is at the heart of the single most sustained narrative in *Dispatches*, the story of Mayhew and Day Tripper at Khe Sanh. At one level this narrative coherence is clearly Herr's stylistic reflection of the ways in which Khe Sanh, as a recognizable space in a largely undifferentiated war, became a "story" simultaneously to the press and to Command. The "narratable" qualities of the battle of Khe Sanh are presented as its distinctive characteristic. Khe Sanh, Herr, tells us "seemed to make sense" (105). It fit traditional formulas of battle. "Khe Sanh said 'siege,' it said 'encircled Marines' and 'heroic defenders.' It could be understood by newspaper readers quickly" (105). The story Herr files seems to differ from such accounts in content rather than form, reflecting Herr's stated preference for the grunt's point of view over that of generals. Herr uses extended dialogue and a quiet attention to incidental, novelistic detail to introduce us to two grunts—Mayhew, a short blond kid trying to grow a mustache who sings commercial jingles, and Day Tripper, a tall black man from Detroit who has recorded an elaborate short-timer's calendar on the back of his flak jacket.

It appears to be a story of unlikely friendship; apparently divided by race and size and attitude, Mayhew and Day Tripper are presented as inseparable. The conflict which gives Herr's "story" shape supports this idea. Mayhew, to Day Tripper's astonishment, extends his tour of duty for four months.

> "I just went over and extended."
>   The smile vanished on Day Tripper's face. He looked like he didn't understand for a second, and then he looked angry, almost dangerous.
>   "Say again?"
>   "Yeah," Mayhew said. "I just saw the Old Man about it."
>   "Uh-huh. How long you extend for?"
>   "Just four months."
>   "Jus' four months. Tha's real fine, Jim."
>   "Hey, man   "
>   "Don't talk to me, Jim." . . .
>   "Oh man, don't call me that." (130)

By calling Mayhew "Jim," Day Tripper depersonalizes their relationship, marking Mayhew as a stranger through black vernacular practice. If "Jim" means simply "man," and not necessarily "white man" (like Mr. Charlie, for example) in African American vernacular, Day Tripper's move to generic naming (calling him out of his name) reopens the distance race is expected to create between them. By extending his tour, Mayhew has threatened the very source of their bond—the understanding that they will see each other through. Day Tripper's anger eventually subsides and when Mayhew contradicts another white grunt by calling him "Jim," Day Tripper's laughter marks their making up. As a set piece, it is a story of guys "making it," surviving under terrible conditions with wit and humanity and thus becomes another version of the events at Khe Sanh which would be "understood by newspaper readers"—particularly as the conspicuous good news story of interracial, foxhole brotherhood in Vietnam.

But the centering of this implicitly racialized narrative crisis at the moment of going home has far more subtle and interesting implications. In the "Postscript: China Beach," Herr runs into some Marines from Khe Sanh and discovers the somewhat inevitable facts that Day Tripper made it back home but that Mayhew had been killed in May, after his original April 20th rotation date. The circumstances of this discovery are conspicuously odd in that neither Herr nor the Marines can remember Mayhew's name. Herr describes him using the very details which make Mayhew seem "known" to us —"He was a little cat with blond hair, and he was trying to grow a mustache" (165). The group of Marines try to come up with his name, but as close as they get is that "it started with an M." Day Tripper's angry misnaming ultimately figures Mayhew's fate. Dead, Mayhew can only be represented as an absence. All the information that seemed to give him such a powerful presence just a few pages before becomes random and incidental, adding up to nothing.

Herr's rendering of Mayhew as forgotten has a political subtext which suggests the degree to which many of the Americans who saw combat in Vietnam were inherently forgettable. "Some journalists," Herr tells us,

> talked about no story operations, but I never went on one. . . . Those were the same journalists who would ask us what the fuck we ever found to talk to grunts about, who said they never heard a grunt talk about anything except cars, football and chone. (29)

Sex, sports, and cars are prominent topics of Mayhew's conversation at Khe Sanh. Notably absent are any plans for the future. Mayhew's past consists of a father who "got greased in Korea" and a mother who works in a department store (117). The distaste other reporters express toward such "material" is obviously born of the inherent class difference between themselves as educated professionals and the 18-year-old draftee. The Vietnam War draft worked, as Lawrence Baskir and William Strauss put in their study, as

> an instrument of Darwinian social policy. The "fittest"—those with background, wit, or money—managed to escape. . . . The draftees who fought and died in Vietnam were primarily society's "losers," the same men who got left behind in schools, jobs, and other forms of social competition.[39]

Government policy encouraged this class split at both ends of the spectrum. College deferments and other means, both legitimate and surreptitious, allowed the privileged to avoid service while Secretary of Defense McNamara's Project 100,000, which sought to give "the subterranean poor . . . the opportunity to earn their fair share of this nation's abundance," made high school dropouts eligible by lowering the qualifying score on the Armed Forces Qualification Test.[40]

The key role played by Daniel Patrick Moynihan in this "progressive" vision of the draft highlights the way in which class difference became most visible as a racial one. Moynihan saw the "utterly masculine world" of the military as the solution to the "disorganized and matrifocal family life in which so many Negro youth come of age."[41] The idea was to give the underprivileged access to technical skills and training. The result was that young men "from disadvantaged backgrounds were about twice as likely as their better-off peers to serve in the military, go to Vietnam, and see combat."[42] At the start of the Vietnam War, black men comprised 31 percent of American combat troops. In 1965, the year Project 100,000 was announced, black soldiers suffered 24 percent of all army combat deaths.[43]

In *Dispatches*, Herr's encounters with black soldiers are direct encounters with this political crisis. Unlike Mayhew, the black soldiers are not figured as unconsciously ironic markers of social injustice but as those who speak back to the system through vernacular transformation and their alignment with politically and culturally revolutionary figures. Mayhew, in contrast, sings the Oscar Meyer wiener advertising jingle. As David James notes, one of the key effects of representing the Vietnam war primarily through the narrative or antinarrative of the soldier's individual experience has been to conceal "the historical events by which the soldiers came to be in Vietnam" (86). The overlapping iconography of the black soldier and the Black Panther, and the use of black nationalism to voice resistance to racism in the military, or conversely, the pre-1968 "success story" of desegregation in the armed services, marks one conspicuous exception to this rule.

In *Dispatches*, and fairly commonly in representations of the war, black soldiers in Vietnam are represented as engaged with history in a way that white soldiers are not. Mayhew's apparent failure to comprehend the consequences of four more months in country stands in fatal opposition to Day Tripper's elaborate mapping of time. Like the paratrooper who had been "scaled," the nose-beaded nationalist, or even the noncommissioned officer (NCO) facing the terrible doubleness of wearing the uniform back home, Day Tripper has a future in and beyond Herr's text which Mayhew does not share—his presence does not even last to the end of the chapter. The casualty statistics from the war cited earlier should not be obscured by this point, nor certainly is this the intention or effect of *Dispatches*. Black soldiers served and died in proportionately higher numbers, as did white soldiers from economically disadvantaged backgrounds.[44]

"Not much chance anymore for history to go on unselfconsciously," Herr remarks in reference to Saigon, but the constitutive place of black soldiers in *Dispatches* marks another crucial form of this historical self-consciousness, linking the war in country with the violent struggles back home (43). The ambivalence within the portraits of black soldiers carries over into this structural positioning. As Kobena Mercer argues, race has been the privileged term for periodizing the postmodern era. But Herr's racializing of historicity in Vietnam, while more materially grounded than Mailer's, continues in crucial ways the ventriloquistic tradition described by Eric Lott in which white working-class identity is voiced through blackface.[45] Typically in representations of the Vietnam War, white soldiers who served are placed in ideological and class opposition to those who did not, a presumed sign of protest. Black soldiers, in contrast, are imagined as resistant even in uniform, even though Muhammad Ali and the Black Muslims offered a powerful model for refusing to serve. The conditions of black soldiers' service are acknowledged to be more complex than "choosing" to be drafted or to enlist. Herr's biography of Mayhew makes this point as well, but in such a way that Mayhew becomes simply a victim whose one hope would have been to have listened to his more knowing black friend. Where Day Tripper gets his knowledge is persented as understood; he's a black man from Detroit in Vietnam. The sign of this knowledge is his vernacular voice. This understanding speaks to an acknowledgment of Du Boisian double-consciousness that was hard pressed by the Civil Rights and black nationalist movements of the time. But it speaks as well to a national fantasy in which questions of class in American society are deferred to and by the question of race.

IN DAVID RABE'S PLAYS, *THE BASIC TRAINING OF PAVLO Hummel* and *Streamers*, the drama of masculinity enacted by black and white soldiers in Vietnam is placed quite literally at center stage. So, too, these works press the dramatic significance of the vernacular. The desire to inhabit the knowing voice of the solider is echoed and recast in relation to black vernacular. The published editions of both *The Basic Training of Pavlo Hummel* and *Streamers* carry epigrams from boxer Sonny Liston, "Life a funny thing" and "They so mean around here, they steal your sweat." Rabe frames the drama of the Vietnam War with black vernacular expression spoken from an emblematically powerful and combative masculine body. But Rabe ultimately challenges the classical contours of the black/white dynamic invoked again and again by Herr. Appearing with the epigrams from Sonny Liston are quotations from Vietnamese legend and Chuang-Tzu. This is not to say that Rabe's plays are "about" the Vietnamese in any substantive way. Rather, Rabe moves, particularly in *Streamers*, toward a recognition of the broader history of race and nation engendered through war in the Pacific. At the same time, Rabe puts homosexuality openly on stage, saying what goes largely unsaid by Herr. In this context, the domestic fantasies of Mailer's appropriation lose their grounding as Rabe presses the violent fictions of American masculinity "to the ends built into their structure."

The Basic Training of Pavlo Hummel opens with a classic enactment of fragging. Humiliated in a fight over a Vietnamese prostitute with the obnoxious Hummel, a sergeant tosses a fragmentation grenade into the bar. Hummel, acting out fantasies of baseball players and movie-made soldier-martyrs, catches the grenade and holds it in his lap where it explodes. Out of the chaos that ensues, a black soldier, Ardell, appears. "You want me, Pavlo?" Ardell asks. "You callin'?" (7).[46] Conjured out of the destruction of the white soldier, who is mutilated and castrated as much by his own mis-apprehension of the world as by the sergeant's revenge, Ardell answers Pavlo's unspoken call, assuming the role of Virgil in the war's Inferno. This scene emblematizes the figurative use of the black soldier in the Vietnam

War as answering the unaskable questions posed by the war's destruction of bodies and narratives of masculinity, race, identity, and history.[47]

Like the black soldiers in *Dispatches*, Ardell speaks from the gap between the body and the nation. "[A]ppearing, disappearing without prominent entrances and exits," Ardell is both ghostly stage presence and a powerfully embodied critical voice (7). When Pavlo tells him that he was hit in "the abdominal and groin areas" Ardell responds:

> Who you talkin' to? Don't you talk that shit to me, man. Abdominal and groin areas, that shit. It hit you in the stomach, man, like a ten-ton truck and it hit you in the balls, blew 'em away. Am I lyin'? (8)

As in *Dispatches*, obscenity and black vernacular, and the intimate connection assumed between the two, pull the soldier back from the abstracting official language of the military, and move toward the body as the grounding site of a nascent ideological reorientation.

The doubling of Ardell and Sgt. Tower, the black drill instructor, qualifies any easy assumption that black soldiers are inherently resistant figures. Tower instructs the men in familiar arts of war, indoctrinating them into the collective body. "[Y]ou gonna think I you mother, father, sisters, brothers, aunts, uncles, nephews, nieces, and children—if-you-got-'em—all rolled into one big black man. Yeh, Gen'lmen. And you gonna become me" (10). The emphatically phallic "Tower" names the drama of racial transference at the heart of Mailer's "White Negro." But where Mailer presents this racial drag as inherently resistant to dominant social structures, Eric Lott notes just how common it is for white American boys to "go Negro" in adolescence, concluding that "the assumption of dominant codes of masculinity in the United States was (and still is) partly negotiated through an imaginary black interlocutor" (53).

Tower and Ardell offer alternate, competing versions of this interlocutor to the hopelessly adolescent Pavlo. Tower plays the role typically assigned to John Wayne as Sgt. Stryker, the seductive model of physical mastery. But where the war makes John Wayne a figure of corrupting irony, the spectacle of Black Power redeems a masculine ideal. Kobena Mercer notes that "what made /Black Power/ such a volatile metaphor was its political indeterminacy: it meant different things to different people in different discourses" (302). If as Mercer claims "Richard Nixon endorsed it as a form of black capitalism," it is even easier to imagine how black power could underwrite the credibility of "making men" in the military (Mercer 302).[48] Ardell's sunglasses and black-ribboned uniform move his image closer to the Black Panthers, whose emergence Mercer credits with "channeling the indeterminacy of /Black Power/ into progressive positions on the left" (302).

The duality structured by these two black soldiers marks the open ideological split over the war. Rabe and his Vietnam plays have continually confounded critics' attempts to locate an "antiwar" message. On the one hand,

Rabe argues that it is both "presumptuous and pointless" to see plays as anti-war because they do not have "large-scale political effect;" plays cannot end a war. On the other, he hopes there is "more content in these plays than the thin line of political tract" (xxv). By placing black men as the guardians of the masculine identities constituted both through war and resistance to it, Rabe makes *Pavlo Hummel* and, as we shall see, *Streamers*, both more and less than "antiwar" plays. Like Herr, Rabe is less interested in arguing the war out of existence than in representing it as a place in which the ideological drama of American identity was thrown into vivid relief. And like Herr, Rabe privileges the place and the voice of black soldiers in representing the war.

Pavlo Hummel, like *Dispatches* and most representations of Americans in the Vietnam War, displays the key features Eric Lott locates in nineteenth-century blackface minstrelsy: "a dramatic spectacle based on an overriding investment in the body, a figural content preoccupied with racial marking and racial transmutation, and a social context of white working class proximity to blacks" (6). But if, according to Lott, minstrelsy's theft of blackness "silenced and embarrassed" the original black figure Cuff, in *Pavlo Hummel* Ardell reclaims the voice of black bodily authority (19).[49] He looks back at the embarrassed, emasculated white body, and reverses the terms of the "cultural exchange" between male bodies described by Lott. Near the very end, Ardell asks Pavlo what he thinks now of "gettin you ass blown off for freedom's frontier," Pavlo responds "with nearly embarrassed laughter" and a curse "Sheee . . . itttt . . ." (87).

During the course of the play Ardell moves from an ironic, questioning counterpoint to Tower's scenes of instruction to outright rebellion against his authority. "That man up there a fool, Jim," Ardell tells, or tries to tell, Pavlo in the second act (78). Rather than, like Tower, offering his own body as a model of power and potency, which Pavlo and the others mistakenly but inevitably read as the promise of invulnerability, Ardell attempts to make Pavlo look at himself, at his own body. When Pavlo is wounded for the third time and still can only ask, "What happened?" Ardell taunts him with the obviousness of the answer.

> The knowledge comin', baby. I'm talkin' about what your kidney know, not your fuckin' fool's head. I'm talking about your skin and what it sayin', thin as paper. We melt; we tear and rip apart. Membrane, baby. Cellophane. Ain't that some shit. (76)

This question of bodily knowledge, what Ardell knows and Pavlo, contrary to all evidence before him, does not, refigures the relationship of Day Tripper and Mayhew in *Dispatches*. But Ardell's ghostly presence, summoned out of Pavlo's scene of self-destruction, denaturalizes the presence of the black soldier in the drama of white masculinity played out within the Vietnam War.

Race is never discussed directly by Ardell or Pavlo, but Ardell's vernacular dialogue, as well as the specific designation of black and white soldiers in the cast, testifies to the play's interest in "racial marking." Ardell tellingly directs Pavlo's attention to skin: "I'm talking about your skin and what it sayin', thin as paper" (76). The claim made here is at once universally human, physical vulnerability, and directed toward the site which forcefully inscribes race and gender. Pavlo's resistance of his own vulnerability is, as Kaja Silverman argues, a constitutive feature of masculinity—the insistence upon an unimpaired bodily "envelope." Skin is the marker of that "envelope," but also, of course, where race as color is most frequently read. "Cellophane" is the brilliant rendering of whiteness, the naturalized text of privilege which, as Richard Dyer notes, seems to be nothing at all.[50]

Both Silverman, in her description of dominant masculinity, and Dyer, in his analysis of whiteness, stress the constitutive feature of "boundedness."[51] Freud associates trauma, like that suffered by soldiers, "with the disruption of a bound state" (Silverman 60). The Civil Rights movement, desegregation, and most forms of Black Power were clear "disruptions of a bound state," disruptions which furthermore mark the contested and coercive correspondence between ego and political boundaries. The Vietnam War with its communist "invasion," hyperbolic body counts, elusive enemy, domestic "front," and tenuous narratability has been frequently read as a crisis in masculinity, but it is equally a crisis in whiteness. In this sense, Pavlo's literal castration that frames the action of the play speaks as much to questions of race as to those of gender, especially with Ardell posed as the narrator of Pavlo's unbinding. Ardell's lesson, "we tear and rip apart," opens a larger resistance to boundedness which is central to Rabe's representation of the war.

IN *STREAMERS* RABE PUSHES THIS MYTHIC RELATION OF BLACK and white men, in Roland Barthes's terms, "to the ends built into its structure," literally "exploding" the fantasy of meaning and history located in the exchange of voice and body between black and white men. The encounters of Mayhew and Day Tripper and Pavlo and Ardell are utopic even in their failure. In terms that would have been deeply familiar to Leslie Feidler 30 years ago, black men seek to educate and protect white men, a mission which fails through no fault of their own. In *Streamers* a black man not only narrates but authors the undoing of the white man's body when he kills both a white recruit and a sergeant who revels in dreams of World War II.

This bootcamp enactment of friendly fire is racially motivated, but not in any simple or immediate sense. Instead, race is embroiled in a more fundamental critique of realism which Rabe has described as signified by the play's violence.

> Realism is not about how people speak, it's about how events are constructed. In other words, the realistic play is a play in which cause and effect work in proportion. A realistic play says, "You make me

mad, and I'm mad in proportion to your cause." It's derivative of the Newtonian notion of the universe. I think it's not true, it's not how life works, because it doesn't take into account the unconscious. So in *Streamers* when the moment comes, you don't have just the response the play has prepared you for, you have the response that is contained within the characters, in their unconscious: you get a nuclear response rather than a proportionate cause and effect.[52]

Rabe begins by questioning an assumption fundamental to the inspiring placement of black soldiers in the other texts: that "how people talk," the vernacular, is the marker of realism. His emphasis on the unconscious tremendously complicates the relationship between black vernacular voices, bodily knowledge, and historical memory which emerges in the fragmented, postmodern landscapes of *Dispatches* and *Pavlo Hummel*. In this commentary Rabe locates the unconscious within the individual psyches of his characters, but the play significantly externalizes many of the assumptions of the "social unconscious" of race.[53] Violence, figured by the trope of friendly fire, marks this return of the repressed.

If *The Basic Training of Pavlo Hummel* overtly metaphorized the process of "making men" through war and the military, the spare, symmetrical barracks set of *Streamers* recurs to this idea in more apparently realistic terms. But, as Rabe suggests, this realism is intentionally misleading, as is the classical symmetry with which the characters are arranged. *Streamers* tells the story of four soldiers, two black and two white, who have completed basic training and are awaiting orders which they expect will mean being shipped to Vietnam, a state of limbo which in many ways echoes the purgatory of *Pavlo Hummel*. These characters are held in a kind of precarious balance, which is both threatened and maintained by the intersecting claims of race, class, and sexuality. The center of balance is the friendship between Billy and Roger, white and black, respectively, who identify most openly with army life, and consequently with each other, responding to any suggestion of confusion with a shared determination to "straighten up their area" or to strengthen their bodies with push-ups. But even these unifying motions are differently motivated. Roger is a black man whose identification with the army is profoundly pragmatic, "We here ain't we."[54] But his bond with Billy, the white recruit from Wisconsin who hides his college education, is the belief that "Army ought to be a serious business, even if sometimes it ain't" (27). Billy is an idealist who wants to *be* "regular army."

This state of regularity and regulation is disrupted by any mention of Vietnam and by the other two recruits, Richie and Carlyle, who proclaim aloud possibilities repressed in the idealized image of the army and masculine identity: homosexuality and inassimilable racial and class difference. The bootcamp promise represented by Billy and Roger, that the world can be ordered to the contours of a disciplined male body, is continually threatened by reminders that the body can be opened and its integrity revealed to be just another sign of what "should be even if it ain't." The opening of the body is, in fact, the play's opening image. A recruit named Martin's attempts to slash his wrists. Richie both binds Martin's wrists and insists that he must "make up a story" to cover up his suicide attempt (6). Martin can only respond that he vomits every day. "Just think thinking about it is going to make me sick. I thought it would be different from the way it is" (6). In a gesture both conservative and protective, Richie wants to keep this difference secret, offering narrative, "making up a story," as the means to bridge this experiential gap; Martin, in a desperate act of rebellion, writes that gap on his body.

Streamers is obsessed with the male body as the site of negotiation between the "way it is" and "the way it should be," the guarantor of "the dominant fiction" which, as Kaja Silverman argues, not only defines masculinity," but forms the stable core around which a nation's and a period's 'reality' coheres" (41). Martin's suicide attempt is paradigmatic of the alignment of body, masculinity, nation, and reality; it is a bodily inscription of "mental instability," a sign of his inability to sustain belief in the collective corps. Feeling powerless and disoriented, Martin attacks his own body as the only level at which he can intervene in the "reality" which has ceased to offer a "stable core."

Billy, Roger, Richie, and Carlyle each stand in different imagined relation to the "way things should be," the normative, but ideal identity signified by the "regular army." Billy is supposed to be a "regular guy," that is, white and heterosexual, his body offered as the naturalized representation of the dominant fiction; Roger has become a regular guy, as a black man who has successfully completed his basic training and been integrated into the society of the army; Richie needs to become a regular guy, the gay man who is supposed to be "straightened out" by the military. But Carlyle is relentlessly irregular; a member not of the communal "home" Billy, Roger, and Richie frequently claim within the barracks, but of a "transient company." Where Roger and Billy talk about getting out of basic and into the "real army" of the war, Carlyle holds tight to the memory of the "outside" which for him is constituted by black urban society.

Discipline is figured again and again as the agent of normative identity, offering the "binding" Silverman describes as necessary to masculinity. While Billy and Roger do push-ups side by side, Richie and Carlyle are both conspicuously "undisciplined," albeit in radically opposite terms. Richie explains his homosexuality as a function of class privilege, of doing "what I wanted all my life. If I wanted to do something, I just did it. Honestly. I've never had to work or anything" (23). According to the stage directions, Carlyle appears "a black man in filthy fatigues—they are grease-stained and dark with sweat" (6), distancing him from the others who are seen conspicuously mopping floors, taking showers, or meticulously hanging up their laundry. Carlyle, moreover, is under the thumb of the army's disciplinary structure, continuously working "KP" whereas the others, with their higher rank (Spec Three), are exempt from duty while awaiting orders. These initial identifications of both Richie and Carlyle are suspiciously stereotypical, structuring a masculine class hierarchy that valorizes the middle by excluding a decadent upper class signified by homosexuality and an indigent, base underclass signified by blackness. But as the play progresses, the very idea of the embodiment of identity assumed by these stereotypes comes to a crisis. Richie and Carlyle present the dangerously liminal boundaries of the body and its personal and national narratives. The dramatic movement of the play brings Richie and Carlyle together, a relationship that, rather than reifying the center, makes all other identifications untenable.

But long before the dramatic crisis which undoes bodies and assumptions alike, faith in the assuring reality of the body is disturbed by the problem of how the body is read by others. In expressing his desire for Billy, Richie continually suggests that Billy is denying his own homoerotic feelings. Billy rejects him, saying, "whatever you see in my eyes—you're just seeing yourself" (22). Billy seems to be asserting a classic divide between his own, embodied reality and the "perversion" of Richie's misreading, but he later admits the problematic relation of seeing and being. Back home, Billy tells Roger, people thought he was a "busybody,"

> I mean, a lot a people thought like I didn't know how to behave in a simple way. You know? That I overcomplicated everything. I didn't think so. Don't think so. I just thought I was seein' complications that were there but nobody else saw. . . . I mean, Wisconsin's a funny place. All those clear-eyed people sayin' "Hello" and lookin' you straight in the eye. Everybody's good, you think, and happy and honest. And then there's all of a sudden a neighbor who goes mad as a hatter. I had a neighbor who came out of his house one morning with axes in both hands. He started then attackin' the cars that were driving up and down in front of his house. An' we all knew why he did it, sorta. (43–44)

Playing on the language of being "straight," Rabe uses homosexuality as a both a specific instance of and a more general metaphor for the "complications" some see but others say are not there. But the "clear-eyed people" of Wisconsin who define the real in terms of what is not there also suggest Richard Dyer's reading of whiteness, which is "revealed as emptiness, absence, denial, and even a kind of death" (44). The murderous rage hidden within the proverbially normal people of Wisconsin denies the "honesty" of their "clear-eyes" and, like Rabe's description of the play as a whole, explodes realism's logic of cause and effect. The world should be "straight" and "clear" but it is instead ruled by the unseen and illogical, the unconscious. Roger's reply to Billy's tentative questioning of the reality of appearances is to play basketball, to return to the body as a site of reassurance.

Yet as often as the men turn to their own bodies as markers of the reality of their worlds, they are confronted with signs of the illusionary nature of both. The meeting of Roger and Carlyle is emblematic in this regard. Following a discussion with Billy about whether or not Richie really is homosexual, Roger, left alone in the barracks, opens Richie's locker and stares at the pinup hanging on the door, as if looking for some confirmation of Richie's sexual identity. Carlyle enters unseen and startles Roger with the mocking accusation, "Boy . . . whose locker you lookin' into?"

Carlyle:	That ain't you locker, is what I'm askin', nigger. I mean, you ain't got no white goddamn woman hangin' on your wall.
Roger:	Oh, no—no, no.
Carlyle:	You don't wanna be lyin' to me, 'cause I got to turn you in you lyin' and you do got the body a some white goddamn woman hangin' there for you to peek at nobody around but you—you can be thinkin' about that sweet wet pussy an' maybe it hot an' maybe it cool.
Roger:	I could be thinkin' all that, except I know the penalty for lyin'.
Carlyle:	Thank God for that. (Extending his hand, palm up)
Roger:	That's right. This here the locker of a faggot. (And he slaps Carlyle's hand, palm to palm.)
Carlyle:	Course it is; I see that; any damn body know that. (15–16)

There are too many bodies being referred to in this exchange to sustain Carlyle's assertion of a reality that "any damn body" can recognize. Black and white, male and female, heterosexual and homosexual, actual and fantasy, these differences challenge the naturalized recognition of bodies as identities that secure one's place in the world. Carlyle and Roger bond before the spectacle of the Playboy pinup, not, or not only as straight men, but as black men signifying on the threat historically posed by the white woman's desirability. She is not Woman but a "white goddamn woman." But when Roger names the image the property of a "faggot," a more essential transformation of the pin-up's desirability seems to take place. How, Roger seems to have been asking, can he read the meaning of the pin-up in relation to Richie? The naked body reveals too little. With meaning becoming increasingly less self-evident, with no one apparently accepting the pin-up's universal embodiment of male desire, Carlyle reaches out to Roger, slapping palms with a touch that seeks to reassure their shared, embodied reality as black men.

Carlyle lays particular claim to bodily knowledge, literalizing the key assumption about black masculinity operating in the other texts.

> That the black man's problem all together. You ever considered that? Too much feelin'. He too close to everything. He is, man; too close to his blood, to his body. It ain't that he don't have no good mind, but he BELIEVE in his body. (51–52)

Carlyle's anger, which flares up throughout the play and explodes in the murders which form the dramatic denouement, is the most literal sign of his bodily feeling. But again, the literal or realistic is a ruse in *Streamers*. As act two progresses, Carlyle's speeches more and more directly call out the secrets the others seek to avoid, specifically the presence of homosexuality, the instability of whiteness, and the deadly future of Vietnam. His speech about the black man's body is framed by a description of "being cool" in Vietnam "cause I been dodgin' bullets and shit since I been old enough to get on pussy make it happy to know me. I can get on, I can do my job" (51). This is a very familiar fantasy image of the black soldier in Vietnam, one which literalizes Mailer's metaphor of the black man's life as a war in which sexual prowess and the vernacular are his weapons of survival. But this is significantly Carlyle's only sanguine moment in thinking about the war. "And this whole Vietnam THING—I do not dig it" is his first and far more characteristic response to the war (18). Unlike the black soldiers of Herr's text, Carlyle does not have a future beyond the war. He won't be able to "do his job" because, as he has told Roger before "I got no job. They don't want to give me a job. I know it. They gonna kill me. They are gonna send me over there to get me killed, goddammit" (39–40). Roger tries to reassure Carlyle that "it's ain't the way your sayin' it," that they're all going to Vietnam, but Carlyle recognizes that the terms are very different for Roger, Billy, and Richie, with their "little home . . . friends, people to talk to" (39). Constituting community brings with it the possibility of survival. Carlyle, in his isolation, is simple fodder.

The terms of realism and fantasy here are very complex. At one level, Carlyle and Roger represent the split narrative of the black soldier's experience in Vietnam: high casualty rates in the early years of the war and even higher incarceration and court-martial rates (Carlyle ends up in the brig not the war)[55] versus the possibilities of assimilation and advancement through the ranks. (Colin Powell is the very obvious example here.) But, in overtly naming the Maileresque, but also much older, fantasy of the black male body as closer to material reality, Rabe deconstructs the unconscious workings of white fantasy. If Billy uses his friendship with Roger to shore up his own masculine identity which is threatened because the world is neither as "straight" nor "clear" as it is supposed to be, Carlyle deeply threatens Billy's self-image. "I can see your heart, Billy boy," Carlyle says ominously, "but you cannot see mine. I am unknown. You . . . are known" (53). Once again the "knowing" black man articulates the white man's fragmenting sense of reality and the body, but unlike Day Tripper or Ardell, Carlyle is not a benign figure of protection.

The unknown is what Billy fears most, and it is the unknown that once again draws together the unsettling and uncontained possibilities of sexuality, race, and the war. Early in the play Billy asks Roger a question from a game he used to play as a child, "you ever ask yourself if you'd rather fight in a war where it was freezin' cold or one where there was awful snakes?" (10). The choice is at once historical and deeply symbolic. It was "Korea time," Billy explains, alluding to the terrible images of U.S. troops freezing at Chosin Reservoir, just as the snakes look back to the tropical campaigns of the Pacific theater of World War II and forward to the jungles of Vietnam. The ernest boyhood game of choosing between wars defines the familiar contours of Ron Kovic's Cold War childhood. Billy follows his description of the game with an apparent nonsequitur: "I got my draft notice, goddamn Vietnam didn't even exist. I mean, it existed, but not as a war we might get into" (10). Again, as for Kovic, Vietnam is the traumatic site which violates all images and assumptions of American identity yet it is also figured as the logical outcome of the demonized landscape of the Cold War. The nation of Vietnam is acknowledged to have existed before becoming the focus of American self-imagining. But, in 1965 Vietnam suddenly becomes one of the narrative possibilities Fredric Jameson describes as opened up by history, one impossible for young American men to deny.[56]

Billy's admission of a deep fear of snakes, however, resonates across a range of symbolic registers. The snake is, of course, the figure of temptation and seduction, a specifically phallic threat of penetration and fall. Richie later teases Billy with the terrors of the Vietcong who "don't just shoot you and blow you up, you know"—suggesting things worse than death, the quite literal threat of castration (25). "[T]here's these caves they hide in and when you go in after 'em, they've got these snakes that they've tied by their tails to the ceiling. So it's dark and the snake is furious from having been hung by its tail and you crawl right into them—your face" (25). Billy "knows he's been caught" but "the fear is real" (25). The iconography of the primitive, dark, literally earthy and animalistic landscape which stands in for an invisible human enemy trades on the deeply racialized patterns of Western and U.S. myth. It is a nightmare vision of the colonial heart of darkness written through the twentieth-century American extension of Indian Country across the Pacific. But spoken from Richie's mouth the sexual threat of the colonial nightmare is foregrounded. What is so terrifying is the loss of "orientation" in the dark, of literally facing the phallus rather than claiming control over it. The snake in the cave prefigures the impending act of oral sex in the dark which precipitates the play's violence.

This scene, however, works not as a point of confrontation, like Richie's more direct sexual innuendoes, but of reconciliation. "The war—the threat of it—is the one thing they share" (24). Roger is not exempt from the narrative's seductive threat as a black man, any more than Richie is by virtue of his homosexuality. The men enjoy scaring themselves with these images; it's another version of Billy's boyhood game. But the drama of the play will build along these racial and sexual tensions and it is Billy who dies and Roger and Richie who survive. Dyer argues that "at the heart of whiteness" is a fear of the body, the need to control both one's own body and "those bodies whose exploitation is so fundamental to the capitalist economy" (63). Homosexuality becomes the signal figure for the loss of this control, both as the "secret" in Billy's heart and in Richie and Carlyle's "uncontrolled" or "undisciplined" union. But the sexual is always clearly imbricated with the racial, just as the racial serves as the visible marker of an exploitive class structure. The specter of the Vietnam War brings these relations into crisis.

In Act II, scene 2 the four men are once again together in the barracks, when Richie begins to flirt openly with Carlyle, touching him, and finally, asking Roger and Billy to leave them alone. The argument that ensues returns again and again to the metaphor of the house. "We live here" Roger protests when asked to leave. "I live here, too," Richie responds. The military logic of making men, which Roger and Billy have enacted throughout the play, has them building out from their bodies, to their area, to a world. They make a world, or at least a home, a place which is theirs, in the image of their own bodies—an extension of the boundedness fundamental to both masculinity and whiteness.[57] "I don't have much in this goddamn army, but *here* is mine," Billy insists, and what is "his" must be pure. Roger's response is to "turn his back" on Carlyle and Richie in an all too predictable anticipation of the weak compromise of the military's 1993 "don't ask, don't tell" policy toward homosexual soldiers. Roger at first refuses to leave, but he accepts Richie's claim to the space, because he already accepts that neither the army nor the world is what it is supposed to be. Billy cannot accept such a dualistic view of the world. He tells Richie and Carlyle to go out in the field. "It ain't going to be done in my house" (63).

In this moment of crisis Richie and Carlyle threaten to unmake themselves, or, more precisely, each other, as men. "Cause if you really are doin' what I think you're doin', you're a fuckin' animal!" Billy yells when he first sees Richie touching Carlyle (61). Earlier, though, Richie calls Carlyle an "animal" in an openly racist gesture (54). Although Roger does not hear Richie say this, he recognizes the racist potential in Richie's approach to Carlyle. "Richie one a those people want to get fucked by niggers, man. It what he know was gonna happen all his life—can be his dream come true.

. . . Want to make it real in the world, how a nigger is an animal" (63). Here Roger names the terrifying point of union for the conflicting fantasies enacted in the black face tradition down through Norman Mailer and beyond. For Roger, white sexual fantasies of blackness are very real but ultimately can only be ignored. "I been turnin' my back on one thing or another all my life," he tells Billy (63). But Billy's identity rests on a much more active repression which must make the world itself conform to his own image. "I see what I see," he insists, "I don't run, don't hide." "You fucking well better learn," Roger warns and then leaves the room, driven out by the increasingly violent confrontation between Billy and Carlyle over the nature of the reality of their "home" (64).

In mockery Carlyle promises that it is "time for more schoolin'" and switches out the lights.

Carlyle: You don't see what you see so well in the dark. It dark in
            the night. Black man got a black body—he disappear.
            (The darkness is so total they are all no more than
            shadows.)

Richie: Not to the hands; not to the fingers.
            (Moving from across the room toward Carlyle)

Carlyle: You do like you talk, boy, you gonna make me happy.
            (As Billy, nervously clutching his sneaker, is moving
            backward). (64)

At this moment the boundaries of the body begin to dissolve in the darkness. Carlyle's "black body" disappears, an act Dyer attributes specifically to whiteness, and becomes identified only by its masculinity, which remains untroubled by homosexuality in Carlyle's selfish determination to "get his nut." Richie's body in turn threatens to lose its masculinity, defined by fingers and hands which work on and not with a penis. In the dark, whiteness and heterosexuality are disassociated, unmaking normative masculinity and with it Billy's reality. This darkness stages quite literally the figurative darkness of racial and sexual fantasy turned nightmare, like the tunnel boobytrapped with snakes, where bodies and identities are violated.

Clutching his "sneaker," the pathetic sign of the body's discipline and control, Billy cannot allow this in his "house." He throws the lights back on in an effort to put things back in place. Carlyle, returned to his frustrated black body, strikes out with a knife and cuts Billy. "That you blood," he yells. "The blood inside you, you don't ever see it there. Take a look how easy it come out" (65–66). Echoing Ardell, Carlyle tries once again to teach Billy the lesson that identities are not bounded by absolute certainties, that they cannot be seen, that appearances deceive, and that not even the body is integral and whole. Roger's absence from the scene at this point is crucial.

The interracial bond between Billy and Roger is what allows them to literally construct a livable reality within the army. Doing push-ups side by side, their bodies synchronized, they reassure each other of a reality which extends across difference. Denied that reassurance, Billy responds with anger and fear, cursing Richie's homosexuality and Carlyle's race, provoking Carlyle into killing him.

This reading, while accurate, is also too literal, too neat in its delineation of cause and effect. Rabe's description of the play's antirealistic, "nuclear response" refers directly to the second murder, Carlyle's apparently "meaningless" killing of the old sergeant, Rooney, who walks into the barracks at precisely the wrong moment. Rabe walks a fine line with his representation of Carlyle's murderous anger. While it speaks to the deep racial tensions that narratives of foxhole brotherhood conveniently elide, it also runs the risk of speaking to the very racist logic of black animalism that is critically foregrounded in the speeches of both Carlyle and Roger. The most powerful deflection of this racist reading is the confusion that remains after Carlyle is led away in handcuffs. Unlike ritualistic displays such as lynching, which scapegoat social uncertainty and guilt onto black male bodies, Carlyle's arrest does not restore order.

Most obviously, the world-threatening possibility of homosexuality remains. Mopping up Billy's blood, Roger asks Richie why he didn't just tell them he was homosexual.

Roger: All my time talkin' shit, and all the time you was a faggot, man; you really was. You shoulda jus' tole ole Roger. He don't care. All you gotta do is tell me.

Richie: I've been telling you. I did.

Roger: Jive, man jive!

Richie: No!

Roger: You did bullshit all over us! ALL OVER US!

Richie: I just wanted to hold his hand, Billy's hand, to talk to him, go to the movies hand in hand like he would do with a girl or I would with someone back home.

Roger: But he didn't wanna; *He* didn't wanna.

(Finished now, Roger drags the mop and bucket back toward the corner. Richie is sobbing; he is at the edge of hysteria.)

Richie: He did.

Roger: No, man.

Richie: He did. He did. It's not my fault. (77–78)

Richie did, of course, tell them that he was homosexual, and Roger clearly seemed to believe it when he told Carlyle. It is only between Billy and Roger that the truth of homosexuality has to be denied in order to preserve their allegiance to the project of making men. Roger attempts to relocate sexual ambivalence back onto Richie in order to deflect it from Billy. Like mopping up Billy's blood, denying the possibility of Billy's homosexual desire is a way of cleansing Billy's body and the "area" they shared. What is most deeply threatening is Richie's camp sensibility, his insistence that every act is charged with more than one meaning. Roger's pragmatic knowledge of the difference between the way things are and the way they should be draws its limit at compromising the promise of what his relation to Billy was supposed to be: the interracial collectivity, which, as Jeffords argues, is masculinity.

Roger seems about to beat this truth into Richie when interrupted by the very drunk Sgt. Cokes who is looking for his buddy Rooney. Cokes and Rooney represent the historically ideal male bond which had "fought it through two wars already and . . . can make it through this one more" (35). Cokes does not know that Rooney is dead, and Roger and Richie don't tell him. Rooney's death is one token of the Vietnam War. It symbolizes the death of the image of the democratic army which repressed the memory of World War II segregation, only to have it return in the terrible class inequities of the Vietnam-era that became most visible in racial terms. But while Billy wants to "be part of the intimacy they are sharing," Roger and Richie read the sergeants in more debased terms—"better than movies" (44, 47). In this sense Cokes and Rooney are another emblem of the fallen John Wayne, old and besotted with drunken nostalgia.

At play's end, however, Cokes offers an eloquent commentary on the limits of masculinity and its assumptions. Shipped home from Vietnam because he has leukemia, Cokes reexamines his life from the knowledge of the body's limitations and his own dissolution. Consoling the still sobbing Richie that "there's a lotta worse things in this world than bein' a queer," Cokes speculates:

I mean, maybe I was a queer, I wouldn't have leukemia. Who's to say? Lived a whole different life. Who's to say? I keep thinkin' there was maybe somethin' I coulda done different. Maybe not drunk so much. Or if I'd killed more gooks, or more krauts, or more dinks. I was kindhearted sometimes. Or if I'd had a wife and I had some kids. Never had any. But my mother did and she died of it anyway. (81–82)

Cokes's new perspective of impending death sends him back over the narratives of masculinity: heterosexuality and procreation, war and racism, that follow from and, in turn, are supposed to support the integrity of the male body. But this integrity cannot be recuperated. Cokes identifies with his mother not his father, and like her, his leukemia will not be cured, just as the death of Rooney cannot be explained and the Vietnam War will compromise the traditional narratives of American identity.

But Cokes's most detailed questioning of his past concerns an incident during the Korean War which refashions the iconography of the Richie's story about the snakes that scared Billy so badly. Cokes retells, this time regretfully, the story of killing a sniper that he had enacted earlier in the play as a kind of ultimate war story. The sniper pops up out of a "spider hole" and wounds Cokes, who sneaks back up on him.

> I bang him on top of his head, stuff him back into the hole with a grenade for company. Then I'm sittin' on the lid and it's made outa steel. I can feel him in there, though, bangin' and yellin' under me, and his yelling I can hear is begging for me to let him out. It was like a goddamn Charlie Chaplin movie, everybody fallin' down and clumsy, and him in there yellin' and bangin' away, and I'm just sittin' there lookin' around. And he was Charlie Chaplin. I don't know who I was. And then he blew up. (82)

The "spider hole" reconstitutes in more apparently realistic terms the threatening tunnel of snakes. But Cokes obsesses over exactly what Richie's story represses, "the gook," the enemy soldier who is not a part of the landscape but locked by a steel door into the prison house of the war. The dangers here are once again castration and dismemberment. Cokes is shot in the butt and the Korean soldier "blows up," a literalized enactment of the "shattering" of the "bodily envelope" which Silverman describes as signifying masculinity's "coherence" (61). For Cokes the male body no longer signals a coherent reality but farce, "a Charlie Chaplin movie." In persona and genre, the reference to Chaplin could not be farther from the typical Vietnam War reference to John Wayne. Chaplin's little tramp knows that the world is not made in his image but also that there is a gap between reality and the egotistic assumptions of his usually larger and more aggressively masculine opponent. Cokes "doesn't know who he was" in this script and Roger asks if "maybe you was Charlie Chaplin, too," but Cokes says no, reiterating his sense of displacement, "I don't know who I was" (82). In the earlier more celebratory telling, Cokes was, in effect, John Wayne, singlehandedly clearing the sniper's "nest," as in *Sands of Iwo Jima*. But in Chaplin films the big tough guy does not win, and Cokes, old and sick, realizes he has not won either. He regrets killing the sniper: "I'd let him out now if he was in there" (82). Instead of seeing the moral of the story as the necessity of being "on top," Cokes has come to identify with the "gook" in the hole and, in a parallel gesture, reassures Richie that there are "a lotta worse things in this world than bein' a queer" (81). Castration, the violent rupture of bodily and symbolic mastery, no longer signifies terror because Cokes accepts it as inevitable.

This acceptance names the play. "Streamers" refers to the song a paratrooper is supposed to sing, to the tune of "Beautiful Dreamer," if his para-
chute fails to open, a sign of understanding and acceptance.

> Counted ten thousand
> Pulled on the cord.
> My chute didn't open,
> I shouted, "Dear Lord."
>
> Beautiful streamer,
> This looks like the end,
> The earth is below,
> My body won't bend.[58]
>
> Just like a mother
> Watching o'er me,
> Beautiful Streamer,
> Ohhhhh, open for me. (34)

The song is not a death wish but a prayer for life which accepts the limitations of the body and so denies the promise of invulnerability reiterated
through the individual and collective projects of building up a body, an
army, a national defense. Every paratrooper knows the song, but Cokes and
Rooney do not believe any of the men they saw die in those circumstances
actually sang it. Those unlucky soldiers hit the ground desperately trying
to change their circumstances, uncomprehending of the inevitable end
they face. The honored response of singing is reserved for the Korean soldier Cokes killed in the spider hole.

The play ends with one last act of white racial ventriloquism, but rather
than an appropriation of black vernacular, Cokes enacts the Korean soldier's dying gesture.

Roger: You think he was singin' it?

Cokes: Oh, yeah. Oh, yeah, he was singin' it.
          (Slight pause. Cokes, sitting on a footlocker, begins to sing
          a makeshift language imitating Korean, to the tune of
          "Beautiful Streamer." He begins with an angry, mocking
          energy that slowly becomes a dream, a lullaby, a farewell,
          a lament.)

> Yo no som lo no
> Ung toe lo knee
> Ra so me la lo
> La see see oh doe.

Doe no tee ta ta
Too low see see
Ra mae me lo lo
Ah boo boo boo eee
Boo boo eee booeeee.
La so lee lem
Lem lo lee da ung
Uhhh so ba booooo ohhhh.
Boo booo eee ung ba
Eee eee la looo
Lem lo lala la
Eeee oohhh ohhh ohhh ohhhhh.

(In the silence, he makes the soft, whispering sound of a child
imitating an explosion, and his entwined fingers come apart. The
dark figures of Richie and Roger are near. The lingering light fades
to black.) (83)

Cokes's belated compassion for his "gook" enemy brings forward in the play's
closing moments the Asian Other repressed in the American obsession with
black and white dynamics in the Vietnam War. That Cokes's "gook" is Korean,
not Vietnamese, is that much more to the point, a remembrance that many
of the horrors constructed as peculiar to the Vietnam War are in fact as old
as the term "gook" itself which evolved from "goo-goo," the slur used in the
long, brutal U.S. campaign to suppress the Philippine insurgence and lay
claim to military dominance in the Pacific. Cokes's child-like imitation of an
explosion invokes the spectacular end of World War II that secured that
dominance, the Cold War boyhoods it spawned, and Rabe's description of the
play's antirealist sensibility as a "nuclear" response. Like Kingston's *China
Men*, the play looks forward to Vietnam by looking back across the Pacific.

Flanked by Richie and Roger, Cokes pushes quite literally beyond the
boundaries of language and the body: into Korean, into the past, into the
space of the dead, the destroyed, the defeated. The end of *Streamers* rewrites
in more elegant and suggestive terms Michael Herr's desire to "get down
and bite the tongue off a corpse." Richie and Roger literalize the constitutive place of sexuality and race in the vernacular language of the war that
seeks simultaneously to describe the trauma suffered by the male body and
to bind it back up. But Cokes gives up the language secured by his body's
experience in war. His "makeshift language" is not meant to be mistaken
for actual or real or authentic Korean—for any of the terms used to valorize the vernacular prose of *Dispatches* even as its postmodernity is being
celebrated. Cokes's song refuses this kind of nostalgic desire for the real war
even as it makes present the structured absence at the heart of most representations of the Vietnam War.

Chapter 5

HUMPING THE BOONIES

Women and the Memory of War

> As always in reading Mailer's descriptions of
> intercourse, one is impressed by how much
> of a war novelist he has remained.
> — Alfred Kazin

> He's just a man like the rest of us,
> James, who wants to fuck away the pain
> and redeem his body.
> — Larry Heinemann

> Since Dawn got pregnant, Sam had been feeling
> that if she didn't watch her step, her whole life
> could be ruined by some mischance, some
> stupid surprise, like sniper fire.
> — Bobbie Ann Mason

The landmark collection, *Sisterhood is Powerful: An Anthology of Writing from the Women's Liberation Movement*, edited by Robin Morgan and published in 1970, includes a reworking of a contemporary advertisement for the Women's Army Corps. The ad features a smiling, fresh-faced young woman wearing fatigues with surgical scissors sticking out of her pocket and carries the accompanying appeal, "Help run the United States Army." "Girls are one of the secrets of running a modern army," the ad confides, "Willing, cheerful, energetic girls." After making the still familiar promises of education, job training, opportunity for advancement, and "a change of scene," the ad closes with a more curious line of encouragement: "It's great training for running a home someday."[1] Beneath the picture appears a feminist elaboration of the connection the ad asserts between the military and the home. Where the ad presents the military as an enlightened bureaucracy in which "girls" can "become personnel spe-

Women. Don't let my uniform get you uptight. I always wear it when I do the housework. Makes me feel more comfortable, more *me* as a housewife.

You know, underneath the military veneer, I really believe women are somehow more gentle than men.

I agree.

I think we should get out of Vietnam.

I'm against the system, whether it's ABM or IBM.

I want R.O.T.C. and CBW stopped.

The military-industrial complex has existed long enough.

I wish people would stop saying that my politics are motivated by my emotions. That makes it sound so easy. Nobody bothers to listen.

Now men they really have to think a lot before taking a stand. Refusing the draft is like refusing manhood. Peace and non-violence come much easier to us because of our roles as mothers and wives.

That's what everyone said when I resigned from the Women's Army Corps in protest against our involvement in Vietnam. "Woman's nature," they all said. Everyone was so understanding.

A week later I resigned from my husband. This time they said I was sick.

I learned a lot in the Women's Army Corps. Like, you can't seriously expect young men to stop serving (and dying) in the Army while you yourself spend your life serving in the home.

You say "it's a dirty war." You're angry because those who call the shots, the big shots, get others to do the dirty work and the killing for them. I'm angry too. But who gets to do the dirty work at home?

Cleaning and killing. That's what makes us so feminine. And them so masculine.

Sure. There's a certain division of labor which keeps people in their place. That's why McNamara (Mac the Knife) sits on top of the World Bank.

I'm not kidding sister.

If you don't believe me, join the Women's Army Corps and find out.

The Pentagon begins at home.

Florika, a member of New Haven (Connecticut) Women's Liberation, wrote the subversive commentary on this Vietnam-era ad for the Woman's Army Corp. Copyright © 1970 by Robin Morgan. By permission of Edite Kroll Literary Agency, Inc.

cialists, or learn to figure the payroll, or type a decent letter," the added text reclaims the young woman's voice and asserts direct connections between the Vietnam War and domestic space, protest against the war, and the contemporary Women's Liberation Movement.

> I learned a lot in the Women's Army Corps. Like you can't seriously expect young men to stop serving (and dying) in the Army while you yourself spend your life serving in the home.
>
> You say "it's a dirty war." You're angry because those who call the shots, the big shots, get others to do the dirty work and the killing for them. I'm angry too. But who gets to do the dirty work at home? . . .
>
> Sure. There's a certain division of labor which keeps people in their place. That's why McNamara (Mac the Knife) sits on top of the World Bank. . . .
>
> The Pentagon begins at home.

As political analysis, the rescripted ad works from the familiar 1960s conception of "the system" whose seeming disparate parts are asserted to be centrally controlled. As feminist critique, it turns on a denial of the separate spheres of public and private, male and female, which is extended to include Vietnam and the United States. Borrowing a Marxist frame of critique which links labor, capital, and culture, and popularizing it through the use of everyday language (e.g., "dirty work" and "big shots") and its play on the ad itself, this feminist text asserts an immediate and powerful connection between women and war—a connection the original ad attempts to obscure even as it renders it visible.

Only a few cliched reminders of this radicalized linkage of women and war seem to remain in popular representations of the Vietnam War, and those are utterly devoid of the wit and verve of the Women's Army Corps ad. The bitter invective reserved for Jane Fonda as emblem of the antiwar movement or the "Dear John" letter written under the influence of campus radicals mark the special quality of women's betrayal during the war. As Susan Jeffords has argued, representations of the Vietnam War have often functioned as a refuge for traditional conceptions of masculinity openly challenged by the women's movement.[2] "In Vietnam," Jeffords quotes John Wheeler, "masculinity did not go out of style" (53). Rather, Vietnam provided the imaginative territory for what Jeffords calls "the remasculinization of America."

In this chapter I want to reopen the association forged in and around 1970 between gender and war, women's liberation and Vietnam, and trace the contours of its obscured memory in the literature of the war. If, as Jeffords argues, the Vietnam War proved to be one of the most effective symbolic fields for suppressing the legacy of women's liberation, then I would argue it necessarily carries the rich potential for the return of that very repressed. In much the same way that the ad for the Women's Army

Corps grounded a feminist critique of the sleight of hand which assumes women both separate from and indispensable to the conduct of war, the memory of Vietnam is profoundly, if paradoxically, a carrier of the memory of the women's movement's moment of radical self-assertion.

At the center of my analysis I want to propose as an intentionally perverse corollary to the feminist refrain of 1970, "the Pentagon begins at home," the familiar vernacular phrase from the war, "humping the boonies." By linking these catch phrases of women's liberation and war culture, I hope to challenge the exclusion of women from war as a privileged site of cultural and particularly literary representation. As William Broyles argues, the purpose of telling war stories "is not to enlighten but exclude. Its message is not its content but to put the listener in his place. I suffered, I was there. You were not."[3] Susan Jeffords has demonstrated that in representations of the Vietnam War, this exclusion works less along the lines of those who actually served and those who did not than along the gendered lines of those who could serve, men, and those who could not, women.

In this sense, representations of the Vietnam War have continued the twentieth-century tendency to foreground war's claim as the text, context, and subtext of literature. Implicit in Paul Fussell's seminal study *The Great War and Modern Memory* is the assumption that the most profound project of twentieth-century literature has been to re-create language at every level. Word choice and diction, metaphor and symbol, style and structure must be refashioned in order to make literary language responsible to the terrible reality of modern war and the perversity of its memory. For women in the twentieth century, war has emerged as something deeply akin to what Virginia Woolf, at the end of *A Room of One's Own*, calls "Milton's bogie," the literary authority which turns a woman's interest perpetually toward man and away from "a view of open sky."[4] In one sense, the problem is compounded in the case of war. For if Woolf calls for women to "escape a little from the common sitting-room and see human beings not always in their relation to each other but in relation to reality," war claims the position of ultimate reality and inscribes its bodily truth on men as soldiers.[5] Within this logic, women can only know war through men.

The radical feminist insistence that "the Pentagon begins at home" was a strategic and theoretical response to exactly this dilemma as shaped by the emergence of Vietnam and the draft as the central issue of social protest and activism after 1966. Women's issues were being raised within Students for a Democractic Society (SDS), Student Non-Violent Coordinating Committee (SNCC), and elsewhere within what was broadly termed "the Movement" as early as 1964. However, as Alice Echols demonstrates, "the draft resistance movement contributed to women's growing peripheralization within the Movement."[6] In the words of activist Mimi Feingold, "women couldn't burn draft cards and couldn't go to jail so all they could do was relate through their men" (Echols 38). Vietnam posed a double bind for radical feminists in the late 1960s. On the one hand, they rejected the role of "wives, mothers and mourners; that is, tearful reactors to the actions of men" (Echols 56). Yet the war reinforced women's positions as "protected" from the real site of struggle and set the definition of militantism as militarism, a gesture literalized by the Black Panthers and most conspicuously, The Weathermen, in their dedication to "bringing the war back home."

Women's subordinate role in the antidraft movement was emblematized by the popular slogan, "Girls Say Yes to Boys Who Say No," which marked the intersection of the antiwar movement less with women's liberation than with the sexual revolution. Indeed, as obscenity and sexuality have increasingly emerged as the privileged metaphors for war's reality in the twentieth century, women's positions within war narrative have typically been determined by male desire. Paul Fussell celebrates as liberatory "the virtual disappearance . . . of the concept of prohibitive obscenity, a concept which has acted as a censor on earlier memories of 'war.'"[7] But this freedom from "all puritan lexical constraint" and its sexualized gendering of war's memory offers a deeply vexed inheritance to women in their relation to both war and the literature so deeply tied to it.[8] Sleeping with a draft re- sister is little different from the Catherine Barkley role in *A Farewell to Arms* of sleeping with a soldier, reaffirming a traumatized masculinity through female self-sacrifice. The rise in sexually explicit representations of war would seem inevitably marked by an increasingly brutal display of the female body, not only through images of rape or prostitution but also in pointed returns to Hemingway's classic parallel construction of childbirth and war.[9]

During Vietnam, radical feminists made a number of attempts to claim the territory of war as their own site of struggle. In 1968, Shulamith Firestone and the group New York Radical Women enacted a symbolic burial of traditional womanhood in Arlington National Cemetery, in an evocative demonstration of the idea that "the Pentagon begins at home." But in the face of the embodied reality of the war's violence, such gestures seemed inevitably to appear only symbolic and parochial. As Firestone argued in *The Dialectic of Sex*, "contemporary politicos see feminism as only tangental to 'real' radical politics . . . they still see male issues, e.g., the draft, as universal, and female issues, e.g., abortion, as sectarian" (quoted in Echols 62). The most rhetorically successful counter to the association of war, and particularly the draft with "reality," followed the line of argument advanced in the SDS Women's Liberation Workshop of 1967, which declared, "in capitalist society and especially in the United States . . . women are in a colonial relationship to men and we recognize ourselves as part of the Third World" (Echols 44). Feminists were able to move beyond their subordinate role by declaring their solidarity with the women of Vietnam. But the gestures of such solidarity, like those attempts to connect traditional gender roles with the war, seemed to operate best at the level of theater and symbol. For example, as participants in an antiwar demonstration, New York Radical Women "dressed like Vietnamese women, handed out leaflets about women's

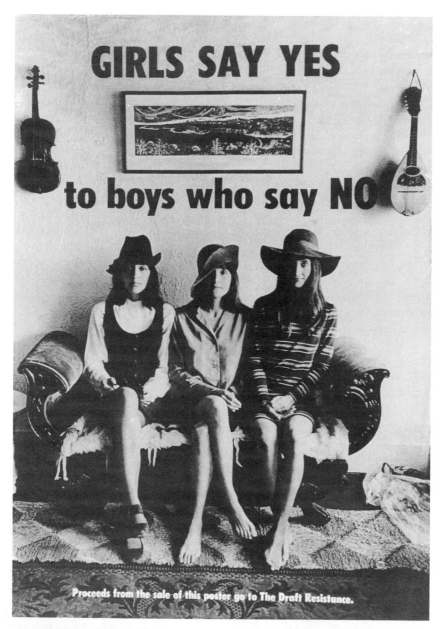

One of few direct claims made for women's role in the anti-war movement. Archival Poster provided by the Center for the Study of Political Graphics.

liberation to women only, and ran through the crowd ululating like the Algerian women in Gill Pontecorvo's 1966 film, *The Battle of Algiers*" (Echols 87). If the Vietnam War seemed to enforce an ultimate and irreducible gender difference, it also raised critical questions about the differences between women which the movement proved unable to adequately answer or even discuss.[10]

Images of both the antiwar movement and women's liberation have been eclipsed in popular memory by representations of American soldiers in Vietnam. But, as I have argued throughout this study, the solipsism of these narratives testifies to the radical social and political conflicts of the war years, even as it attempts to repress them. The critical issues that plagued feminist attempts to think through the relation of women to war during Vietnam continue to operate in crucial if transformed ways in the memory of war. By way of tracing the contours of these relationships within the literature of the Vietnam War, I want to focus attention on resonant meanings of the phrase "humping the boonies," the GI vernacular description for going out on patrol in remote jungle or densely forested terrain. No term better demonstrates the violent inscription of woman's presence and absence in war and war narratives. Humping signifies physical exertion through an overlapping invocation of sex and physical labor and is, in all its associations, an insistently male activity. Yet the conditions and limits of this masculine activity are marked by an implicit feminine presence in both the boonies to be humped and in the home which measures the distance traveled and would mark return. This bifurcation of feminine presence in "humping the boonies" structures yet another manifestation of the trope of friendly fire: woman as the enemy, the embodiment of both an often racialized Otherness and an unfaithful home, a battle manifest in both the literal enactment of rape and violence and in more nostalgic gestures of recuperation.

Moreover, as compelling as the gendered terms of meaning at play in the phrase is its colonial etymology. "Boonies" is short for "boondock," which comes from the Tagalog word "bundok" or mountain, a linguistic legacy of the long campaign of the U.S. military to suppress the Philippine insurgence. Once again, as I argued with Michael Herr's use of the soldier's vernacular, sexual innuendo is racially inflected. The "boonies," like "Indian Country," another legacy of the war in the Philippines, not only marks archetypal uncharted territory but a landscape inhabited by agents actively resistant to U.S. political, military, social, and cultural control. As such, it is a landscape filled with possibilities for American women seeking to follow Woolf's advice and see themselves in relation to a reality beyond the reigning cultural authority. But this historicized conception of the boonies reminds us as well that there is little territory beyond ideology's charting and that other differences besides gender should command our attention.

The course of this chapter will follow the strains of presence and absence delineated for women by the cultural logic of "humping the boonies."

Tim O'Brien's short story "Sweetheart of the Song Tra Bong," Le Ly Hay-slip's memoir *When Heaven and Earth Changed Places*, Larry Heinemann's novel *Paco's Story*, and Bobbie Ann Mason's *In Country* suggest the fuller range of possibilities of such an inquiry that is ultimately concerned not so much with the nature of war as with the gendered conditions of telling war stories. O'Brien constructs an elaborate narrative circumvention of war as an exclusively male territory, in large part through the suppression of the sexualized language of contemporary war stories, sending a bright-eyed American girl into the war zone. Hayslip testifies to the terrible realities of Vietnamese women trapped in the world of the war but more uses the tell-ing of her story to reconcile her two homes—Vietnam and the United States. Heinemann demonstrates in graphic detail the terrible consequences entailed for women by both their presence and absence within war stories. And Mason refigures both the metaphorical relationship of sexuality and war and the meaning of coming home by placing a woman at the center of the story. Collectively, these fictions return to the politicized connections pressed by the women's liberation movement between women and war, the personal and political, sexuality and freedom, and offer the possibility of see-ing women in other than a supporting role to the masculine drama of war.

TIM O'BRIEN'S STORY "SWEETHEART OF THE SONG TRA BONG" offers a brilliant gloss of the gendered cultural logic of war stories. Framed as a tale told by a highly unreliable narrator, Rat Kiley, "Sweetheart" tells the impossible story of a girl who succeeds in "humping the boonies." A young medic at a small station in a remote mountain location of Vietnam sends his girlfriend a ticket to come visit him. Seventeen years old, fresh out of high school, Mary Ann Bell arrives on a chopper in white culottes and a "sexy pink sweater" full of innocent curiosity and good cheer (102).[11] The story presses two conflicting points of impossibility: whether a girl could get to "the boonies" and what would happen if she did. Getting her there, the resourceful young medic, Mark Fossie, explains was expensive and "the logistics were complicated, but it wasn't like getting to the moon" (105). Mary Ann Bell becomes another of O'Brien's travelers, like Paul Berlin in *Going After Cacciato*, who embarks on an improbable but eminently map-pable journey. It is the issue of what happens when she arrives in country that far more seriously strains not simply the imagination but the gendered narrative boundaries of war itself.

Mary Ann Bell's trip to Vietnam violates every operative assumption re-garding how and when and where and why women enter war stories. At first she plays the traditional role, mooning over her boyfriend, flirting just enough with the seven other medics and playing volleyball in "cut-off blue jeans and a black swimsuit top, which the guys appreciated" (106). In short, "she was good for morale" (106). The guys like her but also come to respect her; she asks good questions, "paid attention," and when casualties come in "Mary Ann wasn't afraid to get her hands bloody" (108). She comes to feel "at home" in Vietnam (107). Besides her good-natured flirting and showing off her long legs, however, Mary Ann does nothing to make the camp seem more "like home." She does not cook or clean or offer any little domestic touches. Instead, her attention is drawn out of the camp, away from her boyfriend and his comfortably limited engagement with combat, and toward "those scary green mountains to the west" (106). From the ARVN soldiers camped at the perimeter she learns some Vietnamese, "how to cook rice over a can a Sterno, and how to eat with her fingers" (107). The men tease her about going "native." She badgers Fossie into taking her to the nearby village over his objection that the Viet Cong control it. She seems to know no fear.

"A real tiger," said Eddie Diamond. "D-cup guts, trainer bra brains."
"She'll learn," somebody said.
Eddie Diamond gave a solemn nod. "That's the scary part. I promise you. This girl will most definitely learn." (108)

Eddie's comic bra-size metaphor speaks to the heart of the story's improbability and its power. Mary Ann moves deeper into the war without moving out of her gender identity as a woman. When the wounded come in, "she learned how to clip an artery and pump up a plastic splint, and shoot in morphine," fascinated by the "adrenalin buzz that went with the job . . . [when] you have to do things fast and right" (109). Mary Ann gains confidence and focus; she seemed like a "different person." She learns to shoot and "Cleveland Heights seemed very far away" (109). This difference intrudes into her relationship with Mark. They still sleep together and plan for the future but "her body seemed foreign somehow—too stiff in places, too firm where the softness used to be" (110). At an obvious level, this hardening of her body suggests masculinization, but Mary Ann remains very much a desirable woman to Mark and to all the men. The more telling change is a narrative one—her new uncertainty in the story she had shared with Mark since grammar school: "that they would be married some day, and live in a fine gingerbread house near Lake Erie, and have three healthy yellow-haired children, and grow old and no doubt die in each others arms and be buried in the same walnut casket" (106). After three weeks in country Mary Ann begins to qualify: "Not necessarily three kids, she'd say. Not necessarily a house on Lake Erie. 'Naturally we'll still get married,' she'd tell him, 'but it doesn't have to be right away. Maybe travel first. Maybe live together. Just test it out, you know?" (110). This change, associated in the story with the war, also speaks to the social transformation in traditional mores associated with the sexual revolution and women's liberation movements of the 1960s. Mary Ann has begun to question the inevitable logic of domesticity.

In very subtle and provocative ways, "Sweetheart of the Song Tra Bong" is a story of the women's movement: of one woman's move beyond naturalized gender roles which brings to light deeper assumptions about gender relations and the larger sense of reality. As narrator, Rat is furiously defensive of the story's veracity:

> [T]he one thing [Rat] could not tolerate was disbelief. . . . "She wasn't *dumb*," he'd snap. "Young, that's all I said. Like you and me. A *girl*, that's the only difference, and I'll tell you something: it didn't amount to jack. I mean, when we first got here—all of us—we were young and innocent, full of romantic bullshit, but we learned pretty damn quick, And so did Mary Ann." (108)

"You've got to get rid of that sexist attitude," Rat later chides his listeners, knowing that it is their assumptions about women and not their experience of the war which condition their sense of the possible or the real, their ability to believe the story (117). Like all the stories in *The Things They Carried*, "Sweetheart" is as much about the nature of stories as about the nature of war. At the crucial dramatic moment, Rat plays on his listeners' assumptions. Mark wakes Rat late at night; Mary Ann is gone and he assumes that she must be sleeping with someone else. Rat does a "body count" but all the men are sleeping alone. Rat interrupts his narration to ask his listeners, "Where is she?" One connoisseur of stories immediately knows: she's with the Green Berets that Rat had mentioned at the beginning of his tale who operate out of a hootch at the edge of the camp but generally ignore the medics: "all that's got to be there for a *reason*. That's how stories work, man" (112).

Allegiance to narrative form temporarily overrides gender assumptions, and, in any case, Mark's narrative, "she's sleeping with somebody," stands ready to recuperate more familiar patterns of possibility. But this assumption, too, proves wrong. "She wasn't sleeping with any of them," Rat explains. "At least not exactly. I mean, she was sleeping with *all* of them, more or less, except it wasn't sex or anything. They was just lying together, so to speak, Mary Ann and these six grungy weirded out Green Berets" (112). "Lying down how?" the skeptical and confused listeners ask. "Ambush. All night long. Mary Ann's out on fuckin' *ambush*" (113). That Rat stumbles over the sexual metaphor here is less a mark of his "bad habit" of interrupting the flow of his stories with "little clarifications or bits of analysis and personal opinions" than a measure of how deeply Mary Ann's actions have compromised narrative expectations and even possibility (116). Mary Ann has transgressed the boundaries of common sense in the deepest meaning of the term, the shared assumptions that create a sense of reality.

For common sense would surely suggest that whatever experience Mary Ann gains in Vietnam will necessarily be sexual. Going to Vietnam expands her horizons, her sense of herself and the world. Throughout the 1960s and beyond, sexual freedom has served as both the metaphor and the substance of all too many stories of women's liberation. The narrative that most directly maps the intersection of the Vietnam War and the contemporary shift in gender roles, the film *Coming Home*, plots Sally (Jane Fonda)'s personal growth as the move from the bed of her traditional soldier husband to that of the countercultural antiwar veteran. Sleeping with one of the "Greenies" is the expected way for Mary Ann to move beyond Eddie and escape the home he represents by acting out her fascination with the landscape of Vietnam. Moreover, "fucking ambush" encodes the violent sexual threat of war for women: rape. Common sense would dictate that Mary Ann would need to take one lover as protector from the sexual voraciousness depicted in most representations of the war. In an all-male society women are expected to serve as objects of sexual barter.

But O'Brien plots Mary Ann's move to the Greenies with even more care than her plausible if improbable journey to Vietnam. Crucial here is the emphasis on learning, on acquiring competence and with it respect. Rat's insistence that they were all innocent once but "learned pretty damn quick" in country speaks to the authorial heart of war stories which traces the soldier's journey from innocence to experience, from home to war. By constructing a plausible fiction which takes Mary Ann to Vietnam, O'Brien undoes the narrative presumption that identifies home as the realm of the female and war as the domain of the male. Once in country, she is taken through the deeply familiar routines of learning about the land and the war, its rhythms and demands. The men listening to Rat's story cannot disavow her story without disavowing the terms that authorize their own telling of war stories—how they acquired their own knowledge.

Mary Ann's interest in the land becomes desire and her knowledge translates into narrative possibility, moving ultimately to the story's radical denouement in which Mary Ann humps the boonies. Tellingly, however, the term is never used directly. Rat underlines the weirdness of her arrival by saying, "She shows up with a suitcase and one of those plastic cosmetic bags. Comes right out to the boonies" (102). By implication, the boonies are exactly that place where American women are not. But one of the things that makes her appearance at this remote base possible is that being stationed there involves "no humping at all" (103). In practical terms it is light duty with no officers, but the break in the metaphorical association of "boonies" and "humping" at the beginning of the story is literally and figuratively what makes its narration of the impossible possible. This unhooking of the sexual metaphor is generally characteristic of O'Brien's style which, almost uniquely among veterans writing fiction about the war, does not rely on the hypersexual vernacular of the grunt. If, according to Michael Herr, the feeling of being in a firefight is most closely akin to "the feeling you'd had when you were much, much younger and undressing a girl for the first time," then for Mary Ann to be out on "fucking ambush" is, to say the least, highly ironic (136).[12] But the incongruity in "Sweetheart" rebounds on the male listeners (Herr's "you" literalized in Rat's audience) rather than violently back onto her body. Compare the violent fate of women caught playing soldier in the war zone in *The Short-Timers* or, as we shall see, in Larry Heinemann's *Paco's Story*, novels that contain some of the war literature's most brilliant linguistic plays on and with obscenity.

Within the story both Mary Ann and Rat scrupulously avoid using overt sexual metaphors to explain the desire she feels for the war. Mary Ann uses the term "appetite." "Sometimes I want to *eat* this place, Vietnam," she explains. "I want to swallow this whole country—the dirt, the death—I just want to eat it and have it there inside of me" (121). Certainly there are sexual inferences in this desire to consume; there very well may have to be sexual entendres for her experience to register as a war story. But she cannot respond to the land with the kind of explicit language used by Michael Herr, "kiss it, eat it, fuck it, plow it with your whole body" or even "pucker and submit," without reopening the barely suspended disbelief regarding what women can do in war (Herr 63). Women are typically assumed to be literally, rather than, like Herr, symbolically ravished by war. Rat's metaphor is similar: "Vietnam had the effect of a powerful drug," that is illicit, pleasurable, and dangerous, again like sex, but not quite sex (123).

Rat's ultimate metaphor for Mary Ann's experience echoes across the 1960s' language of sex, drugs, self-discovery, and the war alike; Vietnam becomes her "trip."

> The endorphins start to flow, and the adrenaline, and you hold your breath and creep quietly through the moonlit nightscapes; you become intimate with danger; you're in touch with the far side of yourself, as though it's another hemisphere, and you want to string it out and go where ever the trip takes you and be host to all the possibilities inside yourself. . . . She wanted more, she wanted to penetrate into the mystery of herself. . . . (124)

In a perverse way Mary Ann's trip answers directly Virginia Woolf's call—she moves away from domestic space, away from the future husband who presents himself as her identity and discovers herself in relation to the landscape and within herself. While Woolf would hardly endorse Mary Ann's claim to the masculine art of war and its colonial context, the story presses the textual and material implications of women's liberation. Mary Ann moves quite literally beyond Rat or, by implication, any man's narration. Rat infuriates his listeners by claiming he doesn't know what happened to her, but he finally presents an ending to his story based on rumor and conjecture. Like Sean Flynn in *Dispatches*, "Mary Ann Bell joined the missing" (125)

The story's end makes her absence radically active and thus powerfully denies any nostalgic recuperation of her character.

> But the story did not end there. If you believed the Greenies, Rat said, Mary Ann was still somewhere out there in the dark. Odd move-

ments, odd shapes. Late at night, when the Greenies were out on ambush, the whole rain forest would seem to stare in at them—a watched feeling—and a couple of times they almost saw her sliding through the shadows. Not quite but almost. She had crossed over to the other side. She was a part of the land. She was wearing her culottes, her pink sweater, and a necklace of human tongues. She was dangerous. She was ready for the kill. (125)

Mary Ann's defection marks her as the enemy, but the story refuses to enact the familiar terms which connect women's liberation and the soldier's betrayal. "Sweetheart" is insistently about Mary Ann's self-discovery and its effect on the masculine activity of telling war stories rather than on the lives of the men she leaves behind. The story works directly against the deeply misogynist assumptions that make Jane Fonda such a familiar icon of veteran's feelings of betrayal. Rather than hatred, Rat confesses his love for Mary Ann, because she has ceased to be like "those girls back home . . . clean and innocent" who will never understand what he has been through. "After the war, man, I promise you, you won't find nobody like her" (123). Rat brings to the surface the contradictory structures of war narrative that ask women to heal and absolve men of experiences they are not allowed to know. The Greenies' haunting feeling of being watched asserts Mary Ann's subversive claim to knowledge and experience, just as her necklace of tongues testifies to her violently earned right to tell war stories. Mary Ann has passed Herr's "moment of initiation where you get down and bite the tongue off the corpse" and now sings in a language "beyond translation" (121).

But if gender is denaturalized as a system of absolute difference, Mary Ann's trip to the "far side of herself," especially as likened to "another hemisphere," also suggests more traditional patterns of imperial and racial otherness (123–124). The scene in which Mark and Rat confront Mary Ann in the Greenies' hootch is an orgy of hyperbolic imagery that parodies Kurtz's compound in *Apocalypse Now*: "tribal music," the "exotic" scent of incense mingling with the "stench of the kill," a decayed leopard's head, "strips of yellow brown skin" hanging from the rafters, and a poster that declares "in neat black lettering: ASSEMBLE YOUR OWN GOOK!! FREE SAMPLE KIT!!" (119). Mary Ann emerges out of the gloom, wearing "her pink sweater and a white blouse and a simple cotton skirt" (120). She is the same but clearly not the same. Her eyes are "utterly flat and indifferent," the mark of the proverbial thousand-yard stare.

But the grotesque part, [Rat] said, was her jewelry. At the girl's throat was a necklace of human tongues. Elongated and narrow, like pieces of blackened leather, the tongues were threaded along a copper wire, one overlapping the next, the tips curled upward as if caught in some horrified final syllable. (120)

If this scene is the clearest display of Rat's "reputation for exaggeration and overstatement," it also presents a deeply familiar pattern of horror, of, in fact, *the* horror, Kurtz's vision of the heart of darkness (101).

Mary Ann's desire to "penetrate deeper into the mystery of herself" rebounds ironically on a Modernist legacy that projects the bourgeois unconscious onto the colonized landscapes of Asia and Africa. In a deeply canny revision of Conrad's *Heart of Darkness*, Mary Ann is both Kurtz and the Intended, liberating the woman from the drawing room where she is made to embody the hypocrisy of the imperial project. Mary Ann's "crossing over to the other side," which Rat describes not as joining the enemy's army but as "becoming part of the land," deconstructs the gendering of the boonies as both feminized landscape to be humped and the furthest distance from the home where the woman waits. But Mary Ann's identification with the land displaces the Vietnamese even as it makes manifest the gendered construction of the imperial landscape. The Vietnamese are literally dismembered, figured only as pieces of skin and the tongues Mary Ann has appropriated to voice her own experience. In particular, Mary Ann's claim to the landscape of the war displaces Vietnamese women, whose bodies stereotypically in American representations negotiate the relationship between war and sexuality, material and narrative violence in country. The exclusion of Vietnamese women from the story is a necessary condition of its narratability; their absence underwrites the construction of the boonies as the place where women are not and enables the gap between "humping" and "boonies." The "problem" that racial, national, and cultural difference poses in Mary Ann's liberation from the gendered conventions of war narrative is, not coincidentally, the problem the women's movement itself floundered on in the 1970s.

LE LY HAYSLIP'S MEMOIR *WHEN HEAVEN AND EARTH CHANGED Places* tells precisely the story "Sweetheart" must exclude, the story of a Vietnamese woman. The metaphorical connections between home and war, landscape and sexuality found in O'Brien's tale become graphically material in Hayslip's story of coming of age in the war zone. But *Heaven and Earth* is also, importantly, the story of Hayslip as an American woman. Her memoir is structured by two time lines: the first moves classically from her birth to her departure from Vietnam as the wife of an American in 1972. This story is intercut with another, the story of Hayslip's return to Vietnam in 1986 for her first visit with her family since the end of the war. This double structure, across time and space, from one home to another, from the family of her sons to the family of her mother and siblings, resists the overdetermined logic of home and war which is fundamental to most American war narratives. There is literally a world of difference between Hayslip's war-ravaged home and her status as a refugee and Mary Ann's rebellion against the logic of domesticity. But the stories of these very different women, like the paralleled figures of Cathy and the female Viet Cong soldier to be considered in *Paco's Story*, work together to delineate the boundaries of the American war story.

Hayslip's memoir carries a tremendous burden as by far the most widely read account of the war from a Vietnamese perspective. Often lost in the characterization of *Heaven and Earth* as Vietnamese is its simultaneous status as a Vietnamese-American story. It hardly seems a coincidence that it is a women's story that has emerged to perform this double duty. The terms of friendly fire refuse to recognize the Vietnamese as either allied or enemy soldiers. The shadowy landscape that Vietnamese soldiers typically inhabit in American representations is precisely the space Mary Ann comes to claim in the war story. The gendered terms of female presence and absence within the war story are used in Hayslip's narrative to give voice to the multiple, fraught, and contradictory place of the Vietnamese in "the American War." Hayslip's story is overburdened by representativeness: She is, by turns, not only Vietnamese and American but the cadre and the peasant, daughter and mother, from the country and the city, the victim of the South Vietnamese and the Viet Cong, the French and the Americans.

Hayslip begins her memoir, "For the first twelve years of my life, I was a peasant girl in Ky La, now called Xa Hoa Qui, a small village in Central Vietnam" (ix.).[13] By 13 she concludes, "the insatiable dragon" of war "had swallowed me up" (xiv). The war ruptures Le Ly's narrative of home and girlhood. She is 13 when the Viet Cong first enter her village and the American presence in both men and machines is first seen. It may be a coincidence of Le Ly's life that this new war accompanies the onset of puberty, but it also marks woman's typically sexualized place in war and war narratives. The youngest daughter of protective parents, Le Ly grows up with a dual understanding of her place in the war. She is imbued with the pride of history, learning the ancestral tales of Vietnamese heroes, women as well as men, who defended their country from foreign invasion. When her father recounts to her the litany of children lost by his siblings to the war, whether dead or drawn to the warring capitals of Hanoi and Saigon, he asks the young Le Ly if she understands her job in the war.

> I squared my shoulders and put on a soldier's face. "My job is to avenge my family. To protect my farm by killing the enemy. I must become a woman warrior like Phung Thi Chinh!"
>
> My father laughed and pulled me close. "No little peach blossom. Your job is to stay alive—to keep an eye on things and keep the village safe. To find a husband and have babies and tell the story of what you've seen to your children and anyone else who'll listen. Most of all, it is to live in peace and tend the shrine of your ancestors. Do these things well, Bay Ly and you will be worth more than any soldier who ever took up a sword." (32–33)

But when the war comes to her village, it becomes increasingly difficult to separate the roles of woman and soldier as her father has instructed. As a member of the Viet Cong self-defense force, Le Ly's duties sound very much like those her father has instructed her to fulfill. She keeps watch over the village, signaling the approach of Republican or American troops; she teaches children, tends the wounded, buries the dead. Other girls go off and become Viet Cong soldiers, but as the last child at home, Le Ly is allowed to remain with her parents and perform these "domestic" duties. She earns honor as a Viet Cong hero for faithfully discharging her duty, suffering arrest and beatings at the hands of the South Vietnamese police. But as the war intensifies, duty to family and village and to the Viet Cong no longer seems so easily aligned. The surveillance of the enemy becomes the surveillance of every chance meeting or gesture within her village. Special permission from cadre leaders becomes required to visit relatives or use food for holiday feasts. At one point Le Ly's exasperated parents "decided it was easier to eat all our food outside so that the neighbors could count what we ate and reassure the Viet Cong that we were not feasting in secret" (71). Even in the absence of bombs or soldiers, the war pervades Le Ly's home, symbolically turning her family out of doors.

Hayslip's description of village life testifies to the complexity of the civil war within Vietnam, complexities unimaginable within the American terms of friendly fire. She is careful in her portrait of the Viet Cong, as no doubt she must be given that she is writing as an American citizen but also as representative of a Vietnamese American community which is largely and vocally anticommunist. Indeed, many Vietnamese Americans have condemned her account which, even in its disillusionment with the Viet Cong and the North, does not support the South Vietnamese Republican cause. Hayslip take pains to show how and why the peasants of central Vietnam identified personally and culturally with the Viet Cong and not with the Republican troops. The self-surveillance demanded by the Viet Cong is also necessitated by being caught between the conflicting territorial claims of the Viet Cong and the Republicans. But this makes the Viet Cong's increasing suspicion of the villagers all the more a betrayal. "When the Viet Cong began to condemn us for practicing what they claimed to be protecting [our ancient rights and independence], we began to suspect—at least in our hearts—that the new war we began with high hope was over, and that another sort of war had begun" (71).

Not surprisingly, rape ultimately figures in the Viet Cong's betrayal, alienating the young Le Ly from both her home and any ideological commitment within the war. Even as a young girl she is aware always of rape as the particular threat war poses to women: "that was every girl's risk in Ky La" (10). If the threat of rape, like the surveillance of village neighbors, marks the war's saturation of everyday life, the circumstances of Le Ly's rape dissolves any semblance of agency she had felt in her allegiance to the Viet Cong. Arrested by Republican troops and held prisoner in an infamous military camp, Le Ly ultimately earns release through her mother's skilled use of relatives in the South Vietnamese Army. Her release earns the suspicion and ultimately the condemnation of the Viet Cong cadre. At her trial, Le Ly is never allowed to speak or even be clearly seen. She is never called by name, "only 'a woman' who has done this or that," even when she is finally condemned to death (89). These peculiarities raise doubts as to the legitimacy of the trial even within the Viet Cong's restricted practice of justice. It is unclear in the book whether it is the young condemned Le Ly or the narrating Hayslip who wonders whether the young male cadres Tram, Loi, and Mau had "simply decided to take the people's justice into their own hands" (89). When Loi and Mau rape Le Ly rather than kill her, this would certainly seem to be the case.

Marched across a swamp and into the woods by her executioners, Le Ly is led finally to an open grave. This classic scene of execution offers her a soldier's death which recognizes the legitimacy of her place in the war even in her supposed treason. But just as the trial limited her identity to that of "a woman," refusing to allow her to claim any of her past service to the Viet Cong or her previously praised actions as a member of the village self-defense force, Loi and Mau choose to rape rather than kill her, violently insisting on sexuality as the only grounds of her identity within the war. Hayslip's narration of the rape literalizes the symbolic terms of "humping the boonies."

> Drugged by too much hate and fear and confusion, I just lay back and let Mau do what he had to do. Unlike Loi, he did not spit on me and curse my womanness when he finished. Rather, he seemed like a sad little boy who, believing he was not a man, settled for the imitation of manhood Loi had shown him. That I was the stage for this poor show made no difference; for by now I was no more than the dirt on which we lay. The war—these men—had finally ground me down to oneness with the soil, from which I could no longer be distinguished as a person. Dishonored, raped, ruined for any decent man, my soiled little body had become its own grave. (97)

Rape embodies the mythified connections between female sexuality and the land. The explicitness of Hayslip's understanding of her body as "the stage" for the display of masculinity and the need for soldiers like Mau to lay claim to power by grinding her "down to the oneness with the soil" suggests the pervasiveness of the gendered understanding of humping the boonies. The metonymic link—"the war—these men" enacted in the rape carries as its axiomatic conclusion the link between the land and the female body—"had finally ground me down to oneness with the soil, from which I could no longer be distinguished as a person" (97).

If the rape violently marks Le Ly as woman, Hayslip ends the story of the rape by defining herself as a peasant.

> Both sides in this terrible, endless, *stupid* war had finally found the
> perfect enemy: a terrified peasant girl who would endlessly and stu-
> pidly consent to be their victim—as all Vietnam's peasants had con-
> sented to be victims, from creation to the end of time! (97)

The rape that alienates her from the Viet Cong and active participation in
the war also marks a trope of victimization that is not necessarily bound to
her "womanness." The "terrified peasant girl" comes to stand for "all Vietnam's peasants" across time. Gender names and shapes the perception of
the peasantry, who become the feminized victims of the masculinized war.
But assumptions about the connection between the peasants and the land,
yet another mythified understanding of "oneness with the soil," also shape
the gendered understanding of war. The logic of raping the land and raping a woman in war are circular—shaping and sustaining imperial and
nationalist fantasies which can neither fully subsume or be subsumed by
concepts of gender. The peasants, like women, are figured as outside the
war story, not as active characters within its plots but literally the ground
on which its dramatic events are enacted.

In Tim O'Brien's earlier novel, *Going After Cacciato*, when Paul Berlin
wants to bring a woman into his war story, he imagines the young peasant
Sarkin Aung Wan, the love interest who will also be able to answer the
young American soldier's "nagging question": "Who were these skinny,
blank-eyed people? What did they want?"[14] Sarkin clearly represents the
mythified connection between peasants and the land. She earns her place
in the trip to Paris by leading the unit out of the tunnels into which they
fall early on. Where the Viet Cong soldier they meet underground, Li Van
Hgoc, is trapped in his bunker, terrified to venture out of his assigned place
in the war, Sarkin responds with good-humored peasant mysticism: "The
way in is the way out. We have fallen into a hole. Now we must fall out"
(88). With these words, she leads Paul Berlin and company through the
maze of tunnels from which the soldiers, Viet Cong or American, could
never escape on their own. They emerge in Mandalay, leaving Vietnam and
the war behind. "To go home one must become a refugee," Sarkin insists, a
sentiment she returns to in the Paris peace talks scene (88). This insistence
on home centers the doubling of woman and peasant in ways that, as Hayslip's story foregrounds in its double narrative of travel from Vietnam to
the United States and from the United States to Vietnam, challenge notions
of home as clearly as they challenge notions of war.

The contrast between Mary Ann Bell and Le Ly Hayslip is most pointedly
one of homes: Mary Ann's realizable dream of "a gingerbread house on
Lake Erie [with] three healthy, yellow-haired children" (106) set against the
Le Ly's small family house near the rice paddies which is burned and invaded by the war. In war or peace, the difference in these homes warns
against any simple slippage between the category of woman and the cate-

gory of the peasant. But to engage the full complexity of Hayslip's story, she cannot be placed in simple opposition to Mary Ann: American woman versus Vietnamese peasant. Differences, particularly race, remain, but Hayslip is also an American woman as her married name testifies. The obvious contrast between the fanciful, even fantastic quality of O'Brien's tale and the testimonial realism of Hayslip's might seem to argue against any connection between them. But fiction and nonfiction prove equally shaped by the narrative conventions of humping the boonies. Mary Ann Bell discovers the imaginative power to move beyond her domestic place and into the boonies, the narrative space of the Vietnamese emptied by the trope of friendly fire. Le Ly Hayslip is violently pressed into that same space, through the colonial inscription of the timeless, unchanging, victimization of the peasantry, but she ultimately moves into Mary Ann's space of suburban, American domesticity. Their lives and the privileges attached to them are not commensurate, but both demonstrate that the material distance between these women and their homes can be traveled. The purpose of such a trip, as Hayslip's narrative so powerfully shows, is not to testify to the universal appeal of the American dream but to the necessity of connecting the separate spheres of "the World" and "the War" if peace is to be realized.

As critical as the rape is both to Le Ly's life and to a critical understanding of the gendered logic of war stories, it is but the beginning of a larger story of women pressed into service of the sexual economy of the war. Condemned by the Viet Cong and exiled from her village, Le Ly goes to the city, like two of her sisters before her. Although she tells no one of her rape, Le Ly's work, both in domestic service and on the street, is universally sexualized. As a peasant girl fresh from the countryside, she finds work as a housekeeper, but she is immediately vulnerable to the sexual advances of her employers, both welcome and unwelcome. The girls from Le Ly's village who went North for training as soldiers had returned home transformed: "they wore their weapons the way Saigon girls wear their jewelry" (66). Le Ly learns that becoming a city girl wearing jewelry is in fact the obverse of wearing weapons and barking orders. In Danang, all her opportunities for work are tied to the increasing numbers of American troops in country. She sells trinkets outside the PX, gets a job at a hospital, becomes a hostess at a club and a waitress at the enlisted men's club, but more and more her narrative is structured by a series of relationships with American servicemen. These relationships follow a distinct pattern: the American offers much needed help, Le Ly is seduced by gratitude or need, and then the man becomes violently possessive.

Her first relationship with an American is typical. Red is a sailor working as a medical tech at the hospital where Le Ly has a job as an orderly. Ironically, their friendship begins when Red arranges a transfer to get her away from a lecherous Vietnamese sergeant. Once Red and Le Ly become lovers, not surprisingly, his "attentions" change. When Le Ly asks why they never go out with his friends, Red replies, "Look at you. . . . You look like you just came off the farm. . . . You look like—well, a damned Viet Cong or something" (281). If she cannot be a soldier, then Le Ly must learn quite literally to wear jewelry. She paints her fingernails, puts on makeup and false eyelashes "to make my narrow, Vietnamese eyes look bigger, rounder, and more American," and uses some of her paycheck to get her hair done in a beehive like the "tea girls" Red eyes on the street. "Rouged and teased in my red *ao dai*, I could see the new Le Ly was much closer to what he wanted" (282). Red is now proud to show her off and rents an apartment for them. Personal relationships between Vietnamese women, especially displaced peasants, and American serviceman are inevitably marked by unequal economic status, but this relationship becomes overtly commercial when Red tries to get Le Ly to go to work as a topless dancer, where all the GIs can see "Red's girl." As in the rape, Le Ly is once again to become the "stage" for a pathetic demonstration of masculinity. But overall Hayslip's narrative shows that if "rape was every girl's risk" in her village during war, the sexual economy of war, from prostitution to marriage, seems the fate of every girl driven from the country to the city.

Le Ly refuses Red's crude demand, but her shame at the prospect of topless dancing does not keep her from acknowledging the economic advantages she has gained through Red. "After Red, I at least knew how to fix myself up and act the way Americans expected. It was now within my power to find a really good paying job that could bring me into contact with people who could help me find a better life" (294). Dressing now for American eyes, Le Ly must endure the notice of men on the street, American and Vietnamese. Such notice, both admiring and contemptuous, is always sexual in nature. Indeed, each of three following relationships with Americans described in the book, including her ultimate marriage to Ed Hayslip, begin when she is seen and approached by the man on the street (295, 322, 326). The distinction between a personal relationship which could become legitimated through marriage and street walking, open prostitution, is a tenuous one, although fiercely maintained by Le Ly. Once transformed into the Vietnamese woman suitable for American servicemen's eyes, Hayslip becomes a very public commodity and grows "used to getting wolf whistles and cat calls . . . on the street," just as she becomes emboldened in fighting off sexual harassment at work (295). But the lines between harassment and seduction, work and love, sex and opportunity are anything but clear. The unifying goal of her economically determined personal and work life is the creation of domestic space, a home for herself, her son, and her mother. But the home in Ba Ly made unlivable by the war is never reconstituted in Vietnam. Le Ly's relationships with Americans always involve housekeeping separate from her mother and son. Instead, these relationships become an extension of her earlier experiences in the battle zone in which she is once again violently possessed or thoughtlessly abandoned.

At the end of *When Heaven and Earth Changed Places*, Le Ly gives up her home entirely, marrying Ed Hayslip, and taking her sons to the United States. Lost between the narratives of war and return is the story of making a home in the United States. That story is told in the second volume of Hayslip's memoir, *Child of War, Woman of Peace*. It is striking but perhaps not surprising that she cannot leave the war behind, nor does the structure of her narrative change much in telling the story of life in the United States. Following the death of her husband, the almost ritual enactment of relationships between Hayslip as a Vietnamese woman and white American veterans is continued, underscoring the fraught logic of domesticity which makes woman signify home. As a Vietnamese woman, however, Hayslip's enactment of the women's classic role of seeking to make love heal the wounds of the war is doubled explicitly onto a national model in which the marriage of an American man to a Vietnamese woman will mark an end to the war. This plot is hardly original. The story of the Japanese war-brides promoted in *Life* and other popular magazines and fictionalized in films such as *Sayonara* (1957) were key moments in the reconstruction of American attitudes toward an occupied and domesticated Japan following World War II.[15] But the fictive example from *Going After Cacciato* of Paul Berlin and Sarkin Aung Wan facing each other across the Paris Peace tables suggests the failure of such personal models of national reconciliation following the Vietnam War. These failures are narrative and political, as Hayslip reminds us by setting the story of her failed relationships with American servicemen against her 1986 trip to Vietnam and the complicated conditions of traveling to a nation still unrecognized by the United States.

The most sensational and in many ways most telling of Hayslip's relationships in the United States is the last she describes. Cliff Parry is a self-professed rich veteran who promises to support the writing of Hayslip's memoir and to bankroll her fledgling East–West foundation to build clinics in Vietnam. Parry sets her up in a mansion and tearfully confesses his terrible past as an assassin in the Phoenix program. "The CIA was into a lot of bad shit in those days—drugs, gun-running, white slavery, you name it. Hell, one time another agent waxed the Vietnamese girl I was shacked up with. We were supposed to avoid close contact with any Vietnamese nationals outside channels, so they killed her—slashed her pretty face from ear to ear, can you believe it? I was really pissed . . ." (291). Parry's stories about the war are unique in Hayslip's two memoirs, marked by the GI vernacular and obscenity which by the time she becomes involved with Parry in 1986 had become deeply familiar in American culture through movies, novels, and memoirs. Spoken in what has become the authentic, if increasingly cliched, vernacular of the vet, Parry's stories are in the end very likely fictions. Parry is revealed as a con man, who takes the house Hayslip owns and leaves her owing money on the mansion. Hayslip never knows if he even served in Vietnam. But the powerful narrative of the guilt-ridden, suffering veteran and forgiving Vietnamese woman, with its promise of national and personal reconciliation, proves as seductive to Hayslip as it is to Parry, who attempts suicide when his heartfelt masquerade is about to be revealed.

Other men with whom Hayslip becomes involved, such as her second husband Dennis, do suffer posttraumatic stress disorder and feelings of anger, betrayal, and guilt. But just as was true in Vietnam, Hayslip is fighting a decidedly different "war" from the men around her. Her struggle is for economic self-sufficiency and security. The relationship between heterosexuality and economics is far less determined in the United States. While relationships with men frequently cost Hayslip financially as well as emotionally, her economic status is not dependent upon such relationships in the way it ultimately seemed to be in the war zone. Hayslip finds she can earn more money than the men in her life can provide.

But the "good jobs" Hayslip finds in Southern California turn out to be no less tied to economics of war than when she is working for the U.S. military in Danang. At National Semi-Conductor, Hayslip notes, "[t]wo types of women worked on the assembly line—all Vietnamese. The first were *nha ngoi*—'tile roofed women'—who came from privileged families in Vietnam and left only because of the communist takeover. . . . The rest of us were *gai nha la*, or 'thatched roof girls': poor, uneducated farm girls who knew nothing of the city, or knew it only as housekeepers, tea-girls, or prostitutes" (153). The implications of this social division are complex. Hayslip at once testifies to the social divisions within Vietnam which shaped the war and to the American dream in which such divisions can be overcome. (She proceeds to describe how the *gai nha la* pool money to invest in businesses.) But these differences in Vietnamese station are leveled not simply by American business opportunities and "good jobs" but by the very "machines of war" which displaced these women in the first place. Hayslip is shocked when she learns that the work she had been doing on the assembly line at National Semi-Conductor is part of a Navy contract to build bomber systems. A friend tries to reassure her that with "no war on" the government will just sell the systems to Germany or Korea. Hayslip, however, remembers not only the bombs that fell on her village but the fierce Republic of Korea troops that had fought on the South Vietnamese side. In Vietnam the abstract logic of the global economy of the military industrial complex was made manifest. The connection between arms as commodities and as weapons is found not only in memories of battle but in present domestic space. Hayslip is "astonished to think that by accepting a job that was good for my family" she has become embroiled once again in the "machinery of war" (158).[16] Later, when she renews a relationship with a romantic American officer who had abandoned her in Vietnam, she is similarly stunned to realize that he plans to support them following retirement from the military by working as a private arms trader. Whether from the vantage point of Vietnam or the United States, from past or present, Hayslip comes to an astonishingly immediate realization that "the Pentagon begins at home."

If war breaches the sovereignty of the American home, the domestic crosses back into the war zone as well. When Hayslip returns to the Vietnam in *When Heaven and Earth Changed Places*, the U.N. Mission of the Socialist Republic of Vietnam gives her a short list of things that could be carried from America into Vietnam. "It did not read like a tourist's guidebook, but a shopping list for Sears: one bicycle, two radios, one sewing machine, one hundred yards of material, five cartons of cigarettes" (24). These conspicuously domestic items are what Hayslip must in the end "hump" to the economic "boonies" of Vietnam under U.S. embargo. Carried from one home to the other, the tools of domesticity and a peacetime economy are rendered gender neutral by the ravages of a long fought war and an ill acknowledged peace. Tim O'Brien's story "The Things They Carried," which names the collection in which "The Sweetheart of the Song Tra Bong" appears, enumerates in stunning detail the things American soldiers hump—military gear, personal items, hopes, fears, dreams, fantasies; everything, in short, except what Hayslip carries home: the commonplace items of American domesticity which are needed to rebuild Vietnam.

LE LY HAYSLIP'S MEMOIR HAS BECOME A MUCH READ CORrective to American narratives of the war. Her story demonstrates clearly how gendered the gaps in those narratives are, even, or especially, the gaps determined by national, ideological, and racial difference. Larry Heinemann's *Paco's Story* also makes horrifically present the constitutive absences of O'Brien's "Sweetheart": rape, the Vietnamese woman, feminine betrayal, and, most especially, the vernacular description of war as sexuality. *Paco's Story* critically foregrounds the classic construction of woman as the enemy in both a graphically described rape of a female Viet Cong soldier and the literally physical proximity of the memory of rape to the desire for "home" signified, and ultimately betrayed, by a white American woman. Such patterns of misogyny, both unconscious and critically self-conscious, are a prominent feature of representations of the war, as critics such as Kali Tal, Jacqueline Lawson, Cindy Fuchs, and Jeffords have documented.[17] What distinguishes Heinemann's treatment of this all too common idea is the gendering of memory and its narration and the complex play of racial, class, and sexual difference regulated by and through gender in this memory.

Paco's Story posits a narrator and a reader with identities both specific and collective. The narrator is a ghost, really the collective ghosts, of those who died at Fire Base Henriette when an American officer calls in a massive artillery strike on his own position during an intense battle with the NVA, killing everyone but Paco. Paco's story is spoken out of an apocalyptic scene of friendly fire.[18] The narrating ghost is an insider, a veteran, a speaker of the relentlessly masculine language of the war that Michael Herr captured so well. But unlike Herr, Heinemann's narrator does not universalize a "you," constructing a reader in his own image endowed with the same experiences, reactions, and assumptions. Heinemann's narrator tells his story to a figure named "James," a marker which, as Heinemann suggests in the "Foreword: A Word to the Reader," denotes not only gender but class and, by implication, race.

> The "James" comes from the custom of street folks engaging total strangers by calling them "Jim" or "Jack" or sometimes "Jake" in a jivy sort of way—if you were looking for directions or exact change for the bus or a light for your smoke, say. But since Paco's story requires language more formal than street-corner patois, I thought "James" more apropos. I also had in mind the tongue-in-cheek punch line "Home James."[19]

"James" marks a site of difference, a naming of strangers, which Herr himself invokes in the story of Mayhew and Day Tripper. In Herr's usage, Heinemann's "custom of street folks" is read as a marker of racial difference. As I argued in the last chapter, by calling Mayhew "Jim," Day Tripper names him as white, attempting to invoke the racial gulf which presumably would divide them in the United States. In his portrait of Mayhew and Day Tripper, Herr explicitly presents the way in which the issue of class in American discourse is most often translated into racial terms, but the narrative contract between Herr and the reader is based on white middle-class models that marks an assumed difference from the Mayhews of this world. The discourse enacted in *Paco's Story* is class bound: a shared working-class identity that becomes crucial in the rape scene and more generally in deployment of the embodied, sexualized language of the war.

"Humping" in particular is glossed as a term of labor.

> A body never gets used to humping, James. When the word comes, you saddle up your rucksack on your back, take a deep breath and set your jaw good and tight, then lean a little forward, as though you're walking into a stiff and blunt nor'easter, and begin by putting one foot in front of the other. After a good little while you've got two sharp pains as straight as a die from your shoulders to your kidneys but there's nothing else to do for it but grit your teeth a little harder and keep humping. (9)

The pain of humping is the same pain Paco's friend Gallagher remembers pervading his father's body after a day's work driving a Chicago city bus. At times "this look of pale and exhausted astonishment would come over [the father], like he just woke up and couldn't bring himself to believe where he was"; the "same look as come over that poor fuckin' fool . . . when he drew himself out of that bunker and took a good long look at what was left of his arm" (124). Heinemann explicitly links the alienating labor of working-class existence with the radical alienation of war's traumatic power to, in Elaine Scarry's words, "alter (to burn, to blast, to shell, to cut) human flesh."[20]

The soldier may "hump the boonies," but his body will memorialize that humping as trauma. The soldier's body humps, but it is also humped.

If Gallagher's father beat his own embodied feelings of oppression onto his sons with a belt, Gallagher seeks to reclaim the active mastery promised by humping the boonies through rape. The rape of the female Viet Cong soldier foregrounds the gendered understanding of war's reality that must be circumvented in order for Mary Ann to hump the boonies in "Sweetheart." The ability of a woman to fulfill the soldier's role is proven by the two American soldiers killed by the woman who is recognized as "hardcore VC." The punishment enacted upon her body, in turn, seeks to reaffirm the gendered difference of American men's privileged claim to the role of soldier (175). The memory of the rape, which is narrated over eight pages, begins with the image of Gallagher dragging the woman prisoner by the hair to "this brick-and-stucco hooch off to the side" (175). The recognition of his intention is immediate and many of the men follow: "there's a bunch of guys in that company want a piece of *that* gook" (emphasis in original; 175). Although the language of this line carries no specific gender inflection, her femaleness shapes the intonation and meaning expressed in the underlining of "that" and in "piece." The foregrounding of gender does not deny the significance of the racial marking of the violence to her body. In effect, it underscores the American presumption that the enemy will be racialized, a presumption encoded in the word "gook" and its historical reach back to the war in the Philippines.[21] The revenge to be enacted here is intensified by the gendering of racial Otherness, promising it will be more violent than any knowledge of her abstractly as the enemy, or immediately as the one who killed two of their buddies, could elicit. She is "*that* gook" because she is a woman.

This brutal but fairly familiar scene refers next to the woman's terrified reaction: "And the whole time the girl looked at [Gallagher's] red and black tattoo out of the corners of her eyes like a fretted, hysterical dog" (175). The narrator continues, "She could not see much because of the way Gallagher had her by the hair" (176). Left at this point, the woman's fear and the horrific restriction of her point of view serve only to reinforce the ritual of bonding and mastery which gang rape constitutes. The dragon tattoo is in many ways an overdetermined sign of this masculine power which Gallagher and the others are about to rewrite on the woman's body. But the history of Gallagher's "Bangkok R&R tattoo" complicates this assumption of gender and racial difference. The tattoo is first of all a marker of an enlisted man's working-class identity displayed in sharp contrast to the captain's West Point ring or the lieutenant's Dartmouth degree—the lieutenant who literally turns his back on the rape and his men. Paco and the other men are fascinated by Gallagher's tattoo: "a goddam work of art, everyone said, a regular fucking masterpiece" (174). The tattoo figures a shared and deeply embodied sense of identity; it signifies the body that "humps." The dragon, however, also denotes "the boonies" as it testifies to the long history of the

American military presence in the Pacific and the Orientalist fantasies (and cottage industries) it has spawned. Whatever power such a self-identifying gesture might promise, however, is subject to question even as a confirmation of heterosexual masculinity; the tattoo parlor is part of a "Bangkok fag whorehouse that caters to guys with a tattoo fetish" (135). "What the fuck do you think I am," Gallagher protests when the old man has four male prostitutes model their art for him (135). Gallagher wants to claim a self-evident masculine identity, to write it indelibly on his body, but the setting suggests that all identities are subject to negotiation and even reversal. The body which humps can also, in turn, potentially be humped, not only in terms of class and labor but of gender and sexuality as well.

The narration makes this point manifest when it halts the story of the rape to reconsider the violent constriction of the woman's point of view.

> (Take your hand, James, and reach around the top of your head, grab as much hair as you can grab in one hand and *yank*, then press that arm tight against the side of your head and look over, hard, at your arm out of the corners of your eyes. That's as much of Gallagher's arm as the girl saw.) (176)

Here the gendering of narrator and reader as specifically male is used to foreground what usually goes without saying. The narrator stops his story with a parenthetical time out and calls on the reader to enact the role he has not been playing in the telling of the story, to literally manipulate his body into an approximation of the woman's point of view. But James is asked to become Gallagher as well as the woman, grabbing and yanking his own hair, further disrupting the passive identification that allows the reader to condemn the events being narrated even as he experiences the textual pleasure of suspense and fulfillment. This narrative self-consciousness opens the grounds for a gendered critique of the gendering of narrative that allows a space for women readers, as both agents and narrative possibilities, which is foreclosed by Herr's presumption of a heterosexual, male reader: "you."

Heinemann presses the terms of this masculine presumption even further with a second narrative interruption. "(If the zip had been a man, we would have not bothered with the motherfucker, you understand that don't you?" (176). This parenthetical aside continues for nearly two pages, describing what would have happened to a man, how they would have beaten him and then cut his throat. The description is every bit as detailed and graphic as that of the rape and the language is just as sexual.

> —the zip's eyes that big and his poor little asshole squeezed tighter than a four-inch wad of double sawbucks. The cocksucker would have been pounded on till his face was beat to shit; till our arms were tired— "Anybody else want a poke at him?" (176–177)

Heinemann implicitly invokes the possibility of male rape here: "asshole," "cocksucker," "poke," reminding the reader that it is not impossible to humiliate and torture a man in the same terms the woman faces. But it is "understood" between the men, between the narrator and James, that this will not happen. It is the female body that has been culturally demarcated as the proper ground for the vicious enactment of collective male power and identity. Male rape inevitably entails the possibility that the master can himself be mastered in terms typically denied in the heterosexual presumption of gendered domination. "You've got to understand, James," the narrator repeats at the end of the aside, "if that zip had been a man we would have punched on him, then killed him right then and there and left him for dead" (177). James, the male reader, inevitably does understand. The cultural codes of gender are very clear on this point, so clear that, again, it traditionally goes without saying. The narrator's insistence that "you've got to understand" is an imperative to go beyond the presumption that men only rape women and to consider the meanings entailed and suppressed by this fact.

Only after these long asides does the narrative reach the point at which Gallagher gets the woman into the hootch and the expected brutality begins. Unlike the "Eurasian angel," the female sniper killed by the lusthog squad in *The Short-Timers*, this woman does not symbolize the ideal object of Western male desire. Her body is not described as female in any usual sense; breasts, buttocks, pubic hair go unmentioned. "She was nothing much to look at" is the only comment, with no specific illustration even as insult (177). But look Paco does as the men prepare each other before her bound, bent-over body.

> There was considerable jostling and arm punching, jawing and grab-ass back and forth and everybody formed a rough line, so just for that moment Paco got to stand there and take a long look. A peasant girl, not more than fourteen, say, or sixteen. And by the look of her back she had worked, *hard*, every day of her life. She was not beefy, though. None of the Viets were big, but then sharecropping doesn't tend to turn out strapping-big hale-and-hearty offspring. Ask someone who knows shit from shit and Shinola about farming, James, and he will tell you that sharecropping is a long, hard way to get down to business and get some. (179)

What Paco reads on her body is not gender but class. The look of her back echoes the look and feel of his own, riddled with shrapnel scars from the war, aching and tired from his backbreaking work at the diner and that of Gallagher's father whose "bend in the back" is the reward of a lifetime's labor (124). Paco does not make this connection, but "James" should, especially if he is, in fact, from the narrator's neighborhood as described in Heinemann's "Note to the Reader." The toll Paco's labor takes on his body is described over and again. The difference which is enacted as gender denies the potential commonality formed by a lifetime of labor for someone else's gain: "sharecropping sucks . . . you can't spend your life sharing the crop with *yourself* much less split it between you and the Man" (179). Herr's communal male "you" here defines a shared working-class experience which does not have to be male at all.

This prospect of a shared world is destroyed by the remaking of gender through rape. The woman's back is rewritten when Gallagher "commenced to fuck her, hard, pressing his big meaty hand into the middle of her back" (180). The red mark Gallagher first makes on the woman's back is the part of her body Paco sees as he remembers raping her himself, "remembers feeling her whole body pucker down" (180). As the others take their turns, Paco is held "fascinated by the red welt in the middle of her back" (182). The welt is the mark of gender difference as created by the violent performance of masculinity. She is no longer a soldier or sharecropper, identities Paco can share, but the enemy as female, irreducibly other and violently specified as "*that* gook."

While I have argued that the narrative framing of the rape calls these negotiations and impositions of gender identity into consciousness, the framing of the narrative present in which Paco remembers the scene is even more complex and troubling. The memory of the rape comes to Paco as he lies on his bed listening to Cathy, a student at the local teacher's college, having sex with a boyfriend next door. Paco "is furiously jealous—Marty-boy's clean haircut and the undulating smoothness of his back (not a mark on the son-of-a-bitch, James)" (172). Out of this jealousy comes desire. Paco "has the incredible, shivering urge to sneak into Cathy's room and stalk up behind Marty-boy, grab him by the hips and yank him off," and to take his place in Cathy's bed and in her body. "He imagines, too, that he slides into her as easily as a warm, clean hand slips into a greased glove, that she whimpers grotesquely, encircling him to her like warm covers" (173). Although in one sense Paco's fantasy is rape in its denial of Cathy's conscious volition, the purpose seems less to subdue or punish Cathy than to become like Marty-boy with the smooth, scarless, undulating back. The iconography here is significantly masturbatory; Paco's penis as well as his back is covered in scars. The smooth skin, "warm hand," and "greased glove" all suggest masturbation more than intercourse and thus underline his continued isolation and alienation.

That woman is the prescribed release for this solitary existence and its physical and mental anguish is made explicitly clear.

> He's just a man like the rest of us, James, who wants to fuck away the pain and redeem his body. By fucking he wants to ameliorate the stinging ache of those dozens and dozens of swirled-up and curled-round, purple scars, looking like so many sleeping snakes and piles of ruined coins. He wants to discover a livable peace—as if he's come

upon a path in a vast evergreen woods, come upon a comfortable cabin as solid as a castle keep, and approached, calling, "Hello the house," been welcomed in, given a hot and filling dinner, then shown a bed in the attic (a pallet of sweet dry grass and slim cedar shavings) and fallen asleep. (173–174)

Woman becomes romantic refuge here, the redemptive green world reached through sex where the war is forgotten and the soldier's body healed. Heinemann's livable peace is deeply connected to Hemingway's "separate peace," but woman is significantly disembodied in this construction. Male desire mythifies the female body into a masculine version of domesticity—the cabin in the woods, the castle keep—not only a place where the veteran belongs but one that belongs to the veteran. Woman becomes another version of Hemingway's "clean well-lighted place." The crucial Hemingway connection, however, is to *A Farewell to Arms*, one of the most powerful twentieth-century constructions of woman's role in the soldier's attempt to escape war. Catherine Barkley represents the human equivalent of Switzerland, a place beyond war, in short, "home." Catherine gives herself completely to Frederic Henry. "There isn't any me," she tells him, "I'm you. Don't make up a separate me."[22] Their story is, of course, tragic; she is violently reembodied through childbirth and a slow, painful death, but she remains to the end self-sacrificing. Heinemann's fairy tale imagery likewise acknowledges the unreachable nature of such a romantic refuge, but at the same time it reinscribes this very impossibility as a never-ending quest, much like another classic imagining of the landscape of the eternal feminine, the "fresh green breast of the new world" held out at the end of *The Great Gatsby*.

The intrusion of the memory of raping the Vietnamese woman undermines this fantasy at every level. It violently refigures the innocence claimed for the desire to "fuck the pain away." Most important, it denies the conception of women as separate from war, marking instead the female body as the figurative and literal battleground. The narrative proximity of "wish-fulfillment and realism, . . . desire and history" outlined by Jameson is exactly what romance traditionally seeks to avoid.[23] In this scene "desire and history" are brought dangerously close together, both in narrative terms as Paco's desire to "come home" through a woman carries him back to the war as rape and because of the physical proximity of Paco to Marty-boy and Cathy. Lying on his bed, Paco "can practically slide his hand and arm out his windowsill, over the nicotine burns and coffee cup rings, lean out a little and fingertip-touch the top of her hair" (172). But rather than reaching out to Cathy, Paco's body registers the memory of the rape: "He winces and squirms; his whole body jerks, but he cannot choose but remember" (174). The masturbatory gestures of his fantasy about crossing the distance to Cathy's room is violently refigured (174). The landscape of home, identified as the female body, is overlaid with the landscape of war, which is also identified as the female body. The bifurcation of female presence and absence which structures the separate spheres of home and war does not utterly collapse; the Vietnamese woman and Cathy are not the same, nor is the violence of their inscriptions commensurate, but they are no longer the opposites demanded by the logic of humping the boonies.[24] The absolute alterity of the boonies is severely compromised. Coming home Paco lands in the small town of *Boone,* Texas—its name a marker of both the continuing homage to the figure of Daniel Boone, the solitary hunter ever in advance of the feminized home, and of the town's liminal status as the "boondocks" of American culture.

The most complex sign of this radical proximity between home and war, male and female, desire and history is discovered the next night when Paco sneaks into Cathy's room and reads her diary. She tells of her initial attraction to Paco, which later turns to revulsion. Then he comes across an entry about a dream in which she has sex with Paco and then he sits on her and "peels off his scars as if they were a mask" and begins to lay them across her skin; "he lays them across my breasts and belly—tingling and burning—lays them in my hair, wrapping them around my head, like a skull cap. And where each scar touches me, I feel the suffocating burn, hear the scream" (209). Cathy's dream combines the imagery of the rape with that the apocalyptic battle that Paco alone survives. Paco's desire to "fuck away his pain" becomes literally the desire to hand over that pain and his memories—his scars—to her.

Susan Jeffords sees Cathy's dream as "a record of the non-veteran's inability to understand or feel the pain of those who fought in the war," a failure which makes them complicit in the war's guilt. Jeffords quite rightly notes that "[f]or Heinemann, rape is the figure for the violence of the war." But, she continues, "in a novel in which everyone is guilty, rape loses its gendered force and seems to achieve status as a collective metaphor of American involvement in Vietnam."[25] In the explicit gendering of the narrative, however, Heinemann foregrounds "rape's gendered force." Cathy's dream is less an admission of her guilt than a violent reaction to her gendered role as victim and/or refuge in the narrative of war. Her diary is a female counterpoint to the masculinized ghost/James address of the rest of the novel. She is superficial, immature, narcissistic, and fickle—everything, in short, that the classic "good woman" who would save the soul-sick veteran is not. Rejecting self-sacrifice, she refuses to put her body between Paco and his pain.

The power of this refusal is deepened by Cathy's difference from two other characters who emblematize the more traditional figure of the war narrative's good woman. The first is a very literal enactment of the Catherine Barkley ideal, a nurse in the field hospital where Paco's terrible wounds are first treated. "The nurse went about her work with that calm and soothing patience some women have who understand full well the need for physical kindness and its effect" (54). Smelling of Ivory soap, the nurse cleans and soothes and, not incidentally, excites Paco's body. His first bath gives Paco a deeply embarrassing erection—"the woman a nurse, a stranger after all, an officer, for Christ's sake!"—which the nurse "discourages" with professional cool (54). But this angelic professionalism evolves into a wet dream when, on his last night at the field hospital, the nurse "wiped her hands of soap and encouraged an erection" (55). "A good long time she masturbated him, sucking languorously, and soon enough he felt the pause and urge of terrific inevitability" (56). After his climax, "she cleaned him up and dusted him with talc" (56). She comes to Paco in a morphine haze and is quite literally too good to be true; a figure, like Catherine Barkley, for whom there "isn't any me," only the power to reassure the soldier of his integrity, virility, and physical wholeness.

Paco's first concern about the nurse's officer status fades rapidly under the power of her "swirling tongue" and "warm fingertips," but the second good woman of the novel suggests that class actually plays a significant part in this desire for a woman who could heal the soldier's traumatized body and mind (56). Like the nurse, Betsy Sherburne appears only as a cameo figure. She is sitting in the diner when Paco first comes in and is hired as a dishwasher. The wild rich girl of this small Texas town, Betsy has gotten caught in a thunderstorm with the top down on her Jaguar and runs into the diner soaking wet, clothes clinging to her. "Snap!" the narrator tells us, "just that quickly Betsy has never been more beautiful than she is right now and never will be so again" (99). When Paco makes his entrance at her moment of singular physical perfection, it is the Hollywood cue that they are made for each other. Betsy sees Paco as well and fantasizes about taking him to bed. It is a coupling that promises a very happy ending. Her beauty would redeem his scars and her Jaguar would transform his drifting into play, just as the money it promises would release his body from menial and painful labor. Paco, in turn, would rescue her from a world of meaningless privilege, linking her to the embodied "reality" signified by both his class and veteran status. Betsy "sees herself drawing on his scars as if they were Braille, as if each scar had its own story" (101). But the novel is not a movie, however much energy Heinemann has invested in setting such a scene. Paco and Betsy never act on their attraction.

Unlike Betsy or the nurse, Cathy does not occupy a position of such clear privilege. Her father is an architect, but the affluence this might suggest is undermined by her more visible immersion in the same materially bound world in which Paco lives. She is, in fact, his next-door neighbor, living in her aunt and uncle's shabby hotel while attending Wynadote's Teacher's College. Her "threadbare underwear," costume jewelry, and pink talc are as different in kind from Betsy's expensively casual appearance as they are from the nurse's uniform. Cathy is ambitious and self-protective; she is, in short, "on the make" in precisely the overlapping terms of sexuality and material gain the term implies. She uses her body to manipulate the consuming male desire she recognizes all around her. In her diary she writes:

All those guys staring at me. The men teachers, too. Makes me feel like a piece of meat. When I walk across the campus what is it they imagine under the ski jacket and sweater, not to mention the armful of books, but I figure I've got the pick of this litter. And his name is Martin Hubbard. He stares plenty hard, too, but he's the one who'll be getting an eyeful soon enough.

Marty-boy, Lynette calls him. But she doesn't fuck, so she's not any competition. (201)

Rather than giving her body to a man, Cathy trades on the commodification of her body, which she sees enacted irregardless of the part she plays, good girl or bad, in that economy. Paco "laughs to himself" as he reads this, presumably feeling one up on Marty-boy at last, but at the same time "his groin stirs," marking the irrelevance of Cathy's motives to her desirability (201). Marty-boy gets his "eyeful" and in return, Cathy writes, "he'll do anything I ask" (204). Cathy recognizes sex as a system of competitive, economic exchange. Her dream of Paco's laying of his scars onto her body is an acknowledgment of the particular exchange of bodies which defines the coming home narrative. Where Betsy, the figure of redemptive possibility, dreams of reading Paco's scars, Cathy writes her own desires and her fears (101). Her diary shows her to be literally self-centered and as such it places her in radical opposition to the role traditionally scripted for women by war.

Reading Cathy's nightmare, Paco "feels as if he's met his wraith," a deeply suggestive image in a novel narrated by ghosts (209). It drives him from the town, back out on the road, but not because the dream marks Cathy's rejection of Paco's desire; rather, it renarrates from the woman's perspective the meaning of coming home. What haunts Paco finally and most unalterably is not his wounds or her rejection but the memory of the rape. It literally stands between Paco and the traditional narrative of coming home. Where Susan Jeffords argues that Paco is constructed as a victim just like the Vietnamese woman, a body raped by the war, it is precisely the difference of her rape which compromises the carefully orchestrated gendering of going to war and coming home.[26] After Gallagher kills the woman, the ghosts confess, "[w]e looked at her and at ourselves . . . and knew that this was a moment of evil and that we would never live the same again" (184). The moral language of "evil" enforces a sense of responsibility unexplainable by circumstance. If, in general terms, the representation of the rape is emblematic of Heinemann's drive toward an embodied realism that seeks to destroy the comfortable images of familiar war stories, it is also a deliberate disruption of the gendered boundaries of those stories.

IN *PACO'S STORY*, WOMEN FRAME THE VETERAN'S MEMORY, pain, and guilt. Bobbie Ann Mason's *In Country* reverses this traditional structure. If the metaphorical relationship between sexuality and war typified by "humping the boonies" regulates, from a masculine perspective, women's presence and absence in war narrative, *In Country* rethinks this relationship through the desires, possibilities, and fears defined by female sexuality. Mason's protagonist, 18-year-old Samantha Hughes, attempts both of the female roles suggested by the stories of O'Brien and Heinemann: humping the boonies herself and having sex with a veteran. Both fail as attempts to transcend difference, but at the same time her experience presents the possibility of thinking through difference in less exclusionary terms. Framed as a road trip from her small Kentucky town of Hopewell to the Vietnam Veterans Memorial in Washington, DC, Sam's quest moves toward a meeting, if not a reconciliation, of daughter and father, woman and war, past and present, personal and public memory, local and national. But unlike many of the spectacles of "healing" associated with "The Wall," *In Country* seeks to map this movement through the 1960s rather than by "putting the past behind us."

This historical context is crucial to the novel's treatment of the Vietnam War as both personal and public memory. Part II of *In Country* begins by locating Sam's interest in the war within a particular cultural moment.

> It was the summer of Michael Jackson's *Victory* tour and the Bruce Springsteen *Born in the U.S.A.* tour, neither of which Sam got to go to. At her graduation, the commencement speaker, a Methodist minister, had preached about keeping the country strong, stressing sacrifice. He made Sam nervous. She started thinking about war, and it stayed on her mind all summer. (23)[27]

Coming of age in 1984, the Vietnam War is figured in the novel quite literally as Sam's birthright. Sam's graduation not coincidentally figures her uncomfortable relation to the past and the future in a present marked by the resurgence of traditional patriotism associated with Ronald Reagan's reelection. If there is a significant difference in style and content, especially to Sam, between popular music and the minister, together they testify to the renewed popularity of nationalistic cultural terms—terms which directly ("Born in the U.S.A."), indirectly (the minister), or associatively ("Victory") reference the war. Images of the military, from Jeeps and fatigues to video games such as Space Invaders, are fashionable once again. These icons are presented with no apparent connection to the history of the war in Vietnam, the protest against it, or the continuing struggle of veterans with its legacy, a legacy represented in the novel by Agent Orange. But contextualized by Sam's search for connections to Vietnam and the 1960s more generally, such mythologized icons are suggestively historicized. Sam lives in a kind of cultural double time: playing her mother's records by the Kinks and the Doors alongside MTV, driving a VW and watching cable television, smoking dope and going to the mall, obsessed by a "new" Beatles song played on the radio and watching remakes of horror movies. But as a deeply intuitive critic of nostalgia, Sam interrogates rather than accepts such connections.

In this milieu it seems almost inevitable that Sam will focus her curiosity on the Vietnam War, but her relationship to the war is immediate and personal as well. Sam is quite literally a war baby, conceived during the one month of marriage before her father was sent to Vietnam and born a month after her father returned in a body bag. But her search to understand this connection runs immediately into the veteran's claim to exclusive knowledge of the war and the "protective" desire to keep Sam from knowing too much. Again and again, when Sam asks about the war she is told, "Don't think about it," "It doesn't concern you," "hush"—enforcing upon her the passive female role of war narrative. Threatened by her questions, Sam's uncle Emmett tells her at a key moment, "Women weren't over there . . . so they can't really understand" (107). But Sam refuses to accept this exclusion. "Well, Mom took care of you all those years, and you think she didn't understand? . . . And what about me? I feel like there's a big conspiracy against me. Like something the CIA would be in on" (107). She goes on to point out that women did serve in Vietnam as nurses, but her real point of contention is that the war exists at home as well, and that women are made to be part of something they are not allowed to "know." The pervasiveness of this conspiracy is upheld by the fact that it is not just Emmett or the veterans who try to quiet her questions but her mother, her boyfriend, and her grandparents. The difficulty of either defining or denying the relation of women to war structures the novel. As much as *In Country* has been recognized as a novel about the Vietnam War, it is also insistently a novel about female sexuality which returns again and again to embodied and politicized particulars: birth control pills, pregnancy, abortion, motherhood. Sam must think through both what the war means and what it means to be a woman at the precise historical moment in which the 1960s have become "the past."

The presence of the 1960s in the Reagan-era 1980s is marked ironically within the novel. As Sam's mother Irene tells her, "the sixties never hit Hopewell" (234). Irene is actually quoting her brother Emmett, who returned from Vietnam radically disillusioned yet unable to register any effective protest against the war in Hopewell where the patterns of everyday life seem unchanged by the social revolutions of the time. He goes to California, becomes a hippie, and returns with a bus full of "freaks," but his fundamental challenge to the society that sent him to Vietnam goes largely unnoticed. Most conspicuously, when he and some friends fly a Viet Cong flag from the clock tower atop city hall, they are arrested for trespassing, but no one recognizes the flag. For Irene, however, Hopewell's imperviousness to the social protest of the 1960s has less to do with the war than with her desire to escape from the past, from home, from family, from, in essence, traditional women's roles, and as such is implicitly tied to the women's movement.

Women's liberation is never mentioned directly in the novel. It is a far more unmentionable topic in Hopewell than the war which can be discussed over dinner alongside wedding plans. But Irene's attempts to tell Sam about the 1960s, her father, and the war are marked by a continual slide between references to the war and women's roles. Living now in Lexington, with a new husband and baby, Irene is at continual loggerheads with Sam: Irene wants Sam to come to Lexington and go to the University of Kentucky; Sam wants to enlist Irene in her excavation of the past.

> "You *have* to go to college, Sam. Women can do anything they want now, just about."
> "You just want me to get out of Hopewell and forget about Emmett, the same way you want me to forget about my Daddy," Sam blurted out. "You want to pretend the whole Vietnam War never existed, like you want to protect me from something. I'm not a baby." She glanced at the baby, who was tugging away obliviously. (167)

Arguing across Irene's literal baby, nursing at her breast, Irene offers Sam some details about the past but finally holds up the baby itself as the answer to Sam's questions about the war and the past.

> "Just look at her. I was nineteen, not much older than you. Imagine yourself with this little baby. How would you handle it? But I can't live in the past. It was all such a stupid waste. There's nothing to remember." (168)

It is unclear whether the "stupid waste" is the war or having a baby at 19, the loss of family or the burden of family. Irene refuses to sentimentalize the past for Sam, to reassure her that as a baby Sam was worth every price paid by her mother and father. Yet no resentment toward Sam is involved. Irene speaks to Sam as a woman rather than as her child. Where Sam wants to demystify war, Irene seeks to demystify motherhood. Again and again in the novel, questions about one lead to answers about the other. For Irene the Pentagon truly does begin at home.

For Irene home is also quite literally the "boonies." She identifies her own sense of entrapment with place more than with roles. "God it took me forever to get out of this place," she tells Sam, referring to both Hopewell and the house Sam and Emmett now live in but Irene owns. Irene had moved to Lexington once before, with a hippie named Bob, but returned because "we had the house and they still wanted me at the old job, and everybody was mad at me. And I felt guilty because I felt I owed something to Emmett because he'd gone over there for my sake" (171). In a sense, Irene could not leave Hopewell. The expectations of her family and the community regarding her place are unchangeable; job, house and her roles as daughter and sister, remain unchanged, waiting, expecting, demanding her return. In large part this reflects Hopewell as the social boonies, unaccepting of the changes in mores which were supposed to have revolutionized American society in the 1960s. Irene's sense of debt to Emmett marks her place in war narrative as well, to keep the home that will mark the soldier's return from the boonies. But Emmett's struggles with posttraumatic stress disorder represent his own inability to fully come home. Irene cannot make it happen for him and after years she finally does move away, unwilling to be forever responsible for her brother.

That marriage and a child were finally the means of Irene's escape from Hopewell is not necessarily ironic. When Irene discovered she was pregnant, "she ran [Sam] right off to the doctor and got birth-control pills for [her.] She didn't even ask" (43). Even though she delights in her baby, much to Sam's disgust, she rejects the idea that her daughter will follow in her footsteps, telling Sam that "a woman can do anything." The pill is the crucial marker of this possibility for both Irene and Sam, protecting her from the accidental pregnancy which plots her friend Dawn into early marriage and motherhood. For Irene the pill is less a marker of the sexual revolution, a social shift which has taken place to some degree in Hopewell by the 1980s, than of women's liberation and its legacy's insistence on "choice."

Again and again in the novel, the war is linked to images of female sexuality and Sam's resistance to traditional women's roles. Dawn's pregnancy precipitates many of the most pointed of these connections.

> Hopewell was having Flag Days. . . . All the flags flying from the stores that week made Sam preoccupied with the Vietcong flag Emmett had flown from the clock tower years before. She felt like flying a Vietcong flag herself. She was feeling the delayed stress of the Vietnam War. It was her inheritance. It was her version of Dawn's trouble. The pregnancy test had turned out positive—the test strip turned pale pink. Dawn was afraid to tell Ken. (89)

Sam's desire to protest is named "the Vietnam War," but Dawn's very female "trouble" is more than a metaphor for Sam's inheritance. At stake are the very connections which the women's movement attempted to assert in the 1960s between war and gender, public and private spheres. Hopewell's "Flag Days" may not be Arlington National Cemetery, but it pledges allegiance to a pervasive if more nebulously defined national tradition that entails both war and childbearing—one Sam seeks to resist. In this way the war becomes a metaphor for her embattled desire to claim control over her own life and body. "Since Dawn got pregnant, Sam had been feeling that if she didn't watch her step, her whole life could be ruined by some mischance, some stupid surprise, like sniper fire" (184).

When Dawn becomes pregnant, she is faced with a "choice" not unlike that which sent Sam's father off to war 18 years before. Girls don't go to war and boys don't get pregnant, but each event constitutes a rite of passage in which children become adults by conforming to culturally prescribed gender roles, be it as soldier or wife and mother. At this level, however, while childbearing and combat are both liminal experiences which involve the crossing of boundaries, these boundaries are still mutually exclusive, enforcing the basic gender distinction that women nurture and men kill.[28] When Sam urges Dawn to have an abortion, this difference collapses. The more conventional Dawn won't consider abortion; her own mother died soon after Dawn was born, due to the pregnancy that destroyed her health. Dawn feels compelled to bear this child even at personal sacrifice. Dawn's reaction to the word abortion, "I'll pretend I didn't hear that" (141), parallels Sam's grandmother's reaction when Sam asks if she could go back in time, would she tell her son not to go to Vietnam. Mamaw exclaims, "Oh, Sam. . . . People don't have choices like that" (197). Dawn and Mamaw accept, indeed take comfort in, a naturalized social order which binds change and continuity through generation. Dawn is tired of "playing Mommy," taking care of her father and brothers, and sees marriage and becoming an actual "mommy" as a route of escape. Sam sees only the repetition of the past. "She'll be like my mother, stuck in this town, raising a kid" (187). Mawmaw embraces this repetition, consoling herself with Sam, the "miracle baby" who replaced the lost son, Dwayne. Fighting wars and having babies are figured as deeply entwined historical inevitabilities. Sam, like her mother, insists on "choice," affirming the implicit but profound connection to the ideas of women's liberation.

Dawn and Sam call themselves the "baddest girls in Hopewell," each growing up wild in one-parent households. The death of Dawn's mother from childbirth and Sam's father in war are culturally parallel. But unlike Dawn, Sam uses her socially marginal position as a "bad girl" to rebel against the gendered cultural constructions of childbirth and war. Sam doubly rejects this heritage of gender roles by advocating abortion, and thus rejecting compulsory motherhood, and by her insistent desire to learn what the war was like, further rejecting the limits placed on female experience and understanding.

Sam's rebellious sexuality and desire for knowledge of the war merge in the novel's most profoundly ambiguous and troubling image: dead babies. After her first mild flirtation with the veteran Tom and learning of Dawn's pregnancy,

> Sam dreamed she and Tom Hudson had a baby. In the evening, the baby had to be pureed in a food processor and kept in the freezer. It was the color of candied sweet potatoes. In the morning, when it thawed out, it was a baby again. In the dream, this was a happy arrangement, and no questions were asked. But then the dream woke her up, its horror rushing through her. (83)

Sam's dream unites the mythified oppositions described by William Broyles in his much quoted essay, "Why Men Love War."

> The love of war stems from the union, deep in the core of our being, between sex and destruction, beauty and horror, love and death. War may be the only way in which most men touch the mythic domains of our soul. It is, for men, at some terrible level the closest thing to what childbirth is for women: the initiation into the power of life and death.[29]

But where Broyles affirms a sense of elemental truth, a bodily passage into the timeless "mythic domains of our soul," Sam's dream responds to this cultural reification of the "terrible level" at which war and childbirth are joined as gender difference. In the dream, the common ground between childbearing and war becomes the terrible mutability of the human body which can be destroyed and reconstituted in endless cycles of birth and death. For Sam this cycle is not natural but constructs the terms in which her own life and body are written into a social order she struggles to resist. Sam herself replaced Dwayne, although not a perfect likeness—"Everybody expected a boy, of course, but we loved you just the same," her grandfather tells her (199). But the idea of literally taking his place, living on the farm, jiggling yet another baby on her knee, repulses her. In her father's combat diary the "[u]nreal thought. A Baby. My own flesh and blood" is his purpose in war (204). "It's all for [Irene] and the baby, or else why are we here?" (202). Sam's gestation becomes the social and cultural justification of historical cycles of violence and death, and, much more immediately, for keeping women at home.

Sam's peevish jealousy of her mother's new baby further feeds her morbid imagination.

> The baby was like a growth that had come loose, Sam thought—like a scab or a wart—and Irene carried it around with her in fascination, unable to part with it. Monkeys carried dead babies around like that. A friend of Emmett's knew a lot of dead-baby jokes, but Sam couldn't remember any she had heard. In Vietnam, mothers had carried their dead babies around with them until they began to rot. (164)

Here Sam's initial horror at the mutations of the female body in pregnancy gives way to a more profound appreciation of motherhood's truly ambivalent nature. As the extreme case of war makes vivid, mothers have no supernatural power to sustain the lives of their children—a truth Sam's own mother actively denies, snatching the *Newsweek* cover shot of a Vietnamese woman holding a dead child from Sam's hands and burning it. The cheap catharsis of dead-baby jokes and the quadriplegic jokes told on the local college radio station indirectly voice the cultural anxiety about veterans as either "baby killers" or castrated, unable to reproduce. But these ideas rebound on Sam as well. First, because of her association with Emmett; "There were a lot of stories floating around about Emmett. Emmett was the leading dope dealer in town. Emmett slept with his niece. Emmett lived off his sister. Emmett seduced high school girls. He had killed babies in Vietnam" (31). But also far more directly, out in the swamp Sam thinks, "Soldiers murdered babies. But women did too. They ripped their unborn babies out of themselves and flushed them away, squirming and bloody" (215). The most terrible acts of war carry their domestic double.

This doubling speaks to the logic at the heart of humping the boonies, separating women from war at the same time they are scripted within its narrative structure. Unlike *Paco's Story* or a number of other narratives, *In Country* does not divide the female presence between past and present, Vietnamese and American, battle and home. The only country of *In Country* is the United States; the boonies are the cultural boonies of smalltown Kentucky life. Sam does want to know what Vietnam was "really like," but within this narrative the only way to do so is to discover the war which has "come home." It is almost inevitable that Sam will attempt the traditional form for this quest by sleeping with a veteran. The mutual sexual attraction between Sam and the veteran Tom seems to offer her a way to cross this divide between herself and the war, promising the desired union of male and female, sexuality and war, past and present. But significantly, Mason reverses the metaphorization of war as sexuality; instead Vietnam becomes the metaphoric language for Sam's sexual discoveries. Leaving the veterans' dance with Tom, "She felt she was doing something intensely daring, like following the soldier on point" (124). At stake here is not any sense of "danger" represented by Tom as veteran but the unknown territory of "men" as opposed to boys her own age. "Men were a total mystery" to Sam (184).

Sam is also clearly seeking an authoritative source for evaluating the continual comparisons she draws between the war and her immediate surroundings—orange lights are like napalm, the patchwork quilt on Tom's bed stands in contrast to a soldier's poncho. As she tells Tom, Vietnam always seems like a postcard, an endlessly duplicated, generic image of palm trees and rice paddies. She wants to know what it was like to be there and Tom's body is marked by having been there. Sam wonders about the stiff way he holds his back and later in bed feels shrapnel under his skin; Tom's body seems to offer her a literally sensual text of the war. Sexual intimacy carries the promise of other forms of intimacy: a sharing of experience in which her questions will be answered. But the sexual is not simply a conduit to war; Sam has also used her interest in the war as a way "to go after Tom," an adventure motivated by her own sexual desires (103).

But when Tom proves to be impotent, a psychological wound secretly carried from Vietnam, sex becomes yet another symbol of the way in which the experience of war seems irrevocably to divide men and women. The most obvious source for Mason's Tom is Hemingway's Jake Barnes. As Sandra

Gilbert has argued, the modernist literature that emerged from World War I describes again and again the wounded, symbolically if not literally, emasculated man who returns from the war to confront women empowered, set free by the social dislocations wrought by the Great War. Male rage against the war turns against the female who apparently reaps its benefits. Hemingway's Brett Ashley becomes in Gilbert's words "a kind of monstrous anti-fertility goddess to whose powers the impotent bodies of men had ceaselessly been offered up."[30] Although many feminist critics have challenged Gilbert's contention that women actually did feel empowered by the destruction of men and masculinity in the war, her reading of *The Sun Also Rises* is a useful counterpoint to understanding Mason's purposes in rewriting this plot.[31]

Although Sam feels frustrated to the point of tears when confronted with Tom's impotency and his refusal to talk about it, it is true that the Vietnam War is in one sense a source of empowerment for her. It is the death of her father which gives her life the qualities she prizes most highly. As Sam's grandmother says to her,

> "I keep thinking about Dwayne and how everybody's life is different without him. If he had lived, he'd have a house down the road with Irene, and you would have grown up there, Sam, and I'd have knowed you a lot better, sugar. And you'd have some brothers and sisters."
>
> Sam shudders at the idea of growing up on a farm, doing chores and never getting to go to town. (13)

Sam clutches at the idea that her father might have resisted such a traditional role, as Emmett has done, but at her grandparents' farm she pictures her father there, "discussing blue mold and whether to take risks on wheat prices" just like her grandfather. The legacy demands in turn that her mother "wouldn't have gone to Lexington" and that Sam herself would by now be "jiggling a baby on her knee" (195). Her father's death precipitates her mother's attempt to break away from "home," an overlapping inscription of place and gender roles. In this sense, Sam's quest is less for the absent father than to become the daughter of the mother Irene becomes after Dwayne's death.

Mason avoids the extreme logic of the oppositions Gilbert describes between men and women, combat and home, impotence and power which inevitably define the female as the enemy. In *The Sun Also Rises*, Jake's impotence is the ground zero of the novel's construction, an irreducible, unavoidable, physical fact which structures all the novel's events and relationships. Manhood for Hemingway has a singular, apparently biological and thus "natural" definition: the erect penis as the phallic center around which gender and sexuality is organized. Tom's impotence is not figured so absolutely. For Jake Barnes, Brett Ashley's desire measures his own sense of impossibility. For Tom, Sam's desire, although it cannot heal him directly ("I thought" he tells her, "it would be different with you . . ."), allows him to at least discuss new possibilities (128). Tom describes for Sam the salt-water pump that could be implanted allowing him to simulate an erection. And although cost and fear seem likely to stand in the way of such a move by Tom, the possibility of change remains. For Sam, Tom's impotency is con-fusing and frustrating, but her frustration is not sexual per se. She returns again and again to the possibilities aroused by Tom's love making which she finds more erotic and satisfying than intercourse with her teenage boyfriend Lonnie.

Dwayne's diary finally offers Sam the immediacy of contact with the war she fails to find through Tom. In the diary, the war does become real for Sam in a way she had never faced, inscribed in the reality of the body and regis-tered with the immediacy of the senses. The diary "disgusted her, with the rotting corpse, her father's shriveled feet, his dead buddy, those sickly-sweet-banana leaves" (206). But to a degree even more disturbing than the reality of the war is the presence of her father inscribed in these pages, written in pencil in the dark. The repulsive sensuality of Vietnam mimics that of her grandfather's farm: "the mangy dog, the ugly baby, the touch-me-nots, the blooming weeds, the rusty bucket, her dumb aunt Donna" (206). Irene will later press Sam to understand this connection in social and class terms. Look at the names on the Memorial she tells her, "You'll see all those coun-try boy names. . . . Bobby Gene and Freddie Ray and Jimmy Bob Calhoun. . . . Boys who didn't know their ass from their elbow" (236–237). As Christian Appy has shown, rural areas had by far the highest rates of enlistment and induction.[32] But Sam first must think through her own inscription in the diary and both of the worlds, Hopewell and Vietnam, it makes real. In an immediate sense she has finally become her father's daughter: "[S]he real-ized her own insensitive curiosity was just like her father's. She felt humili-ated and disgusted. The diary made her wonder what she would do in his sit-uation. Would she call them gooks?" (205). She attempts to distance herself from him, condemning his ignorance and racism, but what fuels her disgust is finally her fear of identification with him.

If Sam recognizes herself in her father, she also finds herself scripted more abstractly into the diary and the war. "*July 4*. Letter from Irene. Baby kicking strong," reads one of the first entries (201). Before Sam is even born she is identified with the nation's birth and identified as the "unreal" figure of mediation between male and female, home and war. "Irene seems too far away to be real," Dwayne writes after his first firefight. "But it's all for her and the baby, or else why are we here?" (202). Irene and the baby make sense of war through their absence from it. "I try to play like [Irene's] here in this hole with me but it won't work. . . . And I wouldn't want her to be here and see this. I can't forget what I'm here for" (203). Angered and con-fused by her discovery of just how deeply she is in fact a part of the war,

Sam attempts to press the possibilities of this presence. "If men went to war for women, and for unborn generations, then she was going to find out what they went through"; she sets out to hump the boonies (208).

By going to Cawood's Pond, "the last place in western Kentucky where a person could really face the wild," Sam seeks to confront as directly as she can her relationship to her father's experience (208). Her trip to the swamp is both an escape from and a running toward her knowledge of her father, of war, and of herself. By reenacting a soldier's experience, she paradoxically hopes that by trespassing directly on the male domain of combat, she will discover that she is different from her father and, by extension, all men. But every attempt she makes to enforce gender distinctions fails. "If it were up to women, there wouldn't be any war. No, that was a naive thought. When women got power, they were just like men. She thought of Indira Ghandi and Margaret Thatcher. She wouldn't want to meet those women out in the swamp at night" (208). Sam then turns to soldiers and tries out the William Broyles argument: "Men were nostalgic about killing. It aroused something in them" (209). She tries to explain Emmett in these terms: "He was all the time reliving the war. Men want to kill. . . . . It was their basic profession" (209). But then she finds herself thinking about the egret Emmett always looks for at Cawood's Pond, like the ones he saw in Vietnam. Sam likens the egret to a stork. "The stork bringing her. Emmett went over there soon after, as though he were looking for that stork, something that brought life" (211).

Sam's attempt to "hump the boonies" is doomed to failure as an effort to transcend gender difference, as the sexual suggestion of the term itself implies. She ultimately realizes that "this nature preserve in a protected corner of Kentucky wasn't like Vietnam at all" (214). But in her attempt she learns a great deal about the ways in which "the Pentagon begins at home." If her attempt to place herself within the landscape of war leads her on a seemingly endless meditation in which gender roles divide and collapse, this process is dramatized most fully when morning comes and she hears footsteps approaching. At that moment, Sam is filled with the very real fear of a woman alone in an isolated place—the threat of rape. Even in her fear, Sam recognizes the irony: "What an idiotic thing to happen, she thought—to face the terror of the jungle and then meet a rapist" (217). Although the threat of rape reinforces once again that she is a woman, and therefore not a soldier, these moments of waiting in fear are the closest she will get to knowing what it was like to stand watch against an unknown and unseen enemy. At the same time, however, as *Paco's Story* makes terribly explicit, rape is in fact the ultimate guarantee of the logic of humping the boonies.

If the threat of rape seems to invoke the violent antipathy between women and war, in the novel this threat immediately gives way to another metaphorical reversal of this relationship. When the feared rapist turns out to be Emmett, he offers Sam one war story in hopes of bringing her back home. In the story, Emmett alone survives a mine blast and hides from an NVA patrol under the dead bodies of his friends. Sam watches in awe as Emmett breaks down. "Emmett's sorrow was full blown, as though it had grown over the years into something monstrous and fantastic" (224). At the pond, Emmett gives birth to his sorrow; "[f]rom the back he looked like an old peasant woman hugging a baby" (226). Mason's use of combat and child-birth as reciprocal metaphors reveals the equally ambivalent qualities of both states. If motherhood is not wholly nurturing, combat is not simply de-structive. The experience of combat is largely felt as defensive, motivated by the practically maternal feeling of what J. Glenn Gray called in *The Warriors* "preservative love"—the soldier's desire to protect those immediately around him.[33] When Emmett realized Sam was gone, he tells her, "It was like being left by myself and all my buddies dead" (225). This connection is less a "flashback," an overwriting of the present with the physical and emo-tional reactions of the war, than a revelation of how deeply the experiences of home and war, family and battle are implicated in each other.

Judith Stiehm has noted that "for many Americans, especially women, combat is not so much an abstract idea as it is fiction."[34] Sam struggles against the mediating fictions of her culture, the dissimulations of movies and television, but the novel ultimately takes as its ground the acceptance of metaphor, the structuring of relevant comparisons, as the only possible basis of communication and knowledge. In the novel's closing scene, Sam finds her own name engraved on the Vietnam Veterans Memorial. This rec-onciliation is earned not by denying the differences in age and gender that separate Sam from the Sam Alan Hughes who died in Vietnam but by Mason's insistent illustration that the logic of humping the boonies must invoke a controlled female presence in order to keep American women at home. Searching for her father in the forbidden male territory of the war becomes a way for Sam to think through her mother's challenge that she become a different kind of woman. The novel ends with a metaphorical rather than narrative closure. Sam realizes that she "is just beginning to understand. And she will never really know what happened to all these men in the war" (240). But when she acknowledges this her emotions are so powerful that "it feels like giving birth to this wall" (240). In this revi-sionary image the daughter gives birth to the father, the future to the past, the living to the dead, radically rewriting the logic of both "humping the boonies" and "the Pentagon begins at home."

CONCLUSION

In the fall of 1996 one of the most famous images of the Vietnam War returned to the front pages of newspapers across the county. A small girl runs naked, crying, down a road in Vietnam. Her long, rail-thin arms are held out from her sides in the awkward pose of terrible pain. She was nine years old and had been burned by naplam that had dissolved her clothes and eaten into her flesh. On Veteran's Day 1996, the little girl in the picture returned to American consciousness when 33-year-old Kim Phuc traveled from her home in Canada to lay a wreath at the Vietnam Veterans Memorial.

It is tempting to see the story of Kim Phuc as the return of the repressed for American narratives of the Vietnam War. In the original photograph it is the American GIs who are in the background and the crying, displaced Vietnamese children who are seen front and center. The naked child, both female and Vietnamese, is for once allowed to occupy the center stage of war and history. This framing offers rich possibilities for challenging the traditional structure of American war stories, the ways in which the war has been defined, remembered, and used as a cultural force. This challenge is tempered, however, by the image's sentimental familiarity—the terrible vulnerability of the girl's nakedness, the purity of the children's victimization. The image of the burned girl made Americans see the pain the war inflicted on Vietnamese people, but her image also brushed aside the complex national, social, economic, and ideological struggles that defined the war's meaning within Vietnam. The child's pain is universal; the war's violence was local on a terrible scale.

In giving that emblematic Vietnamese child a name, a history, and a place in the war's memorialization, the 1996 story of Kim Phuc's return would seem a fitting point of conclusion for my study, a way of moving beyond the solipsistic terms of friendly fire. But there is a danger in offering such an "answer" to the limits of American narratives and identities. Kim Phuc's life since being wounded testifies to the terrible burden of being made to embody history. Phuc's parents had moved from their village, allowing their daughter to grow up without the burden of being identified as the girl in the picture. But in applying to go to medical school in Saigon, that identity was discovered by the bureaucracy of the Socialist Republic of Viet Nam. Phuc's personal ambitions were subordinated to her value as an iconic figure for the nation. Instead of going to medical school, she was given a secretarial job in the provincial government where she would be available for interviews, "to remind foreign visitors of how Vietnam suffered."[1]

In an interview just before her appearance at the Vietnam Veterans Memorial, Phuc refused to see any similarity between being made to embody the horrors of the American war for the Communist government of Vietnam and her ceremonial return to American consciousness.[2] For Phuc there may indeed be no comparison, but for critical readings of the Vietnam War and its legacy it is necessary to recognize the continuing appropriation of bodies and images to sustain narratives of nationalism and ideology, righteousness and criminality, forgiveness and memory. In her brief remarks at the Vietnam Veterans Memorial Kim Phuc sought to put the war behind: "I do not want to talk about the war because I cannot change history." Her life was not, she argued, bound in the end by the war or her wounds. She left Vietnam, immigrated to Canada, married, and had a son. Personally and publicly she dedicated herself to building peace rather than remembering war.

In an example clearly intended as symbolic, Phuc said, "Even if I could talk face to face with the pilot who dropped the bombs, I would tell him we cannot change history but we should try to do good things for the present and the future to promote peace." But as is typical of American responses to the Vietnam War, such a symbolic possibility had to be literalized. One John Plummer came forth from the crowd at the Wall that Veteran's Day, claiming to be the American who called in the air strike on Trang Bang in which Kim Phuc was burned. An Associated Press article about Phuc and Plummer's meeting ran under the headline "Screams Silenced: Two victims of Vietnam War bombing reconcile."[3] This headline takes one of the few images of what the war did to the Vietnamese and, in a depressingly familiar gesture of solipcism, turns it into another scene of friendly fire, one more story about what the war did to Americans. The article featured the picture of the nine-year-old Phuc and another of the 33-year-old Phuc, smiling broadly, with her head on the shoulder of the 49-year-old John Plummer. The picture is a very familiar image of personal and national reconciliation in which the soldier "comes home" to the forgiving woman. It little matters that there was no actual romance between them. The romance was generic. But like Le Ly Hayslip's final romance with a tortured

American veteran, this story turned out to be a fraud. John Plummer was not personally responsible for Kim Phuc's burns.[4] Such frauds speak to the intense desire to expiate guilt that can only be imagined as personal and to the expectation that such confessions will pave the way to a happy ending to the American War in Vietnam. This desire for happy endings seems inevitably to lead to the repetition of the same old war stories over and over again.

Andrew Lam has a tellingly titled short story, "Show and Tell," which offers a different turn on the use the famous picture of Kim Phuc as a child. In "Show and Tell," a shy boy, Cao Long Nguyen, joins an eighth-grade class late in the semester. He speaks little English, is identified by the sympathetic teacher as a "refugee," and put into the care of the story's narrator, Robert Mitchell. The story revolves around a series of class presentations, "eighth-grade show and tell," beginning with Robert's family tree, "half a tree" as the class bully Billy points out, as Robert only knows his mother's family.[5] When Billy gets up the next day to give his presentation, his predictable taunting of the new kid takes on a particular historical edge. He begins by showing his father's uniform jacket from the Vietnam War.

> Then [Billy] opened one magazine and showed a picture of this naked and bleeding little girl running and crying on this road while these houses behind her were on fire. That's Napalm, he said, and it eats into your skin and burns for a long, long time. This girl, Billy said, she got burned real bad, see there, yeah. (119)

Billy goes on to show other famous pictures, of the burning monk and of dead bodies in black pajamas along a road, suggestive of My Lai. All these pictures have strong antiwar associations, but Billy uses them to tell a different story. "My Daddy says if it weren't for them beatniks and hippies we could have won, Billy said, and that's when the new kid buried his face in his arms and cried . . . "(119).

Lam's canny version of "Show and Tell" illustrates both the general and specific burdens placed on Kim Phuc's body. If the stark immediacy of the picture would seem to "speak for itself," Lam demonstrates that every picture must be told as well as shown, and in that telling claims are made to power, authority, and history. Billy's presentation, like Robert's very different "half a family tree," makes claims to familial and national genealogy. Billy binds himself to his father and, through his father's uniform, to the nation over the bodies of both Kim Phuc and Cao Long Nguyen. These Vietnamese children, who both eventually seek to claim new lives in North America, are made to once again to tell an exclusionary version of American identity.

But Cao strikes back. He goes to the board and draws his own familial and national history. He draws boys racing on water buffalos, a house by a river, the ocean and then calls on Robert to help. Cao can't tell Robert what he wants, but Robert "just kinda knew" (120). Robert begins to "tell" what Cao "shows" through his illustrations: the Viet Cong taking his father away, his father's death, the boat, arriving in San Francisco. Their collaboration attacks the assumption that it is Cao's sole responsibility to stand up and represent the "other side" of the war and the war story, an assumption shared in many ways by jingoistic attacks on him as the "enemy" and liberal desires to hear his story. Robert has already used his imagination to fill in his "half a tree," not by inventing an unknown paternal history but by embellishing an eccentric maternal one. Robert's telling of Cao's history binds him not to the past but to the present and future, to the possibilities for change by embracing Cao's need to create a new life. Together Cao and Robert free themselves from the pervasive nostalgia for a war that either could have been won or never should have been fought.

"Show and Tell" could have been one more story of friendly fire in which the American boys fight each other over the body of Cao and against the background of the war. Such a showdown begins in the cafeteria on Cao's first day at school. When Robert tells Billy to leave Cao alone, Billy offers a bold but formulaic attack on Robert's masculinity. "Then in this loud singsong voice, he said Bobby's protecting his new boyfriend. Everybody look, Bobby's got a boyfriend and he's going to suck his VC's dick after lunch" (116). In the face of this public attack, Billy and the reader expect Robert to repudiate Cao in defense of his own image, but Robert's response is in many ways more surprising than his later ability to narrate Cao's mural: "So I said, don't mind if I do. I'm sure anything is bigger than yours and everybody in line said Oooh" (116). Billy's presentation on the Vietnam War the following day is a response to this challenge to his own prospective masculine identity as much as it is an attack on the "alien" presence in the classroom. In a classic example of what Susan Jeffords calls "remasculinization," Billy uses the war to reestablish his place in the admittedly juvenile social order of eighth grade, but the terms of the struggle played out there are identical to those of traditional war fiction. Through his queer relation to familial and masculine identity, Robert is willing to play the role of a different kind of man, one not bound to the logic of patriarchal succession and heterosexual mastery. This defiance of the codes of gender and sexuality, as much as those of race and nation, liberate him from fear and enable him to share Cao's story. It is the possibility of such a future sharing which I have tried to work toward in this book. I hope, like Robert placing his crazy aunts up against Billy's soldier father, to eventually make new stories and new interpretations possible.

A very different invocation of Kim Phuc's body, with very different resonances for my project, appeared in the form of a political cartoon published about the time the story of Kim Phuc's "reunion" with John Plummer was circulating. Under the caption "Report Says Nike Workers in Vietnam Paid Starvation Wages and Suffer Corporal Punishment and Forced Running Inflicted by Managers," the cartoon depicts an endless line of young women working an assembly line producing shoe soles marked "Nike." Prominently positioned above their heads a poster represents the awkward pose of the burned, nine-year-old Kim Phuc. Below her reads the familiar Nike slogan, "Just Do It." The cartoon both illustrates and complicates many of the arguments I have made in this book. It redraws the relationship of past and present, then and now in a radically disruptive way. It refutes accepted boundaries of war, insistently crossing the line between combatant and noncombatant, male and female, labor and battle which I have discussed at length. But it also challenges my instance that the United States lost the war, even as it suggests how an absorption in the past can blind us to the present. The reestablishment of diplomatic ties to the Socialist Republic of Viet Nam have occasioned less a confrontation with the shared history of the war than a capitalist free for all. To be sure, the same old ideological battles could be fought over this representation. Does the specter of Nike in Vietnam suggest that the free market will out in the end? that Ho's legacy was one of nationalism before communism? that the United States did more good than harm in Vietnam because, after all, they want us back? that American imperialism continues unabated?

More fundamentally, how appropriate is such a comparison? The use of Kim Phuc's image as a metaphor for the exploitation of Vietnamese women laborers would inevitably strike many people as obscene, as did the comparisons of My Lai and the Holocaust. It is a certain degree of misfit which gives such comparisons their power. We are forced to justify the how and why, the personal and cultural logic that makes us appreciate or denounce such connections. Comparisons which fit too well become myths—naturalized narratives and images which, as Barthes suggests, are so familiar that they need no justification. It now seems perverse that so many young American men could uncritically think that war was like a John Wayne movie; in 1965 it was the most natural thing in the world.

This is why I believe that literature is an important, even an essential place to study the Vietnam War. In my readings of these novels, plays, and memoirs, I sought out such questionable comparisons. When Bobbie Ann Mason connects the 18-year-old female Sam to the Sam Alan Hughes who dies in Vietnam; when Tim O'Brien allows the fantasy of escape from Vietnam to falter in the Shah's Iran; when A. R. Flowers has a black veteran link his veterans' benefits to the failed promise of 40 acres and a mule; when Michael Herr cites hearing Jimi Hendrix in a rice patty as his "Credentials"; when Maxine Hong Kingston links leaving the country to avoid the draft to the "driving out" of Chinese laborers after the completion of the transcontinental railroad, the reader is forced to negotiate narratives of history, categories of identity, and the limits of narrative possibility. Like Cao Long Nguyen's chalkboard mural, these fictions offer us the space to imagine and interpret as well as remember.

The Vietnam War strained the mythified American understanding of then and now, here and there, us and them. But the need to make comparisons and connections across time, space, and identity remains. John Balaban's haunting, graphic poem, "After Our War," ends with a very literary question: In the wake of the war's devastating violence, "Will the myriad world surrender new metaphor?"[6] New metaphor rather than new truths is what these works offer. These elaborate fictions do not tell us what happened in Vietnam but ask us what the war was like, drawing on the experiences and images of today to remember and understand the past. Through analogy, allegory, and allusion these shifting, self-reflexive narratives do not so much make the unfamiliar familiar, or even defamiliarize the everyday, as they insistently ask us to consider the very act of designating the difference. Every aspect of the war that might seem distinctive raised spectral memories from the American past: from the West and the Phillippines, memories of conquest and empire. But home of course changed as well. In grunt vernacular there was "the world" and "the war," the United States and Vietnam. Throughout this book I have sought to question the familiar logic of this opposition that assumes the Vietnam War to be a peculiar, anomalous event in American history, one increasingly imagined as long ago and far away. I have tried, in short, to "bring the war back home," to recognize its meaningful presence here and now.

NOTES

Introduction

1. Michael Herr, *Dispatches* (New York: Vintage, 1991) 73.

2. According to Christian Appy, *Working Class War: American Combat Soldiers and Vietnam* (Chapel Hill: University of North Carolina Press, 1993), "the army reported 126 fraggings in 1969, 271 in 1970, and 333 in 1971. These increases are particularly steep when one recalls that in the same years the total number of American troops in Vietnam dropped from over 500,000 to under 200,000. Among reported fraggings, about 80 percent of the victims were officers and NCO's (246)." Appy cites a 1968 Pentagon report which "concluded that 15 to 20 percent of all U.S. casualties were cause by friendly fire" and that fraggings "accounted for 5 to 10 percent of friendly fire deaths" (185).

C. D. B. Bryant, *Friendly Fire* (New York: Putnam, 1976) is a moving journalistic account of one family's struggle to uncover the truth about their son's death by friendly fire.

3. Richard Slotkin, *Gunfighter Nation: The Myth of the Frontier in the Twentieth Century* (New York: Harper Perennial, 1993) 12.

4. Susan Jeffords, "Born of Two Fathers: Gender and Misunderstanding in *Platoon*," in *Search and Clear: Critical Responses to Selected Literature and Films of the Vietnam War*, ed. William Searle (Bowling Green, OH: Bowling Green University Press, 1988), and *The Remasculinization of America: Gender and the Vietnam War* (Bloomington: Indiana University Press, 1989) esp. 138–141.

5. Amy Kaplan ends her important essay on American exceptionalism in literary criticism with a brief but pointed critique of the failure of either *Apocalypse Now* or Eleanor Coppola's documentary about the making of the film *Hearts of Darkness* to reflect its own colonizing presence on location in the Philippines, even while overtly applying Conrad's classic critique of European imperialism to the American presence in Vietnam. I would further argue that within *Apocalypse Now* the trope of

friendly fire, by keeping the gaze fixed on Willard, Kurtz, and the other Americans, enables the ahistorical slide between "natives" whether Filipino, Vietnamese, Montagnard, or Conrad's fictional Africans. See Amy Kaplan, "Left Alone with America: The Absence of Empire in the Study of American Culture," *The Cultures of United States Imperialism*, ed. Amy Kaplan and Donald Pease (Durham: Duke University Press, 1993) 18–19.

6. See John Carlos Rowe, "'Bringing It All Back Home': American Recylclings of the Vietnam War," in *The Violence of Representation: Literature and the History of Violence*, ed. Nancy Armstrong and Leonard Tennenhouse (New York: Routledge, 1989). "The familiar ethnocentrism and racism of imerialism are . . . reinforced, even reinvented with a difference, by way of claims for the radical ambiguity and undecidability of the Vietnam War, especially in its 'significance' for American Culture" (198). Rowe's analysis of the "American recyclings" has deep resonances with my figuration of friendly fire and I owe much to his analysis of the critical complicity of readings of the war in continuing the war's cultural violence. See also his introduction, with Rick Berg to *The Vietnam War and American Culture* (New York: Columbia University Press, 1991) 1–17.

7. In "Vietnam: The Remake," J. Hoberman offers an insightful discussion of the spectacle of Vietnam War films which subsumes political and historical questions. The article appears in *Remaking History*, ed. Barbara Kruger and Phil Mariani, Dia Art Foundation Discussions in Contemporary Culture, No. 4 (Seattle, Bay Press, 1989) 174–196. Within popular culture, Charlie Sheen's career slide since *Platoon* and *Wall Street* has featured a number of self-parodies, particularly in the *Hot Shots* films. The poster for the first of these films shows Sheen in full Rambo display—bandana, bare chest, crossed ammo belts, and machine gun. At one level, the parody reveals the structural and iconographic similarities between *Platoon* and *Rambo*, but the joke also works to dispel tensions which might carry more significant historical and political possibilities.

8. Tim O'Brien, *Going After Cacciato* (New York: Dell, 1992) 240.

9. Larry Heinemann, *Paco's Story* (New York: Penguin, 1989) 127–128.

10. Heinemann 109.

11. Elaine Scarry, *The Body in Pain: The Making and Unmaking of the World* (New York: Oxford University Press, 1985) 81.

12. Scarry 62, 121.

13. Scarry 118–119.

14. For an insightful discussion of the Vietnam Veterans Memorial's institutionalization of both conservative, neo-Cold War, and subversive cultural memory, see Donald Pease, "Hiroshima, The Vietnam Veterans War Memorial, and the Gulf War: Post National Spectacles," in *The Cultures of United States Imperialism*, ed. Amy Kaplan and Pease (Durham: Duke University Press, 1993) 557–580.

15. H. G. Reza, "Technicalities of War: In the Trenches of Hollywood, Warriors Inc. Aims to Ensure Accuracy on the Battlefield," *Los Angeles Times*, July 30, 1998, C1. It is perhaps worth noting that the largely celebratory article about Dye and Warriors Inc. appeared in the Business section of the *Los Angeles Times*.

16. Scarry 121.

17. Kaja Silverman, *Male Subjectivity at the Margins* (New York: Routledge, 1994) 15–51.

18. I do not mean to deny the difference between history and fictional narrative. But I would agree with Hayden White, ("Interpretation in History," in *Tropics of Discourse: Essays in Cultural Criticism* (Baltimore: Johns Hopkins University Press, 1985), that "the differences between a history and a fictional account of reality are matters of degree rather than kind" (78, n. 27). With White and Fredric Jameson, I would emphasize that historical narrative actively produces meaning in ways deeply similar, if not identical to, those working in fiction. See *Frederic* Jameson, *The Political Unconscious: Narrative as Socially Symbolic Act* (Ithaca: Cornell University Press, 1981).

Chapter 1

1. Quoted in Clayton R. Koppes and Gregory D. Black, *Hollywood Goes to War: How Politics, Profits, and Propaganda Shaped World War II Movies* (New York: Free Press, 1987) 67.

2. David Lamb, "Vietnam's Hold on America," *Los Angeles Times*, March 5, 1992, A1.

3. Discussions of the image of John Wayne in representations of the Vietnam War include Richard Slotkin, *Gunfighter Nation: The Myth of the Frontier in Twentieth-Century America* (New York: HarperCollins, 1992) 512–533; Michael Andregg, "Hollywood and Vietnam: John Wayne and Jane Fonda as Discourse," in *Inventing Vietnam: The War in Film and Television*, ed. Anderegg (Philadelphia: Temple University Press, 1991) 15–32; Tobey C. Herzog, *Vietnam War Stories: Innocence Lost* (New York: Routledge, 1992) 16–24; Jacqueline E. Lawson, "'Old Kids': The Adolescent Experience in the Nonfiction Narratives of the Vietnam War," in *Search and Clear: Critical Responses to Selected Literature and Films of the Vietnam War*, ed. William J. Searle (Bowling Green, OH: Bowling Green University Popular Press, 1988) 34; Lawrence Suid, *Guts and Glory: Great American War Movies* (Reading, MA: Addison-Wesley, 1978) 91–109. Virginia Wright Wexman, *Creating the Couple: Love, Marriage and Hollywood Performance* (Princeton, NJ: Princeton University Press, 1993) 67–129 does not discuss Vietnam but includes a revisionist feminist discussion of the John Wayne mythos. Gary Wills, *John Wayne's America: The Politics of Celebrity* (New York: Simon and Schuster, 1997) is a provocative and thoughtful study which appeared too late for me to take it fully account in my reading.

4. Barry Bearak, "Feeling on Top of the World," *Los Angeles Times*, February 28, 1991, A1. One of the most pointed demonstrations of the way in which the burial of the Vietnam War during the Gulf War enacted the return of John Wayne appeared on the editorial page of the *Los Angeles Times* on March 8, 1991. In an editorial David Lamb noted, "Most of the U.S. troops in Saudi Arabia are too young to know it, but what the Gulf War was really about was Vietnam. It was about burying the past and feeling proud again to be a soldier" ("Liberating Kuwait Buries the Past, Resurrects Pride in Being a Soldier," M1). This pre-Vietnam pride is embodied quite literally by John Wayne. Just above Lamb's editorial was a box headlined "Yellow Ribbons? Look to John Wayne," in which Harry Shearer reassured Americans that the yellow ribbons used to signify support for troops in the Gulf, in pointed repudiation of the protest against the Vietnam War, refer not to the Tony Orlando song but to Civil War tradition and the 1949 John Wayne/John Ford Western, *She Wore a*

Yellow Ribbon. The lyrics to the film's title song followed, framed by the image of Joanne Dru in her fetching mock-cavalry uniform on the left and John Wayne as Capt. Nathan Brittles on the right. Once again, Shearer's ironic tone does little to challenge John Wayne's embodiment of American identity. Standing opposite John Wayne, Joanne Dru in sassy cavalry drag becomes oddly contemporary in a war in which everyone from the President to the man in the street spoke of our "fighting men and women." Women not only donned uniforms in Desert Storm but simultaneously returned to the traditional female role of waiting, grieving, welcoming home—precisely what Joanne Dru had to learn in *She Wore a Yellow Ribbon.* Woman as "home" was spectacularized not only in yellow ribbons but in the numerous stories about photographers who would mail free "sweetheart" photos overseas and about the deprivations of fighting a war in an Islamic country without *Playboy*, whorehouses, or exposed female limbs in USO shows. For a time, John Wayne's power to suspend American social contradictions was quite consciously restored.

5. Larry Heinemann, *Close Quarters* (1977; New York: Penguin, 1986) 53.

6. Michael Herr, *Dispatches* (New York: Vintage, 1991) 71. All further references are cited in the text.

7. Peter McInerney, "'Straight' and 'Secret' History in Vietnam War Literature," *Contemporary Literature* 22 (1981): 193.

8. Herzog, *Innocence* 16–24.

9. Slotkin, *Gunfighter* 638.

10. See Slotkin, *Gunfighter* 512–533.

11. Eric Lott, *Love and Theft: Blackface Minstrelsy and the American Working Class* (New York: Oxford University Press, 1993) 101.

12. It was during the first half of 1962 that, in the words of historian Guenter Lewy, *America in Vietnam* (New York: Oxford University Press, 1980), the "successful ending of the war in Vietnam became an article of faith that was beyond challenge" (24). This optimism was based on reports from Diem's government regarding the successful establishment of over three thousand strategic hamlets, the backbone of pacification in the South Vietnamese countryside. After Diem's assassination, it "became clear that many of these hamlets existed on paper only and were part of the misinformation the GVN was feeding the Americans" (24).

13. Sam Peckinpah's first film, *The Deadly Companion*, premiered in 1961.

14. Tag Gallagher, *John Ford* (Berkeley: University of California Press, 1986) 253.

15. Roland Barthes, *Mythologies*, trans. Annette Lavers (New York: Hill and Wang, 1983) 128. All further references are cited in the text.

16. P. F. Kluge, "First and Last a Cowboy," *Life* 72 (January 28, 1972): 46.

17. David Thompson, "John Wayne," *A Biographical Dictionary of Film* (New York: William Morrow, 1976) 601.

18. Eric Bentley, *Theatre of War* (New York: Viking, 1972) 308.

19. Bentley 308.

20. Tobey C. Herzog, "John Wayne in a Modern Heart of Darkness: The American Soldier in Vietnam," in *Search and Clear: Critical Responses to Selected Literature and Films of the Vietnam War*, ed. William J. Searle (Bowling Green, OH: Bowling Green University Popular Press, 1988) 20.

21. Kathryn Kane, *Visions of War: Hollywood Combat Films of WWII* (Ann Arbor: UMI Research Press, 1982) 84.

22. Richard Slotkin, "Myth and the Production of History," in *Ideology and Classic American Literature*, ed. Sacvan Bercovitch and Myra Jehlen (New York: Cambridge University Press, 1987) 84.

23. MacAvoy Lane animates this irony in his series of prose poems, *How Audie Murphy Died in Vietnam* (Garden City, NY: Anchor Books, 1973).

24. Richard Slotkin, *The Fatal Environment* (Middletown, CT: Wesleyan University Press, 1986) xii.

25. Suid offers a considered and detailed account of John Wayne's image as soldier, including the earliest account of his status as icon in Vietnam literature (100).

26. Suid 99–100.

27. Richard Wheeler, *Iwo* (New York: Lippincott and Crowell, 1980) 161–162.

28. Ron Kovic, *Born on the Fourth of July* (New York: Pocket Books, 1977) 54–55. All further references are cited in the text.

29. Thomas Doherty, "Full Metal Genre: Stanley Kubrick's Vietnam Combat Movie," *Film Quarterly* 42 (Winter 1988–1989): 25.

30. Jeanine Basinger, *The World War II Combat Film: Anatomy of a Genre* (New York: Columbia University Press, 1986) 170.

31. Basinger 170.

32. Basinger 170.

33. Basinger x.

34. By "classic" I am referring primarily to the Westerns made with John Ford and Howard Hawks. The films directed by Andrew MacLaglen coopt the ambivalence of the Ford and Hawks films into a more simplistic celebration of violence and individualism. The opening of *Cahill—US Marshall*, for example, features John Wayne placing five men under arrest by outshooting them without even getting off his horse. As the son of actor Victor MacLaglen, the director is very conscious of Ford's delineation of the genre, working with and against it. But, made in the 1960s and 1970s, these films are contemporary to Vietnam rather than cultural precursors of the war.

35. Gallagher 244.

36. It is worth noting that in *Stagecoach*, as the Ringo Kid, John Wayne is the outlaw who has escaped from prison to see that justice is done, although he is never truly judged or figured as being outside or opposed to the community. In *The Man Who Shot Liberty Valance*, Wayne must move outside the law in a secretive manner because the criminal Valance operates outside the Marshall's jurisdiction. Law here is fundamentally ineffectual and corrupt and Wayne cannot be reintegrated as in *Stagecoach*.

37. Gallagher 252.

38. "Sensuous human activity" is Marx's term. See Carolyn Porter's gloss in "Reification and American Literature," in Bercovitch and Jehlen 194.

39. John Hellmann has an insightful discussion of the importance of JFK's emphasis on physical fitness and its relationship to both the Peace Corps and the Green Berets. See *American Myth and the Legacy of Vietnam* (New York: Columbia University Press, 1986) 44.

40. N. Bradley Christie, "Re/Reading *Born on the Fourth of July*," presented at the Popular Culture Association, St. Louis, April 1989.

41. Slotkin, "Myth" 86.

42. Gustav Hasford, *The Short-Timers* (New York: Bantam, 1980) 1. All further references are cited in the text.

43. Lawson 34.

44. Suid 98.

45. In *War Without Mercy: Race and Power in the Pacific War* (New York: Pantheon, 1986), John Dower documents the vicious circle of propaganda, Allied and Japanese, which fed the Japanese soldier's reticence to be taken prisoner (see pp. 67–68). Dower's study is very important in its investigation of American atrocities, racism, and propaganda against the Japanese, revealing how much of the Vietnam War was not unique in American experience and thus discouraging the idea that Stryker and Gerheim were training their men for fundamentally different wars.

46. Wheeler 234.

47. Suid 108.

48. Thomas Myers *Walking Point: American Narratives of Vietnam* (New York: Oxford University Press, 1988) writes that in war literature, "Black humor . . . is an offensive weapon, the inflation of a historical configuration already in perceived bad taste to the bursting point in order to make its hidden assumptions recognizable" (108).

49. Myers describes Hasford's Marines as embodying a "form of violent American class consciousness" (113).

50. Slotkin, "Myth" 84.

51. Dower 152.

Chapter 2

1. Michael Herr, *Dispatches* (New York: Vintage, 1991) 3.

2. Herr 3.

3. Fredric Jameson, *The Political Unconscious* (Ithaca, NY: Cornell University Press, 1981). All further references are cited in the text.

4. Roland Barthes, *Mythologies* (New York: Hill and Wang, 1983) 128.

5. My reading of the Chinese maps draws on Benedict Anderson's discussion of the introduction of Western mapping techniques and the inscription of borders on both maps and landscape in nineteenth-century Siam. See *Imagined Communities: Reflections on the Origin and Spread of Nationalism*, rev. ed. (London: Verso, 1991) 171–173.

6. Maxine Hong Kingston, *China Men* (New York: Vintage, 1989) 47. All further references are cited in the text.

7. James Corner, *Taking Measures Across the American Landscape* (New Haven: Yale University Press, 1995) 18.

8. Denis Cosgrove, "The Measures of America," in Corner, op. cit., 11.

9. M. Consuelo Leon W., "Foundations of the American Image of the Pacific," *boundary 2* 21:1 (1991): (17–29).

10. As Michael Rogin argues, the "distinction between European powers that held colonies and the United States, which generally did not, wrongly locates the

imperial age in the late nineteenth century instead of three centuries earlier, at the dawn of the modern age." "The American empire started at home," Rogin reminds us, challenging the fallacious historical and academic division between domestic and international politics which would sever the conquest and settlement of the West from the acquisition of territories in the Pacific. See "'Make My Day!': Spectacle as Amnesia in Imperial Politics," *Representations* 29 (Winter 1990): 108. All further references are cited in the text.

11. Richard Hofstader notes that the "evolution of sentiment" during the Spanish-American War from a popular "Free Cuba" movement to the signing of "a peace treaty ratifying the acquisition of the Philippines by conquest" was accomplished under the aegis of "duty" and "destiny"— Americanist terms which placated both those uncomfortable with empire and those who clamored for it. See "Cuba, the Philippines and Manifest Destiny," in *The Paranoid Style in American Politics and Other Essays* (New York: Knopf, 1965) 162–163, 174.

12. Jameson 83

13. Tim O'Brien, *Going After Cacciato* (New York: Dell, 1992). All further references are to this edition.

14. Thomas Myers, *Walking Point* (New York: Oxford University Press, 1988) 171. Compare John Hellmann, *American Myth and the Legacy of Vietnam* (New York: Columbia University Press, 1986): "*Going After Cacciato* dramatizes the heroic pathos of a youth struggling in his mind toward some viable escape from the landscape of a seemingly meaningless war" (161). All further references will be cited in the text.

15. Jameson 83.

16. Jameson argues that the historical situation of a text is not causal but limiting as it "is . . . understood to block off or shut down a certain number of formal possibilities available before, and to open up determinant new ones" (148).

17. "O'Brien's narrative cannot return to Vietnam because it never leaves." Myers 174.

18. See James A. Bill, *The Eagle and the Lion: The Tragedy of American-Iranian Relations* (New Haven: Yale University Press, 1988) 30–41, 98–105; Richard W. Cottman, *Iran and the United States: A Cold War Case Study* (Pittsburgh: University of Pittsburgh Press, 1988) chaps. 3–4; Mark Hamilton Lytle, *The Origins of the Iranian-American Alliance* (New York: Holmes and Meier, 1987) 138–152, 213–218).

19. In February 1946, in the famous "Long Telegram," George Kennan, "The Sources of Soviet Conduct," *American Diplomacy 1900–1950* (Chicago: Chicago University Press, 1951), first articulated a strategy of containment to meet the perceived Soviet policy of aggressive expansion: "Soviet pressure against the free institutions of the Western world is something that can be contained by the adroit and vigilant application of counter-force at a series of constantly shifting geographical and political points, corresponding to the shifts and maneuvers of Soviet policy . . ." (120). The Truman doctrine, the first application of the containment strategy as policy, awarded economic and military aid to Greece and Turkey in February 1947 in order to combat external Soviet pressure and internal challenges by communist guerrillas.

20. Frederick Merk, *Manifest Destiny and Mission in American History* (1963; New York: Vintage, 1966) 261.

21. The scale and variety of GI resistance to the Vietnam War is documented

in the special issue of the journal *Vietnam Generation* 2(1), ed. Harry W. Haines, *G. I. Resistance: Soldiers and Veterans Against the War*, and in David Cortright, *Soldiers in Revolt: The American Military Today* (Garden City, NJ: Anchor Press, 1975).

22. This has a more general relevancy than my discussion of John Wayne might suggest. For example, Richard Slotkin, *Regeneration Through Violence* (1974); Richard Drinnon, *Facing West: The Metaphysics of Indian Hating and Empire Building* (1980); Arthur Kopit, *Indians* (1969); and films such as *The Wild Bunch* (1969), *Little Big Man* (1970), and *MacCabe and Mrs. Miller* (1971) all challenge the traditional iconography and ideology of the Western as a historical and fictional narrative by making implicit and often very explicit references to the Vietnam War as a space in which the West comes to be seen as a site of violence, racism, and exploitation rather than freedom, democracy, and rugged individualism.

23. Richard Slotkin, *Regeneration Through Violence: The Mythology of the American Frontier, 1600–1860* (Middletown, CT: Wesleyan University Press, 1974) 5.

24. Susan Jeffords, *The Remasculinization of America: Gender and the Vietnam War* (Bloomington: Indiana University Press, 1989) esp. chap. 4, "'Do We Get to Win This Time?': Reviving the Masculine."

25. Joan Didion, *Democracy* (New York: Vintage, 1995) 16. All further references are cited in the text.

26. Edward Said, *Beginnings: Intention and Method* (Baltimore: Johns Hopkins University Press, 1975) 48.

27. Said 152, 162.

28. Said 66.

29. See Elaine Tyler May, *Homeward Bound: American Families in the Cold War Era* (New York: Basic Books, 1988).

30. See Loren Barritz, *Backfire: A History of How American Culture Led Us into Vietnam and Made Us fight the Way We Did* (New York: William Morrow, 1985), for an extended reading of the trope of the City on the Hill in relation to the Vietnam War.

31. Alan Nadel, *Containment Culture: American Narratives, Postmodernism, and the Atomic Bomb* (Durham, NC: Duke University Press, 1995) 273–275. Nadel's discussion of *Democracy* in relation to Cold War containment is an important counterpoint to my own as the the narratives of containment and imperialism, while deeply implicated in each other, are not synonymous.

32. Lily Dizon, "For Thousands of Refugees, Return to Vietnam Looms," *Los Angeles Times*, June 26, 1996, A9.

33. Lisa Lowe, *Immigrant Acts: On Asian American Cultural Politics* (Durham, NC: Duke University Press, 1996) 16.

34. For the sake of clarity I have designated the sustained narratives about Kingston's father, grandfathers, and brother "chapters" and the intervening short sections "allegories." I would note however, that the crucial section on "The Laws," which insists on the legal facts of exclusion, fits neither category.

35. The Japanese American "no no boys" who refused to serve in World War II in protest of the internment are a crucial example which overtly politicizes the doublebind of Asian Americans during the war, caught not between loyalty to two nations but between exclusion and citizenship within the United States.

36. David Leiwei Li discusses the important connection between building the

transcontinental railway and "establishing the 'empire' of the Pacific." See "*China Men*: Maxine Hong Kingston and the American Canon," *American Literary History*, 2 (Fall 1990): 490–492.

37. It should not be surprising that critics such as Lisa Lowe and Sau-Ling Wong, who have emphasized different issues in this debate, agree that considerations of the national and then de- or extra- or postnational meet with literal violence in war, or that the Vietnam War is the exemplary moment of this intersection as the place where American imperialism in Asia became undeniable. See Lowe 3–5, 16–19 and Sau-Ling Wong, "Denationalization Reconsidered: Asian American Cultural Criticism at a Theoretical Crossroads," *Amerasia Journal* 21:1 & 2 (1995): 1–27.

Chapter 3

1. Ralph Ellison, *Invisible Man* (New York: Vintage, 1972) 420.

2. See William B. Gatewood, Jr., *"Smoked Yankees" and the Struggle for Empire: Letters from Negro Soldiers, 1898–1902* (Urbana: University of Illinois Press, 1971), quoting Galloway at 14.

3. Larry Neal, "And Shine Swam On," *Visions of a Liberated Future: Black Arts Movement Writings* (New York: Thunder Mouth Press, 1989) 13.

4. Neal, "Shine" 14.

5. Neal, "Shine" 646, 647.

6. *Black Fire: An Anthology of Afro-American Writing*, ed. Larry Neal and Leroi Jones (New York: Morrow, 1968). The forward by Jones (signed Ameer Baraha) opens with the words, "These are the founding Fathers and Mothers, of our nation." Neal asserts, "most of the book can be read as if it were a critical reexamination of Western political, social, and artistic values." Houston Baker, *The Journey Back* (Chicago: University of Chicago Press, 1983), discusses the opening and closing statements of *Black Fire* in related terms: "I interpret these statements as conative utterances. The goal they propose is rebirth. But the rebirth they propose is an exclusively lexical one: The words strive to recreate a primordial black logos, or word, through sheer lyricism and assertiveness" (134). A black logos would, of course, make possible a discourse of black history.

7. "We can learn more about what poetry is by listening to the cadences of Malcolm's speeches, than from most of Western poetic. Listen to James Brown scream. Ask yourself, then: Have you ever heard a Negro poet sing like that? Of course not, because we have been tied to the texts, like most white poets. The text could be destroyed and no one would be hurt in the least by it" ("Shine" 653).

8. Larry Neal argues that blacks had most often sought to resolve the tension of being black in America through violence "simply because the nature of our existence in America has been one of violence." An alternative form of resolution lay "in recognizing the beauty and love within Black America itself. No, not in a new 'Negritude,' but a profound sense of a unique and beautiful culture; and a sense that there are many spiritual areas to explore *within* this culture. This is a kind of separation but there is no tension about it. There is a kind of peace in the separation. This peace might be threatened by the realities of the beast-world, but yet, it is lived as fully as life can be lived" ("Shine" 647).

9. Hayden White, *Tropics of Discourse: Essays in Cultural Criticism* (Baltimore: Johns Hopkins University Press, 1978) 2.

10. There continues to be a heated debate over whether or not black men served and suffered casualties at a higher rate than did white soldiers. The most pointed correlation is to class. "Poorly educated, low-income whites and poorly educated, low-income blacks together bore a vastly disproportionate share of the burdens of Vietnam. . . . [M]en from disadvantaged backgrounds were twice as likely to as their better off peers to serve in the military, go to Vietnam, and see combat." Lawrence Baskir and William Strauss, *Chance and Circumstance: The Draft the War, and the Vietnam Generation* (New York: Vintage, 1978). But this fact in no way reflects an "equal" disadvantage. As Christian Appy, *Working Class War: American combat soldiers and Vietnam* (Chapel Hill: University of North Carolina Press, 1993), points out, "the black veterans [in the 1978 Veterans' Administration *Legacies of Vietnam* survey] were significantly more representative of the entire black population that white veterans were of the white population. This reflects the fact that whites and black have different class distributions, with blacks having a much larger proportion of poor and working people and a much smaller middle class and elite. In the Legacies sample, 82 percent of black non-veterans were working class or below, compared with 42 percent of the white nonveterans" (25). At almost every level the statistics are contestable in relation to whether they reflect the fairness or unfairness of Vietnam-era service. Black reenlistment rates were much higher than for whites, a point in which the military took great pride. But this reflects as much the lack of opportunity in civilian society as any enhanced opportunity within the military. Perhaps the most telling statistics are the grossly disproportionate numbers of African Americans who received dishonorable discharges and jail terms within the military justice system. "A 1971 study by the Congressional Black Caucus discovered that half of all soldiers in confinement were black, a finding matched by a National Association for the Advancement of Colored People (NAACP) study in Europe during the same year. The NAACP study also found that a white offender was twice as likely to be released without punishment as a black first offender. . . . The NAACP study found that 45% of all less than honorable discharges went to blacks" (Baskir and Strauss 139).

11. Hayden White: "troping is both a movement *from* one notion of the way things are related *to* another notion, and a connection between things so that they can be expressed in language that takes account of the possibility of their being expressed otherwise" (2).

12. White 2.

13. C. D. B. Bryant, "Barely Suppressed Screams: Getting a Bead on Vietnam War Literature," *Harper's* (June 1984): 68.

14. Clyde Taylor, "The Colonialist Subtext in *Platoon*," *Cineaste* 15 (1987): 8. Taylor argues that if the protagonist of *Platoon* had been black, the act of murdering Sgt. Barnes would have "released the unspeakable text of anticolonialist violence" (9), thus illustrating the black soldier's tropic position, one who expresses the possibility of an alternative discourse of history to the one featured.

15. An opposite but related tactic involves exploiting the "threat" the black veteran might pose to American society. This issue was first fully articulated by Whitney Young in 1967 following a tour of American bases in Vietnam.

After risking his life in the service of his country and experiencing the most advanced form of integration in America's history, the Negro veteran is not prepared to return to the status quo, to regress culturally and socially once he steps foot on American soil. He is grimly determined—by whatever means necessary—to live in an America where his rights are fully guaranteed. In his war experience he has acquired new confidence and new skills, among them the skills of guerilla warfare, of killing, of subversion, and the gamut of tricks of military command. . . if they return to find the conditions they left unchanged, these negro veterans might become an interested audience for the preachers of violence—and one capable of being organized into a major national threat.

"When the Negroes in Vietnam Come Home," *Harper's Magazine* 234, (June 1967): 65.

Young's careful analysis of the circumstances which might encourage black vets to turn to violence becomes a simplistic equation of the black veteran with violence in a number of pulp fictions in which black vets turn terrorist. To take one example, Walter Kempley, *The Invaders* (New York: Dutton, 1976), tells an improbable tale of a white army bureaucrat sent to Saigon to curb the problem of "gangs" formed by mostly black deserters, "[E]very damn one of them thinks of himself as some sort of General who is going back to the States and get an army together and take over." One such gang launches a plot to blow up West Point. This act of violence is without any larger political motive or connection. The violence of the black veteran is presented as an end in itself. They are, of course, defeated in the nick of time.

It is worth noting that in the opening scene of the film *First Blood* John Rambo (Sylvester Stallone) journeys to the Northwest to visit a black army buddy only to discover that he has died. If Rambo is seen as a surrogate of this dead black veteran, then his apparently unmotivated persecution by the cracker-like sheriff and his anarchic violence take on a more familiar dimension.

16. Robert Stokes, "Race Riot at Long Binh," *Newsweek*, September 30, 1968; 35, David Cortright, *Soldiers in Revolt: The American Military Today* (Garden City, NY: Anchor Press/Doubleday, 1975) 40.

17. Stokes 35.

18. Stokes 35.

19. Cortright 207.

20. Conversation with David Willson who served as stenographer to the Inspector General, USARV from September 1967 to October 1968. The Inspector General's office was responsible for investigating all complaints generated by prisoners at Long Binh.

21. Cortright 41.

22. To cite but three notable examples, the term "Black Power" gained its electrifying currency on June 17, 1966, when Stokely Carmichael confronted a crowd with the connection between Vietnam and the civil rights struggle.

"We're asking Negroes not to go to Vietnam and fight but to stay in Greenwood and fight here. . . . If they put one of us in jail, we're going to get him out. We're going up there and get him out ourselves. . . . We need black power." Then shouting to the crowd, he asked, "What do we want?"

"Black power!" the crowd shouted back.
"What do we want?"
"BLACK POWER!" (Thomas Powers *The War at Home* [Boston: G.K. Hall, 1973] 152–153)

In New York on April 4, 1967, Martin Luther King, Jr. declared it was "time to break the silence" and announced not only his opposition to the war in Vietnam, but analyzed the colonial history of the war in Vietnam and the larger pattern of American interventions around the world, implicitly identified the struggle of black Americans with that of Vietnamese peasants, and outlined a specific policy for ending the war. The speech is reprinted in Clyde Taylor, *Vietnam and Black America: An Anthology of Protest and Resistance* (Garden City, NY: Anchor Press/Doubleday, 1973) 79–98.

In "Black Power in the International Context," Larry Neal stresses the connection between the Vietnam War, the "rebellion in the cities" and the necessity of a global vision of black power. "It is no longer a question of civil rights for Negroes; but rather, it is a question of national liberation for black America. This means we see ourselves as a 'colonized' people instead of disenfranchised American citizens. . . . Angola, Vietnam, and Chile are here, and we must deal with that reality in a manner that is understandable to the masses of black Americans." Reprinted in *Visions of a Liberated Future*, 137, 141.

23. Powers 218.

24. To return to an example cited earlier, the narrative of Abraham Lincoln freeing the slaves, a central episode in traditional narratives of American history, would necessarily be transformed if full consideration was given to the large numbers of slaves who freed themselves by escaping from plantations and taking refuge behind Union lines following the outbreak of the war, damaging the southern economy, and forcing the President to respond. Undoubtedly, the Emancipation Proclamation would remain a key document, but the narrative defining its context and significance would be very different. For such an alternative history, see W. E. B. DuBois *Black Reconstruction in America 1860–1880* (1935; New York: Atheneum, 1969) 55–127. In DuBois's words, "Lincoln's proclamation only added possible legal sanction to an accomplished fact" (84). In his award-winning history, *Reconstruction: America's Unfinished Revolution 1863–1877* (New York: Harper and Row, 1988), historian Eric Foner notes, "In many ways, *Black Reconstruction* anticipated the findings of modern scholarship" (xxi).

25. Houston A. Baker, Jr. *The Journey Back* (Chicago: University of Chicago Press, 1980) 136.

26. *The Journey Back* 135.

27. John A. Williams. *Captain Blackman* (1972; New York: Thunder Mouth Press, 1988) 314. All further references are cited in the text.

28. In his series of *New York Times* articles on the black soldier, Thomas A. Johnson, for example, fundamentally revised the usual media approach by emphasizing the black soldier's history of service, sacrifice, and frustration dating back to Crispus Attuks, rather than the much celebrated opportunities military service had offered to blacks since desegregation. As a result, the tensions surrounding black

soldiers regarding the prospect of poor opportunities back home, recruitment by such militant organizations as the Black Panthers, or the increasing racial turmoil within the service after 1968 appear less like gross ingratitude than signs of the limited achievement of desegregation itself. Johnson's articles are a crucial source for any analysis of the black soldier's experience, one Williams himself quotes in *Captain Blackman*. Johnson's articles appeared on the front page of the *Times* on April 29 and 30, May 1, and July 28, 1968.

29. *The Journey Back* 81.

30. See Eldridge Cleaver, *Soul on Ice* (New York: Dell, 1968). "Rape was an insurrectionary act. It delighted me that I was defying and trampling on the white man's law, upon his system of values, and that I was defiling his women—and this point, I believe, was the most satisfying to me because I was resentful over the historical fact of how the white man has used the black woman" (14). Cleaver comes to realize that rape is a repudiation of not just the white man's law but of "being human, civilized" and turns, significantly, to writing instead. But while calling for a healing of "the sickness between the white woman and the black man," he notes "the black man's sick attitude toward the white woman is a revolutionary sickness: it keeps him perpetually out of harmony with the system that is oppressing him" (16).

31. In *The Sanctified Church* (Berkeley: Turtle Island, 1981) Zora Neale Hurston describes Highjohn de Conqueror as the folkloric hero who was not enslaved but followed the captured Africans into the New World where he "took on flesh" and "walked like a natural man." He embodies autonomy from slavery and the promise of freedom. After emancipation he is said to have put his power into the root which bears his name and is used extensively in the art of conjure (69).

32. Houston A. Baker, Jr., *Blues, Ideology and Afro-American Literature* (Chicago: University of Chicago Press, 1984) 87.

33. A. R. Flowers, Jr., *DeMojo Blues* (New York: Ballentine, 1985), 125. All further references are cited in the text.

34. Wallace Terry, *Bloods: An Oral History of the Vietnam War By Black Veterans* (New York: Ballentine, 1985) xv. All further references are cited in the text.

35. See, for example, "The Great Society in Uniform," *Newsweek* August 22, 1966, 46, 48, 57. "Off the battlefield there is a sort of separation of the races—in Saigon where the Negroes tend to seek out their own bars, or in rest areas where whites and blacks often congregate in separate groups. But this is a personal choice rather than imposed segregation. As one Negro GI chuckles: 'We sometimes segregate ourselves from those white guys. We don't like their hillbilly music'" (46). The same point is made in "Only One Color," *Newsweek*, December 6, 1965, 43; "How Negro Americans Perform in Vietnam," *U.S. News and World Report*, August 15, 1966, 63; "Armed Forces: The Integrated Society," *Time* December 23, 1966, 88.

36. I would argue that Flowers alludes directly to the dancing Sambo dolls sold by Tod Clifton in a dream which Tucept has soon after his return to the United States. He dreams of a battle in which all the soldiers are "puppets on a string, buckdancing minstrels dodging slow motion bullets to the tune of Yankee Doodle Dandy. You dance on gossamer strings sometimes seen sometimes not. They move your arms like jerky windmills and buckdance your feet, you fight and strain but still you dance, what a dance they do" (32).

37. Baker, *The Journey Back* 129.

38. Sterling Stuckey, *Slave Culture: Nationalist Theory and the Foundations of Black America* (New York: Oxford University Press, 1987) 11.

39. Robert E. Thompson, *The Four Moments of the Sun* (Washington, DC: National Gallery of the Arts, 1982) 28, quoted in Stuckey 12.

40. Wallace Terry was called to the White House following his generally positive 1967 *Time* magazine cover story on black soldiers in Vietnam. In his introduction to *Bloods*, Terry reports that President Johnson "was pleased by my briefing" (xiv).

41. Baker, *Blues* 4.

42. My thanks to Betsy Erkkila for suggesting the similarity between Crevecoeur's account and that of Woodley. J. Hector St. John de Crevecoeur, *Letters to an American Farmer* (New York: Penguin, 1981) 178.

43. The testimonies contained in *Bloods* detail a number of accounts of black veterans who joined the Panthers on return home. A kind of popular paranoia also circulated that the Panthers were actively recruiting in Vietnam. For a sympathetic account, see Michael Herr, *Dispatches* (New York: Avon, 1977) 190–191.

Chapter 4

1. Elaine Scarry, *The Body in Pain: The Making and Unmaking of the World* (New York: Oxford University Press, 1985) 108. All further references are cited in the text.

2. See Susan Jeffords, *The Remasculinization of America: Gender and the Vietnam War* (Bloomington: Indiana University Press, 1989); Tania Modleski, "A Father IS Being Beaten: Male Feminism and the War Film," in *Feminism Without Women: Culture and Criticism in a "Postfeminist" Age* (New York: Routledge, 1991) 61–75; Kaja Silverman, *Male Subjectivity at the Margins* (New York: Routledge, 1992).

3. Richard Dyer, *Heavenly Bodies: Film Stars and Society* (New York: St. Martin's, 1986) 138.

4. Dyer 138.

5. Dyer 139.

6. Norman Mailer, "The White Negro," in *Advertisements for Myself* (New York: Putnam, 1959). All further references cited are in the text.

7. Silverman, *Male Subjectivity at the Margins*. All further references are cited in text.

8. "The Homosexual Villain," in *Advertisements* 220–227. For a brief but instructive reading of *The Naked and the Dead*, see Joseph Allen Boone, *Tradition and Counter Tradition: Love and the Form of Fiction* (Chicago: University of Chicago Press, 1987) 274–275.

9. Norman Mailer, *Why Are We in Vietnam?* (New York: Henry Holt, 1982) 208.

10. Mailer, *Vietnam* 208.

11. Kobena Mercer, "'1968': Periodizing Politics and Identity" in *Welcome to the Jungle* (New York: Routledge, 1994). All references are cited in the text.

12. On the general relationship between the Vietnam War and postmodernism, see the special issue of *Genre* (ed. Gordon Taylor), "The Vietnam War and Postmodern Memory" 21 (Winter 1988); John Limon, *Writing After War: American War Fiction from Realism to Postmodernism* (New York: Oxford University Press, 1994),

"Vietnam, it could be argued, is the source of a unified postmodern sensibility that has two faces (American postmodernism following French, as America followed France to Vietnam): where reality at its most demented met fabulation at *its* most demented" (5); John Carlos Rowe's analysis of literary postmodernism's most prominent years (1965–1975) describes the literature's fitful relation to political crisis, most especially the Vietnam War, "Postmodern Studies," in *Redrawing the Boundaries: The Transformation of English and American Studies* (New York: MLA, 1992) 178–208; at the end of *Receptions of War: Vietnam in American Culture*, Andrew Martin critiques the popularity of Vietnam as postmodern war (Norman: University of Oklahoma Press, 1993) 153–159.

On the postmodernity of Vietnam War literature and particularly *Dispatches*, see David James, "Rock and Roll in Representations of the Invasion of Vietnam, *Representations* 29 (Winter 1990); Thomas Myers, *Walking Point: American Narratives of Vietnam* (New York: Oxford University Press, 1988) 23, 146–169; Thomas Carmichael, "Postmodernism and American Cultural Difference: *Dispatches, Mystery Train*, and *The Art of Japanese Management*," *boundary 2* 21 (Spring 1994): 221–232.

13. Fredric Jameson, "Postmodernism, or The Cultural Logic of Late Capitalism," *New Left Review* 146 (1984): 84.

14. Jeffords 41–43. Jeffords's keen analysis of the deep structure of gender in Herr, Mailer, and postmodernist critical writings has been crucial to my thinking about the related ways race operates, even while I disagree with her understanding of race as a function of the central organizing role of gender in representations of the Vietnam War (see *Remasculinization* xii, 58). See also her discussion of *Platoon* in "Masculinity as Excess in Vietnam War Films: The Father-Son Dynamic of American Culture," *Genre* 21 (Winter 1988): 497–499.

15. See Mercer, "1968: Periodizing Politics and Identity," op. cit.; Wahneema Lubiano, "Shuckin' Off the African-American Native Other: What's 'Po-Mo' Got to Do with It?" *Cultural Critique* 18 (Spring 1991): 149–186; Philip Brian Harper, *Framing the Margins: The Social Logic of Postmodern Culture* (New York: Oxford University Press, 1994) esp. 3–29; Cornel West, "Black Culture and Postmodernism," in *Remaking History*, ed. Barbara Krueger and Phil Mariani (Seattle: Bay Press, 1989) 87–96, and "The New Cultural Politics of Difference," *October* 53 (Summer 1990): 93–109; bell hooks, "Postmodern Blackness," in *Yearning: Race, Gender and Cultural Politics* (Boston: South End Press, 1990) 23–31; Richard Dyer, "White," *Screen* (Autumn 1988): 44–64, and *Heavenly Bodies: Film Stars and Society* (New York: St. Martin's, 1986) 1–18, 67–139; Eric Lott, "White Like Me: Racial Cross-Dressing and the Construction of American Whiteness," in *The Cultures of United States Imperialism*, ed. Amy Kaplan and Donald Pease (Durham, NC: Duke University Press, 1993) 474–495; Andrew Ross, "Hip, and the Long Front of Color," in *No Respect: Intellectuals and Popular Culture* (New York: Routledge, 1989) 65–101 and "Bullets, Ballots or Batman: Can Cultural Studies Do the Right Thing?" *Screen* 31 (Spring 1990): 26–44.

16. Michael Herr, *Dispatches* (New York: Vintage, 1991). All references are cited in the text.

17. Harper 4.

18. Roland Barthes, *Mythologies*, trans. Annette Lavers (New York: Hill and Wang, 1983) 111.

19. Barthes 115.

20. Limon 6.

21. See Paul Fussell *Wartime: Understanding and Behavior in the Second World War* (New York: Oxford University Press, 1989), on World War II, "while servicemen's language often exhibited such literary qualities as originality and energy, 'literature' languished in respectability, caution, and prudery. It was almost as if the cause of literary 'modernism,' temporarily abandoned by 'authors' and 'artists,' had descended to the troops. It was they during the war who behaved as if continuing the modernist impulse toward subversion and Making New. Their main technique of subversion was, of course, obscenity" (252). For an extended discussion of obscenity and especially "fuck" and "fucking," see 90–95, 251–267.

22. Colonel John R. Elting et al., *A Dictionary of Soldier Talk* (New York: Scribner's, 1984) 120. See also Linda Reinberg, *In the Field: The Language of the Vietnam War* (New York: Facts on File, 1991) 89.

23. Ernest Hemingway, *A Farewell to Arms* (New York: Collier/Macmillan, 1986) 46.

24. Norman Mailer, *The Naked and the Dead* (New York: Henry Holt, 1981) 7, 681.

25. See, for example, Clarence Major, *Juba to Jive: A Dictionary of African-American Slang* (New York: Penguin, 1994) 310; Geneva Smitherman, *Talkin and Testifyin: The Language of Black America* (Detroit: Wayne State University Press, 1977) 60–62.

26. Arthur Norman, "Army Speech and the Future of American English," *American Speech* 31 (May 1956): 107–112. For citations of Norman, see, for example, Colonel John R. Elting et al., *A Dictionary of Soldier Talk* 204; Stuart Berg Flexner, *I Hear America Talking: An Illustrated Treasury of American Words and Phrases* (New York: Van Nostrand Reinhold, 1976) 159; Hugh Rawson, *Wicked Words: A Treasury of Curses, Insults, Put-Downs, and Other Formerly Unprintable Terms from Anglo-Saxon Times to the Present* (New York: Crown, 1989) 257–258. Rawson uses an interesting example from the confrontation between the Ohio National Guard and student antiwar protesters at Kent State University in which women abused members of the Guard by calling them "motherfucker" as a sign of its broad anti-establishment use by the 1970s. Paul Fussell, although not citing Norman, writes, "It was left to the more embittered soldiers of Second World War, especially those then designated 'colored' to improve this [i.e., 'fucking' as all-purpose adjective of 'self-contempt']to *motherfuckin'*" (92–93).

For a highly suspect alternative reading, see Gregory R. Clark, *Words of the Vietnam War* (Jefferson, NC: McFarland, 1990) 147. Clark references "Do Ma": "Colloquial Vietnamese phrase loosely translated as 'motherfucker' (mofo); figurative translation, fuck mother. GI's were quick to pick up on the phrase." It seems telling that while Clark misses the black vernacular connection, he shares Norman's desire to locate the ultimate obscenity outside of white usage.

27. J. L. Dillard, *Lexicon of Black English* (New York: Seabury Press, 1977) 43.

28. Norman 111.

29. Norman 110–111.

30. "Michael Herr, We've All Been There," in Eric James Schroeder, *Vietnam, We've All Been There: Interviews with American Writers* (Westport, CT: Praeger, 1992) 43.

31. David James, "Rock and Roll in Representations of the Invasion of Vietnam," *Representations* 29 (Winter 1990): 85. All further references are cited in the text.

32. Hendrix makes the comment about napalm in an interview included in *Jimi Hendrix*. Prod. John Head. Videocassette. Warner Brothers, 1973.

33. According to Christopher Appy, *Working Class War: American Combat Soldiers and Vietnam* (Chapel Hill: University of North Carolina Press, 1993) "In airborne units—for which training is voluntary—blacks were reported to comprise as much as 30 percent of the combat troops. Moreover, blacks had a reenlistment rate three times higher than whites" (21). See also Whitney Young, Jr., "When the Negroes in Vietnam Come Home," *Atlantic Monthly* 234 (June 1967): 63–69. Hendrix was inducted in 1960. He was discharged following an injury sustained in jump school.

34. Kobena Mercer likewise cites Hendrix's performance at Woodstock as one of the signal moments in his genealogy of the "transracial identifications among postwar youth implicated in collective dissatisfaction from the 'American Dream' through mass protest against the Vietnam War," but reads it as "an ambiguous appropriation of black expressive culture."

> As a countercultural event, and as a commodity spectacle, it constituted its audience as members of a separate, generationally defined, "imagined community," as the predominantly white, middle-class youth who went thought that they constituted a "nation within a nation"—the Woodstock Nation. On the day it was over, Jimi Hendrix performed the "Star Spangled Banner," or, rather his sublime deconstruction of this hymn to national identity gave voice to an antagonism that questioned its own terms of representability.

Whereas the "whiteness" of the "Woodstock Nation" or the counterculture more generally and questions of appropriation are crucial issues, Mercer's implicit identification of protests against the Vietnam War with a white, racially blind, counterculture is exactly what I see deconstructed in Hendrix's performance. See Mercer, "'1968': Periodizing Politics and Identity" 302, 303–304.

35. Dick Cavett for one had trouble grasping this in his famous interview with Hendrix.

Hendrix: All I did was play it. I'm American so I played it. I used to have to sing it in school. They made me sing it in school. It was a flashback. That was about it.

Cavett: This man was in the 101st airborne, so when you write your nasty letters . . .

JH: Nasty letters?

DC: When you mention the National Anthem and talk about playing it in any unorthodox way, you immediately get a guaranteed percentage of hate mail from people who say how dare you.

JH: It's not unorthodox.

DC: It's not unorthodox?

JH: No, no. I thought it was beautiful, but there you go.

(Audience applause. Hendrix looks to the audience and flashes them the peace sign.)

Clips from the interview as well as the performance at Woodstock are included in the documentary film, *Jimi Hendrix*.

36. See Henry Louis Gates, Jr., *The Signifying Monkey: A Theory of Afro-American Literary Criticism* (New York: Oxford University Press, 1988).

37. Wallace Terry, *Bloods: An Oral History of the Vietnam War by Black Veterans* (New York: 1985) 39, 101, 167.

38. W. E. B. Du Bois, *The Souls of Black Folks*, in *Three Negro Classics*, Introduction by John Hope Franklin (New York: Avon, 1965) 214–215. In Wallace Terry's *Bloods*, Haywood Kirkland describes having his unit assigned to the riot squadron during the 1968 Democratic Convention. Haywood had already finished his tour in Vietnam. "I told them I'm not going there holding no weapon in front of my brothers and sisters" (100). He ultimately pleads a recurrence of malaria, and goes to the hospital instead of on duty in Chicago.

39. Lawrence Baskir and William Strauss, *Chance and Circumstance: The Draft, the War, and the Vietnam Generation* (New York: Vintage, 1978) 6, 8.

40. Quoted in Baskir and Strauss 216–217.

41. Quoted in Baskir and Strauss 125.

42. Baskir and Strauss 9.

43. Baskir and Strauss 8. The army did take steps to reduce the numbers of black soldiers in combat units. In 1966, black soldiers comprised 16 percent and in 1968, 13 percent.

44. Christian Appy untangles the complex relationship between class and race in the gross unfairness of military service during the Vietnam War era. Class, designated by income, type of employment, and region, is the correlating factor of service and avoidance. Richard Nixon, *No More Vietnams* (New York: Arbor House, 1985), and the far more sympathetic 1980 Veterans Administration study (*Myths and Realities: A Study of Attitudes toward Vietnam Era Veterans* (Washington, DC: U.S. Government Printing Office) both insist that black men, over the course of the war, served in numbers only proportionate to their presence in the U.S. population as a whole. But Appy examines the multiple levels at which black men suffered the class inequities of the draft more systematically than whites. For example, the reserves and National Guard, a favored form of respectable avoidance, were overwhelmingly white. In 1964, 1.45 percent of the Army National Guard was black; in 1968 it was 1.26 percent. At the other end of the scale, 40 percent of the 240,000 soldiers inducted under Project 100,000 were black. Half of those in Project 100,000 were sent to Vietnam, where they suffered a death rate twice as high as the armed forces as a whole. In Appy's words, "This was a Great Society program literally shot down on the battlefields of Vietnam" (33). See Appy 29–38.

45. Eric Lott, *Love and Theft: Blackface Minstrelsy and the American Working Class* (New York: Oxford University Press, 1993). All further references are cited in the text.

46. David Rabe, *The Vietnam Plays, Volume One* (New York: Grove, 1993). All further references to *The Basic Training of Pavlo Hummel* are cited in the text.

47. In the Hughes brothers' 1995 film, *Dead Presidents*, a white soldier is found alive but castrated, his penis stuffed in his mouth, in a graphically depicted scene. The white medic binds him up and the main character, a black soldier, carries him out. The wounded soldier begs to be killed, a plea the black soldier quietly honors by giving him a second, lethal injection of morphine. In *Dead Presidents* the black man has a life

and a narrative separate from the war and the white man's mutilation, but even here he is still the one with the answer to the white man's crisis. This scene echos Gene Woodley's confrontation with the white GI who has been staked out discussed in chapter 3 (in this volume). *Dead Presidents* was "suggested by a story" in *Bloods*, so the structural similarity to the Woodley scene may be more than coincidental.

48. The role of Lou Gossett as Drill Sgt. Foley in *An Officer and a Gentleman* is particularly telling. As I argue elsewhere, race, and its unspoken appeal, is critical in the film's amazingly successful rehabilitation of the military as a positive cultural institution following the debased images associated with the Vietnam War. See Kinney, "Cold Wars: Black Soldiers in Liberal Hollywood," forthcoming in *War, Literature, and the Arts*.

49. This is taken from Lott's discussion of an 1867 account of T. D. Rice's first blackface performance in which Rice orders Cuff, a Negro street figure, to disrobe and then puts the clothes on himself and wears them onstage to general hilarity while Cuff huddles, naked behind the stage. Lott calls the account the "least trustworthy and most accurate account of American minstralsy's appropriation of blck cultural practice." Lott emphasizes not only Cuff's debasement and embarrassment but the "tittilating threat that he might return to demand his stolen capital" (18–19).

50. Richard Dyer, "White," *Screen* (Autumn 1988): 44.

51. See Silverman 60–64 and Dyer 50–51.

52. David Rabe, "A Harrowing Audience Experience," in Schroeder, op. cit., 209–210.

53. I borrow here from Eric Lott's phrase, "the social unconscious of blackface."

54. David Rabe, *The Vietnam Plays, Volume Two* (New York: Grove, 1993) 27. All further references to *Streamers* are cited in the text.

55. The uprising at Long Binh Stockade discussed in chapter 3 (in this volume) testifies to the high numbers of black soldiers incarcerated in country. The National Association for the Advancement of Colored People estimated that 45 percent of all less than honorable discharges during the Vietnam era were given to black soldiers, another sign of the grossly disproportionate number of punishments handed out to black soldiers by the military justice system. James William Gibson, *The Perfect War: The War We Couldn't Lose and How We Did* (New York: Vintage, 1986) 218.

56. Fredric Jameson, *The Political Unconscious: Narrative as Socially Symbolic Act* (Ithaca, NY: Cornell University Press, 1981) 148.

57. See Silverman's discussion of ideological belief in Althusser as unconscious and enacted bodily.

We might of course attempt to explain the exteriority of ideological belief according to a performative model, whereby meaningful practices and rituals are understood to produce the assent of the individual who engages in them. Such a reading of *Lenin and Philosophy* would be facilitated by Foucault's *Discipline and Punish*, with its account of the discursive construction of the subject by means of the "calculated manipulation" of the body's "elements," "gestures," and "behavior." Within such a reading, belief would emerge as a kind of spiritual extension or registration of an orchestrated corporeality. However, the main thrust of Althusserian argument is to locate ideological faith outside of *consciousness*, rather than the *psyche*. Ideological belief, in other words, occurs at the moment when an image which the subject consciously knows to be culturally fabricated nevertheless succeeds in being recognized or acknowledged as 'a pure naked perception. (17)

The army and Billy and Roger's determination to "be" regular army and to "believe" Billy's "straight" narrative work in precisely this way. Moreover, Scarry's reading of the body as the source of "world-making" and reality would seem to assert belief as extension of an *unorchestrated* corporeality, or at least one orchestrated by more benign models of social organization than those of Foucault.

58. The 1977 Knopf edition of *Streamers* has "bend" at the end of this line (43). The Grove edition has "end." "Bend" seems so much more in keeping with the ultimate enacting of the song, I have used the earlier edition's version in this one case.

Chapter 5

1. Robin Morgan, ed. *Sisterhood IS Powerful: An Anthology of Writings from the Women's Liberation Movement* (New York: Vintage, 1970) n.p.

2. Susan Jeffords, *The Remasculinization of America: Gender and the Vietnam War* (Bloomington: Indiana University Press, 1989) 25–28, 41–43.

3. William Broyles, Jr., "Why Men Love War," *Esquire*, 102 (November 1984): 55–65.

4. Virginia Woolf, *A Room of One's Own* (New York: Harcourt Brace Jovanovich, 1929) 118, 39.

5. Woolf 118.

6. Alice Echols, *Daring to Be Bad: Radical Feminism in America 1967–1975* (Minneapolis: University of Minnesota Press, 1989) 37. All further references are cited in the text.

7. Paul Fussell, *The Great War and Modern Memory* (New York: Oxford University Press, 1977) 334.

8. Fussell 328, 330.

9. The role of Jenny in the mega-hit *Forest Gump* is emblematic in its charting of the woman's experience of the "sixties" as being the abused girlfriend of a series of counterculture, political activist types. Women's liberation seems the only event of cultural history the film does not explore, except indirectly through Jenny's "liberated" sexuality. Tellingly, she dies of AIDS.

10. Echols includes as an appendix to her history of the radical feminist movement the transcript of the "Discussion at Sandy Springs Conference, August 1968" on black women and women's liberation, which testifies to the abstract understanding within the women's movement that race mattered but the utter failure to act on it. One telling statement claims, "We all agree that the women in Algeria, Viet Nam and Cuba, the consciousness of them affects the consciousness we have. But I would be more comfortable discussing this with men whom I know than with black women at this point" (376). Distance would seem to strengthen rather than weaken the appeal of Vietnamese women as revolutionary "role models."

11. Tim O'Brien, "The Sweetheart of the Song Tra Bong" in *The Things They Carried* (New York: Houghton Mifflin, 1990) 99–125.

12. Michael Herr, *Dispatches* (New York: Vintage, 1991). All references are cited in the text.

13. Le Ly Hayslip with Jay Wurts, *When Heaven and Earth Changed Places* (New York: Plume/Penguin, 1990). All further references are cited in the text.

14. Tim O'Brien, *Going After Cacciato* (New York: Dell, 1982) 233.

15. On the larger *Madam Butterfly* narrative of the tragic romance between an Asian woman and an American officer as a structuring metaphor for U.S. relations with Asian nations, and on *Sayonara* in particular, see Traise Yamamoto, *Masking Selves/Making Subjects: Japanese American Women, Identity, and the Body*, chap. 1 [Berkeley: University of California Press, 1999], and Gina Marchetti, *Romance and the Yellow Peril: Race, Sex, and Discursive Strategies in Hollywood Fiction*, chap. 7 [Berkeley: University of California Press, 1993].

16. Le Ly Hayslip with James Hayslip, *Child of War: Woman of Peace* (New York: Anchor Books, 1993). All further references will are cited in the text.

17. See Kali Tal, "The Mind at War: Images of Women in Vietnam Novels by Combat Veterans," *Contemporary Literature* 31 (1990): 76–96; Jacqueline Lawson, "'She's a Pretty Woman . . . for a Gook': The Misogyny of the Vietnam War," in *Fourteen Landing Zones: Approaches to Vietnam War Literature*, Philip K. Jason, ed. (Iowa City: University of Iowa Press, 1991): 15–37; Cindy Fuchs, "This Is My Rifle, This Is My Gun," paper delivered at Popular Culture Association, New Orleans, March 1988; Jeffords, *Remasculinization*. Kali Tal and Jacqueline Lawson edited a special edition of *Vietnam Generation*, "Gender and the War: Men Women, and Vietnam," 1 (Summer–Fall 1989).

18. This is, in one sense, quite literally the same scene of friendly fire which forms the climax of *Platoon*. Years after the war, Heinemann and Oliver Stone discovered that, while serving in different units, they were in the same battle during Tet (conversation with Heinemann, January 1989, University of Pennsylvania).

19. Larry Heinemann, *Paco's Story* (New York: Penguin, 1987) ix. All further references are cited in the text.

20. Elaine Scarry, *The Body in Pain: The Making and Unmaking of the World* (New York: Oxford University Press, 1985) 64.

21. See John Dower, *War Without Mercy: Race and Power in the Pacific War* (New York: Pantheon, 1986) 151–152.

22. Ernest Hemingway, *A Farewell to Arms* (1929; New York: Scribner's, 1986) 115.

23. Fredric Jameson, *The Political Unconscious: Narrative as a Socially Symbolic Act* (Ithaca: Cornell University Press, 1981) 182.

24. A number of works feature this structural use of the Vietnamese woman as the emblem of the war, the past, and guilt and the white American woman as home, the present, and the promise of expiation. In Bruce Weigl's haunting poem "Song of Napalm," the narrating veteran tries to follow his wife's advice and not continually reinscribe the landscape around him with likenesses of Vietnam and the war. But he is ultimately haunted by an image of a girl running down the road, burning with napalm, a personalizing of one of the most famous photograph's of the war. He tries to imagine that she flies away, "So I can keep on living,/ So I can stay here beside you," but it is a lie. "Nothing can change" the terrible violence to

the girl's body, not even his wife's "good love." See W. D. Ehrhart, ed. *Carrying the Darkness: the Poetry of the Vietnam War* (Lubbock: Texas Tech University Press, 1985) 273–274. The hugely popular Broadway musical *Miss Saigon* is the most egregious example, using the *Madam Butterfly* story to oppose the Vietnamese woman and the proper white American wife.

25. Susan Jeffords, "Tattoos, Scars, Diaries, and Writing Masculinity," in *The Vietnam War and American Culture*, ed. John Carlos Rowe and Rick Berg (New York: Columbia University Press, 1991) 212.

26. Jeffords sees the novel's self-consciousness toward gender as ultimately recuperated into collective masculinity (70–71).

27. Bobbie Ann Mason, *In Country* (New York: Harper and Row, 1986). All further references are cited in the text.

28. My discussion is much indebted to Jean Bethke Elshtain's cultural analysis in *Women and War* (New York: Basic Books, 1987) esp. 222–223.

29. Broyles 61–62.

30. Sandra M. Gilbert, "Soldier's Heart: Literary Men, Literary Women, and the Great War," *Signs* 8 (1983): 444.

31. See Jane Marcus, "Corpus/Corps/Corpse: Writing the Body in/at War," Afterword to *Not So Quiet. . . .* by Helen Zenna Smith (New York: Feminist Press, 1989) 295–296.

32. Christian Appy, *Working Class War: American Combat Soldiers and Vietnam* (Chapel Hill: University of North Carolina Press, 1993) 14–15.

33. J. Glenn Gray, *The Warriors: Reflections on Men in Battle*. (New York: Harper and Row, 1970) 83.

34. Quoted in Nancy Huston, "Tales of War and Tears of Women," *Women's Studies International Forum* 5 (1982): 274.

Conclusion

1. Alex Chadwick, "The Girl in the Picture: Interview with Kim Phuc," *Morning Edition*, National Public Radio, November 8,1996.

2. Ibid.

3. *San Jose Mercury News*, April 13, 1997, 27A.

4. Tom Bowman, "Veteran's Admission to Napalm Victim a Lie: Minister says he never meant to deceive with 'story of forgiveness,' *Baltimore Sun*, December 14, 1997, 1A.

5. Andrew Lam, "Show and Tell," in *Watermark: Vietnamese American Poetry and Prose*, ed. Barbara Tran, Monique T.D. Truong, and Luu Truong Khoi (New York: Asian American Writers' Workshop, 1998) 113. All further references are cited in the text.

6. John Balaban, "After Our War," *Carrying the Darkness: American Indo-China: The Poetry of the Vietnam War* (New York: Avon, 1985) 16.

INDEX